Praise for *Once Upon a Revolution*

"It is one of the many strengths of Thanassis Cambanis's fluent, intelligent, and highly informed book, *Once Upon a Revolution*, that he convincingly explains what happened in Egypt over the last four years. It should be read by anybody perplexed by how Egypt's apparent entry into a brave new democratic world was ultimately defeated. This account has the vividness and readability of eyewitness reporting combined with an unsentimental and perceptive judgment about where the opponents of autocracy went wrong."

—Patrick Cockburn, *The New York Times Book Review*

"Cambanis has achieved something altogether remarkable here. Through tracking the thoughts and actions of two rivals in the Egyptian revolutionary movement, complemented by his own acute on-the-street observations, he has produced an account of the rise and fall of the Egyptian Revolution that is at once gripping, illuminating, and wise. *Once Upon a Revolution* is essential reading for anyone seeking to understand the political and religious crosscurrents currently roiling the Middle East, or who wishes to gain an insight into where the region might be headed next. It is also that rarest of 'compulsory' books: one that is a pleasure to read."

—Scott Anderson, author of *Lawrence in Arabia: War, Deceit, Imperial Folly and the Making of the Modern Middle East*

"A comprehensive, straightforward—and sympathetic—accounting of the Egyptian revolution. . . . A cautionary and instructive tale that should be required reading for would-be revolutionaries everywhere, Wall Street Occupiers and Hong Kong umbrella-holders alike, on the extent to which the powerful will go to prevent change and the pitfalls of decentralized revolutionary movements."

—Max Strasser, *Los Angeles Review of Books*

"In *Once Upon a Revolution*, Thanassis Cambanis draws on a decade of reporting in the Middle East to produce a kaleidoscopic narrative of 'the revolution that for an instant felt like it might transform the world.' Through the intertwining tales of two very different revolutionaries, Basem and Moaz, Cambanis conveys the profound moment of hope that existed in Tahrir Square—and the tumult and tragedy that followed. Gripping, vivid, compassionate, and often funny, Cambanis's book captures the political drama and human folly of these historic events in Egypt."

—Patrick Radden Keefe, author of
Chatter and *The Snakehead*

"*Once Upon a Revolution* is a beautifully written, deeply reported, and thrilling book. Thanassis Cambanis has remarkable access to the men and women at the heart of the most important revolution of our times and he uses that access to tell a story that is both compulsively readable and essential to anyone trying to understand people and politics of the modern Middle East."

—Matthew McAllester, author of *Beyond the Mountains of the Damned*

"The characters Cambanis renders in *Once Upon a Revolution* are irresistible; you will cheer for them, cry with them, and feel the weight of their task as they bring down a dictator only to face the harder challenge of reinventing Egypt. Cambanis tells no fairy tales, but grim reality is tempered by the compassion, humor, and hope of the young people in the square."

—Quil Lawrence, NPR News correspondent and
former Baghdad Bureau Chief

"The Egyptian uprising of 2011 was packed with principled struggles and craven opportunism, unexpected triumphs and horrifying reversals. Cambanis works to guide us through this thicket with intense on-the-ground reporting. His readers will understand why Egypt's would-be revolutionaries made the choices—and the mistakes—they did."

—Nathan J. Brown, author of *When Victory is Not an Option: Islamist Movements in Arab Politics* and Professor,
George Washington University

"A warm, deeply human chronicle of the people who drove the revolution and a cool, withering analysis of why they failed."

—*Boston Globe*

"Cambanis's remarkable account of Egypt's 2011 uprising and 2013 counterrevolution is built on his firsthand reporting. . . . Cambanis's analysis is sharp, and he does not hold back when it comes to graphically depicting the Egyptian state's violence against its own people, be they Coptic Christians or Muslim Brotherhood supporters."

—*Foreign Affairs*

"A gripping portrayal of the forces that led to the eruption in Tahrir Square in Egypt on January 25, 2011. . . . The richness of [Cambanis's] reporting informs his book, but it is the narrative nonfiction frame that humanizes the account and makes it more accessible. Wonderfully readable and insightful."

—*Booklist* (starred review)

"In this highly readable book, journalist and author Cambanis recounts the trials and tribulations of that revolution. The work is informed by the author's sustained, on-the-ground, astute observations of the unfolding events in Egypt. A welcome addition to the literature on Egypt's uprising."

—*Library Journal*

"Smart, troubling study of the events surrounding Tahrir Square and their aftermath. . . . A clear exposition and analysis of complex, swiftly changing events. The book gives readers cause to understand why we might support regime change in the Middle East, even if it brings instability and incoherence."

—*Kirkus Reviews*

ALSO BY THANASSIS CAMBANIS

*A Privilege to Die: Inside Hezbollah's Legions
and Their Endless War Against Israel*

ONCE UPON
A REVOLUTION

AN EGYPTIAN STORY

THANASSIS CAMBANIS

SIMON & SCHUSTER PAPERBACKS

New York   London   Toronto   Sydney   New Delhi

Simon & Schuster Paperbacks
An Imprint of Simon & Schuster, Inc.
1230 Avenue of the Americas
New York, NY 10020

First Simon & Schuster trade paperback edition January 2016

SIMON & SCHUSTER PAPERBACKS and colophon are trademarks of Simon & Schuster, Inc.

For information about special discounts for bulk purchases,
please contact Simon & Schuster Special Sales at 1-866-506-1949
or business@simonandschuster.com.

The Simon & Schuster Speakers Bureau can bring authors to your live event.
For more information or to book an event, contact the Simon & Schuster Speakers Bureau
at 1-866-248-3049 or visit our website at www.simonspeakers.com.

Interior design by Erich Hobbing

Manufactured in the United States of America

1   3   5   7   9   10   8   6   4   2

The Library of Congress has cataloged the hardcover edition as follows:

Cambanis, Thanassis.
Once upon a revolution : an Egyptian story / Thanassis Cambanis.
pages cm
Includes bibliographical references and index.
1. Egypt—History—Protests, 2011– 2. Kamel, Basem. 3. Abdelkareem, Moaz. 4. Political activists—Egypt—Biography. 5. Civic leaders—Egypt—Biography. 6. Revolutionaries—Egypt—Biography. 7. Egypt—History—1981—Biography. 8. Social change—Egypt—History—21st century. I. Title.
DT107.88.C36 2015
962.05'5—dc23
2014022751

ISBN 978-1-4516-5899-6
ISBN 978-1-4516-5900-9 (pbk)
ISBN 978-1-4516-5901-6 (ebook)

For Anthony,
whose love and enthusiasm inspired this project
and imbues my every day;

And for Athina and Odysseas,
perpetual revolutions of curiosity and joy.

But what about us? Or let me say what about you? You who reject the injustice of detention but remain free outside the prisons? What will you do? Will you share in the show? Or withdraw from it and wait silently to be taken from your homes? Will you abandon us? Will you be content to wait because this is a temporary situation? . . . Everyone knows that there is no hope for us who have gone ahead into prison except through you who will surely follow. So what are you going to do?

—Alaa Abdel Fattah, "Everybody Knows,"
Letter from Prison, *March 2014*

Remember the tomorrow that never came?
—Keizer, Cairo street graffiti

Even though you can destroy a man, destroying him does not make him cease to exist. On the contrary, if I can put it this way, he begins to exist all the more. These are paradoxes no tyrant can deal with. The scythe swings, and at once the grass starts to grow back. Cut again, and the grass grows faster than ever.

—Ryszard Kapuściński, *Shah of Shahs*

CONTENTS

1.

BREAKING THE WALL OF FEAR

Listen: I didn't mean to write a book about the Egyptian Revolution. When Tahrir Square first erupted, I had to go see it for myself, because I'd been writing about hopelessness in the Arab world for most of my adult life, and January 25, 2011, was the first unequivocally hopeful thing I'd seen. I meant to stay only a little while, but the people I met there were doing something that mattered not just for Egypt or the Arab world but for everyone. They weren't merely trying to overthrow a despicable regime; they were trying to invent a new kind of democracy that would improve on the existing models around the world. They were ambitious idealists. They wanted to take the best of what they saw in democracy around the world and combine it into a system that was fairer, freer, and more efficient.

Egypt's dictators had insisted that their subjects were incompetent, helpless sheep who needed a strong hand. Left on their own, they'd make a mess and starve to death. Egypt's revolution began with eighteen utopian days in Tahrir. A group of people with no previous experience of self-rule created institutions to rule the square. It was nothing short of a new society in miniature. They collected garbage in a country where littering was endemic. They organized security patrols, a jail, food distribution, prayer spaces, entertainment. They even formed a government of sorts, the Revolutionary Youth Coalition, which drafted policy proposals and plotted a political strategy. These individuals had come of age impervious to society's effort to make them passive and helpless. I sought out the people in the square who were taking initiative, taking charge, spewing

1

plans and ideas. They were the ones most responsible for the inspiring eighteen days in Tahrir, and I wanted to see how they would go about seeking change in the years to come. They knew that remaking Egypt was a long-term project with long odds.

I focused on a few dozen activists who gravitated to politics. They came from varied backgrounds and had different areas of expertise: street organizing, human rights, policy, party politics. I followed them as they endeavored to translate Tahrir Square's utopian society into a political system. In the years after Tahrir Square and the fall of President Hosni Mubarak, Egypt hosted a bloody struggle for power and between different ideas of government. The revolutionaries brought a lofty, idealistic tone to the contest, but they were joined and often bested by the established players: the army, the police, Mubarak's elite, and the Muslim Brotherhood, the secretive religious organization that had survived eight decades underground. Many revolutionaries show up in these pages, along with representatives of the establishment and other reactionary forces. I have chosen to place at the center of the story two men from different backgrounds who embodied the revolution's most important aspirations and persisted through setback after setback.

One is a schlumpy pharmacist named Moaz Abdelkarim, a career activist who grew up in the Muslim Brotherhood but whose propensity for joking and asking questions was incompatible with its authoritarian culture. When the revolution began, Moaz was twenty-six years old. He represented the revolution's id or soul, and its Islamist branch. Moaz was personally religious but passionate about pluralism and secular government. At all times, he lived by an injunction to do the right thing regardless of its personal cost. Moaz wore this morality without fanfare, and never set it aside. Like many revolutionaries, he also had trouble thinking beyond the present moment. If the right thing right now conflicted with the right thing for the long run, he always prioritized right now.

The other figure I have emphasized is an architect named Basem Kamel, who avoided politics until he turned forty the year before the uprising. Basem was as shrewd as Moaz was impulsive, as punctual as Moaz was perpetually tardy. Basem had built a business, raised a family, and stayed out of trouble. When finally he started to resist Egypt's corrupt political system, he moved strategically. He had more at risk than those revolutionaries without families, but also more to gain. Basem never did anything without first considering the long-term consequences. Tahrir Square was a powerful symbol, but it wasn't the goal of the revolution; the goal was to bring effective representational democracy to Egypt. Protest was just one tactic to that end. Basem worked hard at politics, unflaggingly, even when no one was paying attention. He cared deeply for the revolution but wasn't carried away by emotion. He represented the revolution's ego or brain, and its secular branch.

Basem and Moaz were hardly ever alone in their political adventures, and there were many equally admirable and equally flawed individuals working alongside them. There are perhaps a few hundred activists whose commitment never failed. Their stories differ in emphasis and detail but fit tightly together in Tahrir's revolutionary constellation. The story of where Basem and Moaz came from and where they ended up tells a large part of the story of why the Tahrir Revolution occurred and why it followed the course it did.

I must be frank. I fell in love with the Tahrir Revolution, but this love didn't blind me to its faults. I admired the men and women I followed through years of revolt and upheaval, but it was not an uncritical affection. They defied the society from which they sprang, but they also reflected it. They embarked on their flawed but inspiring uprising freighted with all of Egypt's legacies. The revolutionaries suffered from a political miseducation and, at climactic moments, from a reflex to avoid conflict. They were almost fatally polite and obsessed with consensus, flaws that sometimes made them lose nerve but more often made them lose coherence. They embodied the human capacity to transcend one's life story, but they didn't defy the laws of physics and human nature. They didn't make magic, even if their story was magical.

This is a primal story of human beings shattering the chains that bind them, and striking against a power that oppresses them. But it's a true story, not a fairy tale, so the power fights back. The heroic revolutionaries suffer from fatal flaws, while their opponents—the people who side with the old regime—aren't all cartoon caricatures of evil. This is a story about universal human aspirations and the timeless struggle of revolutionary youth against wily power; but it's also a story very particular to Egypt. The revolt arose from a proud tradition of Arab nationalism and a specifically Egyptian sense of destiny. Like Americans, Egyptians believe their nation charts a course for all others to follow. They call Egypt "the mother of the world" and hearken often to its birthright as the cradle of civilization. Traditionally, Egypt also occupies the center of the Arab world. In the last century, it has struggled with both the legacy of colonialism and the Israeli-Palestinian conflict on its border. The young activists in Tahrir wanted to reclaim Egypt's historical influence without its bullying. They wanted to resolve their nation's historical conflicts rather than simply sweep them away.

People are constantly expressing sympathy: "How can you write a book about the Egyptian Revolution, when it never stops changing?" Friends also usually extend some kind of condolences for the outcome: so many hopes frustrated, so many innocent people in prison or exile, so many villains back in power. As I write these words today, I cannot predict what will become of the revolution that for an instant felt like it might transform the whole world. Predicting history is a fool's business. What I do know is that the human story at the core of the Tahrir Square Revolution, of ordinary individuals who forced an extraordinary transformation in themselves and their society, is a story for all of us and for all time. It cannot be undone. What must happen for Egypt to shake its history of state oppression is the same thing that needs to happen anywhere for an unfree society to become free: individuals change in their souls, and then gather enough momentum to transform their government and its grinding machinery. We change the way we think; then we conquer the institutions of control.

Such drastic change for the good requires an almost impossible confluence of brilliance and luck. My generation came of age at the end of the Cold War, and was taught that history had ended. Now we were just tinkering with the details of how to reach the destination on which everyone had agreed. We were taught to triangulate, to make reasonable demands. That phony consensus spawned an age of pragmatism. Excessive hope and belief in revolution came to be seen as embarrassingly naïve, because the world evolves slowly; it never makes staggering leaps.

Tahrir reminded us that it isn't always so: that history still makes leaps and retains a capacity for surprise, even if, for Egypt, great change proved out of reach for now.

Revolutions are violent. They create, they destroy, and often they do not end well. It is often said that they eat their children, like Cronos the Titan in Greek mythology. The end of the Cold War misled us into thinking revolutions were romantic affairs. Gentle transitions with names such as the Velvet Revolution accompanied the fall of the Iron Curtain, but they weren't really revolutions: the old rulers more or less agreed to move on when the Soviet Union collapsed, surrendering their power structures intact to new, liberal custodians. But real revolutions aren't courtships; they are wars, sibling rivalries resolved by murder. Real revolutions challenge everything. They shake the foundations of power, and power clings tenaciously. Often the old ways win. Or the revolutionaries prevail but, like the Bolsheviks and the Jacobins and the ayatollahs, create new horrors to replace the old.

Egypt's revolution erupted into the open in 2011, and it will take decades to conclude. Perhaps the best analogue is the French Revolution of the late eighteenth century. It was easy to kill King Louis XVI but much harder to build a republic; it took eighty years and three tries before the idea really stuck. Egypt's uprising showed us the limits of a leaderless revolution: "people power" at its purest. The cell that prompted January 25 and formed the heart of Tahrir was obsessed with unity and legitimacy. Revolutionaries were determined not to replace Mubarak with another dictator. They wanted to topple a tyrant, not take his place. Young leaders at Tahrir believed they could avoid the corruption that usually comes with power, so they attempted a revolution without any of the usual political gambits. They didn't try to take over the government's television stations or any ministries. They didn't revolt inside an army barracks, or infiltrate the police, or establish underground cells, or get explosives training. They didn't have the bloodthirsty hearts of the Bolsheviks who seized Russian factories, or the French who stormed the Bastille. For revolutionaries, they were excessively respectful, moderate, and inclusive: so much so that they composed a beautiful paean to incremental change, consultation, and transparency without actually changing that much of Egypt's system of governance. It quickly became evident that even with the noblest sentiments, a reluctant revolutionary fails easily, outmaneuvered and shunted aside by any Machiavelli.

The Tahrir leaders did, however, invent a completely new approach to political life in Egypt and the Arab world, one that will produce consequences for generations to come. Their idea was that a state could be governed fairly by its own people, with limited power given to elected officials, equal justice for everyone, and an economy that allowed the rich to make their money while taking care of the poor. Their idea was that apparently powerless citizens can organize to overthrow a tyrant who appears all-powerful. The Tahrir revolutionaries killed the lie that people are sheep and the best government they deserve is an ironfisted tyrant who will keep them alive. No Arab leader can again take the population's consent for granted.

Tahrir formed only one political vehicle that included revolutionaries and moderates, secular activists and Islamists: the Revolutionary Youth Coalition, which tried to conduct politics in the name of the youth revolt. From the start, it was fractured by some of the same forces that prompted the original uprising. Members suffered from paranoia about infiltration and surveillance. The religious and secular members never fully trusted each other. Xenophobia had permeated Egypt even before the revolt and grew more pronounced afterward. Most significantly, its rulers had managed a delicate trick. They had convinced the public that the military men in charge were selfless stewards of the national interest, while the politicians who sought to challenge them were self-serving careerists. Decades of steady propaganda portrayed all politics as selfish, and inimical to enlightened governance. That attitude outlasted the revolution, and street activists derided any would-be leaders as power grubbers. The harder the revolutionary youth leaders worked to advance the revolution's aims, the less respect they commanded on the street.

Fearful of alienating the public, the Revolutionary Youth Coalition never decided on an ultimate aim. Did it want to topple the military regime behind Mubarak, creating a true republic where the popular vote trumped the military and plutocracy? Or was it only fighting for mild improvements to elections and the balance of power between the president and the parliament? Ultimately, did the youth of Tahrir want reform or revolution? They never could agree. As a result, organized, richly staffed power centers like the army and the Muslim Brotherhood were able to emerge strongest from Egypt's revolutionary transition.

Tahrir Square seized imaginations far beyond the Arab and Islamic world. The original uprising in January 2011 appealed to a universal desire to root for the underdog, to believe that a group of ordinary people armed with nothing but their determination and a few paving stones could bring down an implacable police state. For an instant, the revolt seemed to have a storybook ending: the tyrant flees the palace, the people demand justice, the poor and hungry embark on a renaissance. Then the Tahrir Revolution became, in its next chapter, a coming-of-age narrative about the difficulty of transforming idealism into practice; about how much easier it is to break something down than to build it up; about dreams, politics, and compromise; and about how an early victory can mask a harder fight ahead.

Like the revolution they embody, the two characters at the heart of this story make imperfect decisions and sometimes tragic mistakes. However, they pursue a dream with undeniable bravery, and in good faith. We can admire and learn from them even when they disappoint. It will take decades to assess the legacy of the revolutionaries of 2011. They could not immediately persuade a majority of their fellow citizens, but still they altered the course of a nation. Naysayers should remember that a revolution remains a revolution even if it fails. And they should remember too what happened to the children of Cronos after he swallowed them: they grew strong in his belly until his sixth child, Zeus, escaped his father's jaws, liberated his siblings, and overthrew the Titans.

2.

THE COUNTRY IS DYING

Basem Kamel counted himself young and lucky: only forty years old and awash in comfort by Egypt's meager standards. He had spent a decade commuting to work six hours away from Cairo. Now he worked in the same city as his wife and three children. The roof and walls around them were paid for, and he had enough for his children's school fees. This was the bounty of Basem Kamel. Egypt was on the verge of revolution, as it had been for as long as modern history had been recorded, but the revolution never came. There were occasional mirages, such as 1952, when the Free Officers expelled Egypt's foreign masters but then enslaved it under an indigenous military dictatorship. Congenitally good-humored and conditioned like most Egyptians to laugh at frustration and ill fortune, Basem would tell his children, referring to his reserves of good cheer rather than money, "We are rich!" His father was the son of a peasant laborer who had fought his way into the middle class, earning enough at a secure university job to build a five-story apartment block for his children an hour's drive from downtown Cairo.

At architecture school, Basem had studied with the pioneers of contemporary Arab aesthetics. He designed ecological dwellings inspired by Egypt's native flora and landscape: modern homes with echoes of the mud hut, the papyrus reed, the desert slope. No one wanted to build them, so Basem settled for the kind of architecture that earned a living wage: cheap, ugly concrete blocks as tall and densely packed as the authorities would allow. He confined his artistic pursuits to watching television specials on Vincent van Gogh and Antoni Gaudí, the Catalan architect.

He took pride in showing up early for meetings, which made him an oddity in Egypt. He strode rather than walked, erect, with an expression of purpose. Basem was taller and slimmer than most men. He cropped his goatee and receding head of hair to the same stubble length, accentuating his oversized oval head. Because of his light skin and soft hazel-brown eyes, people sometimes mistook him for a foreigner. On special occasions he went tieless, wearing fine shirts with the tails fluttering out, a blazer over his jeans, and, weather permitting, loafers without socks. Basem looked the part, but it didn't change the fact that upward mobility had ended for the Kamel family in 1980, as it had for most of Egypt. As an adult, Basem Kamel toiled sixteen hours a day at the architecture firm that he'd founded and that supported most of his extended family. He worked longer hours than his father, though the family's standard of living had distinctly fallen a notch.

One day in 1999, a worker fell from the second-floor scaffolding at a construction site that Basem was supervising in the Sinai. The man's head was mangled; his spine broken. At the hospital, the doctors refused to treat the worker unless Basem paid in advance out of his own pocket. Wheelchair-bound, the laborer never was able to work again. There was no social security, no state pension, so he fed his family by begging. He was Basem's age, hardworking, with children. "If this happened to me, what would I do?" Basem thought. "What would happen to my kids? One accident, and my family would become beggars too." President Hosni Mubarak had possessed all power for nearly two decades. If such a fragile thread separated a bread-winning man from utter destitution, then Mubarak was responsible, and Mubarak had failed. He had to go, and after the accident, Basem was willing to say so to his workers and friends. So long as he never did anything about it, his feeble protest went unpunished.

With a preemptive expectation of defeat, Basem Kamel watched on television in 2005 when a group of Egyptians organized under the Kifaya banner to say "Enough!" and voice their disgust with Mubarak. "They seem like fine people," he told his wife as they sat beneath the low ceiling of their sitting room. "I respect them. But don't they realize that they cannot change anything? This system is too strong." Five years later, he read in the newspaper that Mohamed ElBaradei, the Nobel Prize–winning diplomat, was pondering a return to Egypt to run for president against Mubarak. Basem had hardly remembered that the renowned Arab statesman was Egyptian. Maybe ElBaradei had the stature to make something happen in Egypt. After midnight, when he had dined with his wife after a long day with clients at a building site, Basem turned to the internet. He grew excited as he read. He found a Facebook group that was preparing for ElBaradei's return, but not at ElBaradei's request. These Egyptians were taking their own initiative. The organizer was a well-known intellectual named Abdelrahman Youssef, son of the megacelebrity television preacher Yusuf al-Qaradawi. This Abdelrahman Youssef was famous in his own right for his poetry, for openly taking on Mubarak, and for breaking with his own father to criticize the Muslim Brotherhood.

Basem skulked on the Facebook group, reading the postings with growing alacrity. The members weren't cloaked in anonymity. They clearly didn't care that the ubiquitous secret police could read their subversive critiques and plans. One day the ElBaradei group advertised a meeting in a downtown office. Intrigued, Basem sent a short message to the online administrator.

"Is it safe?" he asked.

The reply was terse. "The country is dying," Abdelrahman Youssef wrote back. "Do as you see fit."

No entreaties, no assurances. Basem thought of his father, whose advice had never wavered over the decades. "Think of your work and nothing else," Basem's father always told his children. "Politics and activism lead only to prison."

For his entire life, Basem had embarked on his projects wholly or not at all. With method and devotion, he had courted his first cousin and childhood playmate; he had ascended to a respectable position as an architect and developer; and he had brought three children to the cusp of adulthood. He didn't want to jeopardize all those accomplishments. Nor, however, did he want to pass to his children an eroding Egypt and an example as passive as that of his own father. As he pondered the online Facebook message from a man he had never met, Basem Kamel grew pregnant with the secret: The country is dying. Do what you must. Do what you must. Forty years of frustration crystallized in a day. All at once, Basem could not imagine forgoing the meeting and its inevitable chain of consequences. For he had never done anything by the teaspoon. And now, he knew, he would do this. For four decades, he had devoted his entire life to securing a single acre for his family. For one probably hopeless meeting, Basem Kamel could easily end up like countless other Egyptians before him: in prison, unemployable, and useless to his family. But the opportunity had beckoned for something greater than this pittance on the fringes of Cairo: a real inheritance for his children, an Egypt that belonged to them or, failing that, a father who dared object to a dreary lifetime of defeat. He told his plan only to his youngest brother, so someone would know where to start looking if Basem never came home.

"The country is dying," he said. "I will do what I must."

3.

ENOUGH

The grievance that smoldered almost imperceptibly for four decades before bursting forth to consume Basem Kamel began with the simplest of swindles: a promise of prosperity in exchange for submission. The Kamel family was one of millions that followed Egypt's mercurial arc from subjugated colony to independent nation. In less than a century, Egypt ricocheted between extremes. It fought its way out of British tutelage, and shot from subjugated third world poverty to liberation. An industrial boom wrenched the population away from feudal farming and spawned a period of great expectations. Basem's father, Mohamed Kamel, considered the routine humiliations a reasonable price to pay for his five children's passage out of rural poverty and into the university-educated middle class. It was too late for Mohamed Kamel to change his ways when he realized that he had assumed far too much of the burden of submission, while the masters of Egypt had enjoyed the prospering in his stead. But his children had taken note and quietly, steadily raged. The pattern repeated in household after household: a series of frissons that collectively gathered enough force to shrug off a regime. A molten seam of anger festered beneath Egypt's crust, waiting to gush forth.

Mohamed Kamel was born in 1937, the same year as the coronation of the teenage King Farouk I. Farouk ate oysters by the hundred in a well-lit palace while his subjects endured the bombardments of World War II in hunger and darkness. Indifferent to the miserable conditions of most

13

Egyptians, the British colonials reveled in the grand bars of Cairo and Alexandria. A tiny number of landowners and foreigners reaped all the profits from the cotton fields and the Suez Canal. Most Egyptians nursed their ambitions and grudges in the shadow of stifling inequality. Unable to share in the riches of the delta farmland, the Kamels moved to Bulaq Aboul Ela, an impromptu neighborhood full of new arrivals on the edge of downtown Cairo. Mohamed Kamel's uneducated father angled his way into a job at the Ministry of Health as the assistant to an X-ray technician, enabling him to send the children to school. Around him, Egypt spun fast. It joined the first of many wars against Israel in 1948. The loss was searing and seminal, but it forged a group of confident officers led by Colonel Gamal Abdel Nasser. They rejected the inequality and corruption that characterized Farouk's reign, in which major decisions were increasingly outsourced to foreign advisers while the royal family's fortune grew. The young officers ousted King Farouk in 1952, and then, a few years later, the British.

These new rulers called themselves the Free Officers; they were military men with efficient minds. At first they were preoccupied not with ideology but with tangible goals, many of them linked with harnessing and redistributing Egypt's wealth to the benefit of people like the Kamels and the rest of the neglected citizenry. They suspended the corrupt parliament and outlawed the bombastic political parties. Nasser favored neither East nor West in the Cold War. He galvanized the region with a call for unity and Arab nationalism, although in his political calculations he always put Egypt first. The Arab world had nothing to be ashamed of, and Nasser proudly feted its riches in rousing speeches. It had vast natural resources and hardworking people. Egypt's economy was equal to Italy's and South Korea's, and no less promising. With self-reliance and common sense, Egypt and Egyptians would take a seat at the world's table. The teenage Mohamed Kamel felt intuitively the promise of this modern age, in which men weren't consigned to till someone else's fields or labor at a day rate. He studied assiduously and joined the Boy Scouts to deepen his self-reliance, even though he was a secular nationalist and most of the other scouts were Islamists.

This new Egypt that Nasser was building was a wondrous thing. On a command from Cairo, irrigation canals extended across the delta. The state laid dams in the Nile River, drew subdivisions in the desert, built factories the sizes of cities. There was no room in this project for critical voices. The Muslim Brotherhood alone had survived Nasser's rise independent of his control. The young dictator instinctively understood that any competition posed a threat, so two years after taking power, he did his best to excise the Brotherhood from Egypt. He executed some of its leaders and jailed the rest. Entire categories of suspicious people were swept up, including the Islamist-infiltrated Boy Scouts. Along with thousands of teenagers, Mohamed Kamel, seventeen years old, was imprisoned without charge. That fall, Basem's father spent thirteen days in jail, even though he had studiously avoided any kind of political activity, Islamist or secular, and he admired everything about Nasser's project and Nasser the man. Before Nasser, such injustices and worse were routine, but Nasser was supposed to be different.

For the Kamel family, the detention marred but did not completely shatter the idyll of the Free Officers' reign. In 1956, Nasser was elected president, making himself a symbol of renewal for Egypt and the entire Arab world, if at a steep price. He wanted his people to believe in themselves as Egyptians and Arabs. Colonial powers had abused Egypt, and rich foreigners had enjoyed unjustifiable privileges. Nasser tapped into this very real source of resentment among the newly independent Egyptian people, stoking xenophobia and fear. He cast a net of suspicion far beyond the British colonial overseers. He confiscated the property of Jews and Greeks, treating them as a potential fifth column, and within a few years in the 1950s these vibrant minority communities all but disappeared from Egypt. Nasser spoke of conspiracies, foreign fingers, hidden hands: tropes that contaminated political thinking in Egypt long after his death.

Still, Colonel Gamal Abdel Nasser had made the Kamels prouder than ever before to be Egyptian. Rationing and privation contributed to new national industries. Egypt was actually building things. It required discipline and, yes, some authoritarianism, to get the right things done. Before Nasser, a tiny group of plutocrats had literally owned the nation, and he stripped away their land and confiscated their money. If they displayed any inkling of dissent, he locked them up too. Things had never been fair for the common man in Egypt, but for the first time, the rigged playing field was tilting in his direction. There was still suffering in the land, but now it was distributed more equitably. The disruption of young Mohamed Kamel's liberty was but a flickering debit on the balance sheet of the shared national endeavor, a cost of doing business in this new Egypt. On the credit side, because Nasser democratized education, a laborer's son like Mohamed Kamel was able to study social work and get a job at Cairo University. In 1965 he wed and bought a house in Imbaba, a pleasant if modest outlying district of Cairo on the western bank of the Nile.

Unfortunately for Mohamed Kamel, the now-paranoid Nasser perceived a rekindled Islamist threat. His name was still on a list, a result of his brief membership in the Boy Scouts. The secret police rapped on his door a few months after he signed his marriage contract. Again Mohamed Kamel was taken to prison, again without any accusation or charge. This secular, conventional man joined thousands of other political prisoners, most of them Islamists. Thirteen days passed, like the first time. Then another thirteen. Incarcerated without trial, Mohamed Kamel's detention stretched into a year and then more. From jail, he watched as Nasser, increasingly erratic and belligerent, readied the nation for a supposedly glorious war against Israel. A better-equipped Israel moved first, and June 1967 was a rout for Palestine, Egypt, and all the Arab nations involved.

Nasser wasn't a cunning genius. Charismatic and charming, the president had fallen in thrall to his own mesmerizing rhetoric. His Arab nationalism hardened into ideology, and his inspiring leadership aged into despotism. His hubris and incompetence catalyzed the war known as the *Naksa*, or setback, the bookend to the 1948 *Nakba*, or catastrophe. The setback brought some small, unintended comforts. In December 1967, thousands of political prisoners were released, among them Mohamed Kamel. He had spent two years, ten days, and seven hours in detention. "I do not like Nasser," he told his wife when he came home, bristling with rage. Uttered only in private to his family, those words were as close as he came to rebellion.

Basem, the Kamels' second child and second son, was born in 1969. His father's job teaching social work was secure and respectable, but the wages penurious: one hundred Egyptian pounds a month. He could make ten times that a short ferry ride away in Saudi Arabia, where the oil money flowed, and the kingdom needed fellow Arabs to staff its new hospitals, universities, and ministries. So he joined the exodus of Egyptian workers to Saudi, moving his family to Jeddah and following Egypt's decline from abroad. Just fifty-two years old, Nasser died unexpectedly of a heart attack in 1970, and despite everything that had happened to him at Nasser's hands, Mohamed Kamel wept. The dictator who twice had thrown him in prison also had ended generations of poverty in his family. "I hate him, but I respect him," Mohamed Kamel said to his wife. "At least he cared about us." He repeated those words many times in the decade that followed, most of which he spent with his family in Saudi Arabia.

Basem Kamel recorded his first memories in Jeddah. As an Egyptian kid in a Saudi public school, the boy was well aware of his status as an outsider and a guest. Mostly he played with the other Egyptian kids. From as far back as he could remember, he had been told that the family's sojourn in Saudi Arabia was temporary, a necessity so that ultimately they could live comfortably back home in Cairo. He didn't think too much about the Saudi system, which offered its citizens no political rights or freedoms but tremendous economic security. At the time, as a child, he didn't think much either of the fact that his father couldn't make ends meet in Egypt but, with the same set of skills, could earn a comfortable living across the border. Working in Saudi Arabia was a blessed opportunity, not a sacrifice; plenty of Egyptians didn't have a marketable trade that could command such a decent salary abroad. Even as a little boy, Basem absorbed his father's work ethic: no drama, no fuss, set your goals, and then do whatever's necessary to achieve them. Basem never had to be reminded to do his homework.

During the decade that the Kamels spent in Saudi Arabia, Egypt whipsawed in the charge of its second charismatic despot in a row. Anwar Sadat unleashed the Islamists against the Nasserists, unreconstructed nationalists who yearned for the days of Nasser; they wrecked each other while Sadat emerged the stronger. The new president spun Egypt forward with a policy called *infitah*, or "opening": opening the Egyptian economy to capitalism, and opening political life, tentatively, to competition. Sadat's turn away from a state-controlled economy created new wealth for the country, but mostly to the benefit of a microscopic new elite. He befriended Washington and made peace with Israel, enraging a citizenry that had been primed with nationalism for generations. He gave the people a tiny glimpse of what it felt like to speak out: one student leader who challenged Sadat at a public debate in the 1970s used the moment as a presidential campaign plank in 2012. Sadat wheeled and wheedled, running circles around Egyptian political bosses who thought they'd found a pliant puppet after the uncontrollable Nasser.

After a decade in Saudi Arabia, the Kamels had eked out enough to return home in 1980 and establish a beachhead. Cairo had metamorphosed while they were away. Millions of peasants without money or opportunity had overwhelmed the city. They occupied all available space, building coffin-shaped apartment blocks on slivers of irrigated cropland around the capital. Cairo's outskirts merged with the center, swallowing the once-isolated suburbs. Along the grand avenues radiating from Tahrir Square, the art deco façades crumbled while the sidewalks, no longer graced with municipal maintenance, buckled and cracked. With nowhere else to channel people, government planners turned to the vast desert plateau southeast of Cairo. The royal family had built its summer dwelling there in the village of Helwan because of the fair breeze. The British had added an observatory. But Cairo was growing too quickly to leave this wondrous escarpment unmolested. Helwan became a factory zone, and around it sprang up military bases, worker hostels, and, finally, subdivisions for the lower middle class. One of these was called Wadi Hof, an inhospitable triangular spit of land between a highway, an army camp, and a factory. It seemed at the end of the earth, but in Wadi Hof's fresh air and open vista, the Kamels saw their chance. They purchased Plot 56 on Street 32 in the empty new subdivision. A fifteen-minute walk led to a train track, and from there one could ride to downtown Cairo in an hour. With unbelievable speed, roads were paved, empty spaces filled in, and families like the Kamels, year by year, added floors to their homes until they reached the new development's zoning limit of five. This was what passed as achieving the middle-class dream. The Kamels planted an olive tree and a grape arbor in the backyard, which was just large enough for a dozen children to play tag.

Baby Basem had been conceived in a time of faltering expectations. By the time he'd learned to walk, his parents had scaled down their hopes. They would build their home in the desert, and they would send their kids to school, but they no longer believed that Cairo would join Paris and London among world capitals, or that their sons were destined to enjoy the same upward mobility their parents had.

In order to maintain his own family in Cairo, Basem's father had to leave them behind in Helwan and depart once more to Saudi Arabia. He worked abroad in Jeddah for a second decade to pay for the house in Wadi Hof. It was a common trajectory for millions of Egyptians of all classes. As he grew older, Basem also mimicked his father's studious avoidance of public life. It was, after all, the harmless and well-intentioned act of joining the Boy Scouts that had turned Mohamed Kamel into a political prisoner; the lesson was that no act was too insignificant to avoid. Basem steered clear of the student union at school.

In 1981 President Anwar Sadat was assassinated live on television during a ceremony commemorating the October 1973 war against Israel. Hosni Mubarak had been standing beside the president. He was immediately sworn in to succeed Sadat, still spattered with his blood. Steady, handsome, and not particularly bright, Mubarak seemed at first the perfect antidote to three decades of larger-than-life dictators. Nasser had sculpted a new Egypt, which Sadat had shoved into the age of capitalism. Perhaps Mubarak, a methodical former air force general, could offer a respite so that Egyptians could catch their breath.

In the Kamel household, the violent transfer of power—the last that Egypt would witness for three decades—was observed mostly by an absence of remark. The television stayed on after the footage of murder and pandemonium, but this was authoritarian state broadcasting, not latter-day cable; instead of news coverage, the government played a loop of patriotic music, and announced a mourning period. "No school for a week!" Basem exulted. No further political implications were discussed.

In the popular imagination, Mubarak was a provincial buffoon, cautious and devoid of ideology. In the quintessential joke, Mubarak's presidential limo reaches an intersection.

"Which way shall we go, sir?" the driver inquires.

"Which way would Nasser have turned?" Mubarak asks.

"Always left," comes the answer.

"And Sadat?"

"Always right."

Mubarak sighs. "Just don't move."

For all his apparent mediocrity, Mubarak shrewdly solidified one-man rule. He waited until he had enough loyalists, and then, in 1987, he fired his only powerful and charismatic rival, defense minister Adel Halim Abu Ghazala. Mubarak won the trust of Washington, and in 1990 he joined the rest of the Arab world in expelling Saddam Hussein from Kuwait. With that, Egypt returned to the region's good graces, despite its peace treaty with Israel. Stability was restored. No waves of prosperity, but no major shocks either. Mubarak's portrait decorated billboards everywhere. His police stood at every corner. The state wanted Egyptians to know they were being watched, not because Mubarak enjoyed the power, but for the people's own good. Basem learned that families could speak carefully at home, in private, about some of the state's failures. Within reason and within limits. They talked about the lack of jobs and the excess of debt, but not about the fact that independent political parties had been illegal since the 1950s. They talked about the fact that certain powerful families close to the regime seemed to grow richer and richer through each period of alleged reform, but not about the glaringly obvious connection of this rotten state of affairs to the one man who now held all the power: President Hosni Mubarak.

The second generation to come of age expecting some practical reward in exchange for the absence of political rights realized that the Arab authoritarian compact was a con. Egyptians had been told they were exchanging freedom for personal prosperity and national power. Instead, they found themselves in a Potemkin republic, crowded into unplanned apartments on narrow lanes, their grown children unemployable in Egypt whether they had a master's degree or merely a strong back.

Basem had grown taller than his father by the time he finished high school, but he had the same even-keeled demeanor. Together they agreed that he should seek admittance to Cairo University's engineering faculty, even though it would require several extra years of courses and part-time work after high school. It was a sound, reasonable plan. Engineers could always find work, in Egypt or, if necessary, abroad.

Basem loved to walk through Wust el-Balad, the historic downtown, scrutinizing the ornate turn-of-the-century buildings of old Cairo. His family's new home, like most of modern Egypt, was an improvised necessity, built with regard only for cost. Aesthetics were a luxury. Cairo and Egypt were awash in the ugly because the ugly was cheap and practical. Nonetheless, Basem nurtured a quiet dream of everyday beauty that was in everyone's reach. He saw glimpses of it in the elegant wall of the Citadel, a bequest of Islamic Cairo's glory age that began in the twelfth century; in the Hanging Church in Coptic Cairo, once a Nile-side village and now a metro stop between Tahrir Square and Wadi Hof; in the pyramids; and in the carefully orchestrated container gardens that families like his cultivated on stoops and balconies barely a few meters square. He resolved to work as an architect, where at least he would control some aspect of his environment, shape some slice of Egypt, and inject a few lines of harmony and joy into the day.

After four years of trying, Basem secured a spot studying architecture. With a prestigious trade and an apartment in the family bloc in Wadi Hof, Basem made an appealing match. He was ready to start a family. Following a common practice for marriage, he proposed to his first cousin Rasha Lutfy. Rasha loved Basem. He made her laugh, and she considered him a promising partner. She accepted immediately. After he graduated from university and finished his obligatory year of military service, the couple signed their marriage contract, moved into the first-floor flat on Street 32, and had their first child.

Basem found a job with a firm that built hotels and other commercial buildings in the Sinai. The pay was good, it offered room for advancement, and it was scarcely a six-hour drive away. He would be able to visit his wife most weekends, a great improvement on his father's lot a few decades earlier, when the only acceptable jobs were across the Red Sea. His dutiful course forward had been charted. With hard work and a little luck, he could expect in two more decades to be able to build another ramshackle apartment building, another hour farther out in the desert, for his own children, and, barring catastrophe, they'd be able to leapfrog up a level and become doctors.

Mindful of his pact with Egypt to keep his head down, Basem worked every waking moment, starting in the early morning and often not stopping until midnight. He loved being in charge of every detail of a building project: the exacting plans, the demands of the client, the unpredictability of the construction. He particularly enjoyed his days on building sites, where he interacted with men of every social class and background. He had a knack for putting people around him at ease, whether it was a Cairo businessman who was financing a project, a Bedouin tribal leader from the Sinai, a fellow engineer, or one of the multitudes of foremen and workers.

After six years of commuting from the Sinai, Basem found a job in Cairo. Each night around ten o'clock he would return home, calling first on his parents on the ground floor and then dining upstairs with his wife, who always waited for him. They had two daughters and a son. Year by year, he saved a bit of money for them and beautified the apartment room by room. At the same time, he numbly watched Mubarak's rule descend into farce, as if it were a televised documentary about some other country.

Across the border, Israel was crushing the al-Aqsa intifada, the popular Palestinian uprising that had started in September 2000. Egyptians marched in solidarity with the Palestinians, and Mubarak's police roamed among them with truncheons and tear gas. University students opposed the simultaneous American invasion of Afghanistan that fall, and hundreds of thousands joined them in the streets. Two years later, America invaded Iraq, more people filled the streets, and more riot police rained down upon them. The regime seemed willing to allow some street protests, so long as no one chanted against Mubarak; it was a kind of steam valve to release societal anger in a harmless way. No one thought about how this activity would affect the popular imagination, expanding the frontier of the possible. People saw what it looked like when they took a street, and they began to understand the elemental math of revolt and regime control. These demonstrations offered a glimpse of how an uprising might look.

Adding to the popular sense of insult and provocation, the president was openly positioning the younger of his two sons, Gamal, to take control of the ruling party. A Westernized banker nicknamed Jimmy, the anointed heir was known to have scooped enormous amounts from the public treasury through kickbacks and corrupt privatizations of state industries. Citizens took pride in the fact that Egypt was a republic, not a Pharaonic dynasty. Yet Hosni Mubarak appeared ready to shred this last vestige of dignity, machinating to bequeath Egypt to his son as if this nation of ninety million, the wellspring of civilization, were just another banana republic. *Tawreeth*, the word for "inheritance," became the call to action for a small rebellion that flourished within the shrinking middle class. Even the military and the secular elite that had most benefited from Mubarak detested the notion of hereditary rule. Since the end of the monarchy, three men had ruled Egypt, and all of them could plausibly claim to have risen on merit from poverty to the top echelons of the military, and all of them could boast passably heroic combat records.

Who was Jimmy Mubarak? A spoiled second son who'd been given the keys to the Egyptian economy, which he had proceeded to loot with his circle of industrialist friends. Egypt's remaining success story was the tiny plutocratic sliver of the population, the only beneficiaries of Jimmy Mubarak's economic reforms. Rich by any country's standards, they had fled the capital into gated communities beyond the Ring Road, their own private Cairos with unwittingly self-parodying names like Mirage City. Everything about Egypt was slowly declining, and it began to feel inevitable that Mubarak would pass the state to Gamal, leaving no possibility for a course correction.

In 2002 an antiwar conference in Cairo brought together for the first time ideologically opposed groups that had traditionally squabbled or ignored one other. Secular and Islamist youth began talking together about Mubarak's inequities, sparking feelings of outrage and solidarity that Mubarak's police state had worked hard to keep from taking root. They were joined by all the major political groups in Egypt: communists, socialists, Arab nationalists, Muslim Brothers, and others. After the conference, they began to attend one another's tiny protests. From the older elite, a small but eloquent group of judges, union leaders, intellectuals, and Brothers spoke openly against Mubarak's plans to hand Egypt to his son. They spawned a vigorous independent judges' movement, as well as a bold citizens' group called Kifaya ("Enough"). Kifaya's founders included Abdelrahman Youssef, the intellectual who later would invite Basem Kamel into the ranks of dissidents, and a who's who of the critical elite.

Basem admired Kifaya but never considered joining. Their protests drew no more than a few hundred people. The regime would send thousands of riot police to surround them, and the effect was smothering. Passersby couldn't even see the protesters behind the phalanx of black-clad Central Security Forces and their Plexiglas shields. For good measure, the Security Forces would beat the protesters without provocation, chasing them away with sticks, often tearing the clothes off the women and groping them. The official Kifaya organization showed both the promise and the limitations of the Egyptian people's opposition. Kifaya's members bravely challenged the increasingly despotic regime, shaming Mubarak and his son by name. But they could agree on only one thing: Mubarak was evil. No common vision for the future united them. At the time, it seemed that Kifaya's defiant message wasn't reaching many Egyptians. The effort seemed marginal and ineffectual. But the activists had shattered taboos and glimpsed a possibility of their own power. They were learning tactics and making connections.

Under American pressure, Mubarak allowed challengers in the 2005 presidential election. A preening lawyer and member of parliament named Ayman Nour dared to run, winning 8 percent of the vote. For his effrontery, Nour was thrown in prison on fabricated charges of forging signatures on his original campaign petitions. Harried and bruised, the Kifaya and judges' movements seemed to fade. The streets were quiet again. But something major had shifted. Although only a tiny number of activists had taken part in the events of 2005 and 2006, a major barrier had fallen. Islamist and secular activists had become friends, and had stood together against police. When thousands of Muslim Brothers were detained in those two years, secular lawyers defended them. Connections were formed between groups such as the Revolutionary Socialists and the left-wing Youth Movement for Justice and Freedom, or the liberal Democratic Front and the Muslim Brotherhood. Friendships followed. They all struggled with the question of how to secure daily bread for the overwhelming majority of Egyptians who lived week to week. They shared a growing concern over the erosion of liberties in a republic whose president had invoked a state of emergency and suspended the constitution continuously since 1967. Under perpetual military rule with emergency power, the state could detain people without charge and try civilians before military tribunals. Heavy policing limited the demonstrations, but the relationships among the protesters deepened.

On April 6, 2008, textile workers in the gargantuan factory complex in the city of Mahalla spearheaded a national strike. The police shut it down with the usual truncheons and gas. This time around, however, the strikers were politicized and streetwise, articulate about their demands, and also physically tough in battles with the police. They won public sympathy, and the state suppression was videotaped and shared online.

Egypt was controlled through a network of military and security services with anonymous leaders and black budgets. Scholars coined the term "the deep state" to describe the security leviathan that had grown unabated through three regimes. Regular Egyptians adopted it, referring sometimes with disdain and other times with pride to the deep state, an apparatus that was far more powerful than any single leader or even any single police agency or military branch. The deep state depended on America's generous underwriting. Washington sent about $2 billion a year to Cairo, most of it for the Egyptian army. The payment grew out of the first peace talks between Egypt and Israel in the 1970s. Equally important to the regime was America's political backing. President George Bush's push for democracy had become an irritant. It was US pressure that had forced Mubarak to entertain a challenger in the 2005 presidential race, and again a year later, to allow a modicum of fairness in the parliamentary elections. As a result, the Muslim Brotherhood won 88 seats.

It might seem like a token amount of the 444 elected representatives, but in the Egyptian context, it was an earthquake. The Brothers would have won an even greater share of parliament if the regime hadn't manipulated the second and third rounds of the voting.

Mubarak's long game was running the way he wanted. Other Arab dictators ran far deadlier states. In places such as Syria and Libya, opposition figures routinely disappeared for years or decades in regime dungeons. Critics were assassinated, their relatives suddenly stripped of their businesses. Mubarak's style was far more effective and, in a way, more subtle. His aim was to eliminate any plausible centrist alternative that stood a chance of capturing widespread sympathy. He didn't want reasonable opponents who could theoretically challenge him by winning over the plutocrats, military men, and police officials who undergirded his regime. But he saw value in keeping some extremists around so that Egyptians would remember that they could have it far worse than Mubarak. A group like Kifaya was hemmed in from the start, and many of the reformist judges were pressed into exile. The Brotherhood, on the other hand, served a purpose as the regime's foil. Known Brotherhood leaders ran for parliament as independents. The Brotherhood was legally banned, but it was tolerated and allowed to function just enough that Mubarak could hold up its leaders as bogeymen: *"Après moi le déluge,"* either this regime or a band of bearded fanatics.

Affronts piled up, great and small. The regime's premier enforcement arm, the secretive and omnipresent State Security Investigations, grew ever less restrained. The clicks of cheap surveillance were audible on phone calls. Shortages and unemployment exacerbated social tensions. Attacks against the Christian minority increased steadily, and the government never seemed to find those responsible. The Coptic Church, an Eastern Orthodox sect, offered the only organized leadership for Egypt's Christians. It represented about 10 percent of the population, but had little leverage and most always deferred to the government. Private companies had to stack their boards with members chosen by State Security. The upper echelons of the public sector were heavy with men whose only qualification was that they were retired generals. Even in newsrooms, clinics, soup kitchens, and other places ostensibly independent from the state, State Security agents paid visits and issued commands.

Mubarak had grown brittle and intolerant, an impregnable dictator who couldn't bear the slightest criticism. Still, he had more nuance than his peers in the Arab-presidents-for-life club. Unlike Syria's al-Assad clan, Iraq's Saddam Hussein, and Libya's Mu'ammar al-Qaddhafi, Mubarak actually desired some trappings of a democratic society. He allowed a far more vigorous free press than any of the other dictators in the region, and the approved opposition was permitted to criticize the government so long as it avoided the president himself. Mubarak meant to keep his citizens pliant, but they grew accustomed to certain limited freedoms. When they crossed lines, however, the punishment struck decisively, as when popular newspaper editor Ibrahim Eissa wrote about the rumors that Mubarak had a serious illness and promptly found himself sentenced to prison. Eventually the journalist's connections won him a pardon, but he said his sentence had "opened the gates of hell for the Egyptian press."

This corrosive cocktail had eroded the patience of Egyptians. Policemen did nothing to unsnarl the quotidian traffic jams but constantly thrust their hands forward for bribes. Bosses connected to the ruling party sent their employees to pay their personal bills. One day a neighbor tried to sexually assault Basem Kamel's seven-year-old niece. When Basem and his brother went to the police, the officer rudely propped his bare feet on his desk, mumbling as he took the report. Eventually Basem's family arrested the perpetrator themselves and delivered him to the authorities. Thus was justice managed in Mubarak's Egypt. The government didn't serve the people; the people served the government. These depredations had been barely tolerable when the country's standard of living had actually been improving, in the 1950s and 1960s. Now the quality of life kept worsening, while the abuse remained constant.

Basem followed it all from a remove on foreign satellite networks. He digested the dissent, silently applauding it but all the while convinced of its noble futility. A mundane event jolted Basem from his personal slumber, readying him for the political awakening to come. For a decade, Basem had worked ceaselessly, forgoing weekends and holidays with his children to push forward the family architecture business he had established. Then, in 2008, a relative died and Basem skipped work to go to the funeral. It was the first day he could remember spending without his phone. The business survived. Basem realized that he could spend time for pleasure. He took his children to the Citadel and his wife to the opera. He looked at the paintings in the Cairo Museum of Art and the antiquities at the Egyptian Museum. These diversions opened him to other thoughts he had avoided.

It was in this receptive state that he had clicked on the dissident Facebook group. Only when he joined the welcoming committee for Mohamed ElBaradei did Basem dare to believe that things could change not merely in his own life but also for all of Egypt. And he began to meet other Egyptian men and women, a small but growing phalanx of dedicated dreamers who had always believed it, or who, like Basem, were now ready to surrender to idealism. They were poor and rich, educated and self-taught, brawny and effete, secular and religious. They were the youth of the revolution (even though many, like Basem, verged on middle age), and in each setback, they discovered another incentive to act.

ElBaradei returned to Egypt after his long career abroad, and he welcomed the volunteers who had conjured up an organization for him. Basem and the others became ElBaradei's aides, raising a professional-class campaign out of a vacuum. One spring day in 2010, Basem came home long after midnight. He had been with ElBaradei. Basem's father, convinced that his son had been arrested, grew agitated and collapsed. At the hospital, the doctors said it was a stroke.

"No more politics," Basem's mother pleaded.

"We won't discuss it anymore," Basem said with a reassuring smile. He didn't plan to stop, but he no longer would tell his parents what he was doing. A few months later, Basem went missing again on a weekend.

"Where is your brother?" his father demanded as the family sat in front of the television.

"At work," his youngest brother said. Just then the newscast showed a group of activists escorting ElBaradei through the provincial city of Fayoum. At the candidate's side was Basem. Mohamed Kamel, foggy since his stroke, noticed nothing. But Basem's mother did. She leaned in close to her youngest son.

"Liar," she hissed.

In the summer of 2010, police in Alexandria beat a young man named Khaled Said to death; the kind of brutal act that had become routine long ago. There were unsubstantiated claims that he had posted an online video documenting police brutality, but later reports suggested that Khaled Said was an apolitical homebody who hung out with stoners and liked to chat online. Plenty of witnesses saw the two cops batter Khaled Said at the internet café near his apartment, and then later in the street. He might have been punished for refusing to snitch on local drug dealers. In any case, such beatings were commonplace in Egypt, although they normally didn't end with murder. The police expected to get away with it. With straight faces, they claimed that Khaled Said had choked to death trying to conceal contraband marijuana in his mouth. There had been an obscene parade of victims like him, decade after decade. But his death struck a chord because he was so manifestly neither a criminal nor a political dissident. He posed no conceivable threat. He was a middle-class boy trying to keep his head down, and that still hadn't been enough. The regime's message turned out to be that nobody was safe, even those who kept their mouths shut and followed the popular adage to avoid attention and "walk by the wall." Egypt's middle-class youth identified overwhelmingly with Khaled Said.

The police's actions were normal for Mubarak's Egypt, but this time the response was not. A Facebook page called We Are All Khaled Said drew hundreds of thousands of members. Egyptians who had avoided politics adopted the cause, joining the veterans from Kifaya, ElBaradei's campaign, the Muslim Brotherhood youth organization, and the other small but dedicated activist groups. Weekly vigils began. The Facebook page became an instant organizing tool, but the government seemed oblivious. Mohamed ElBaradei initiated a petition campaign with the almost meek demand that Mubarak's regime follow its own laws in the next election. Incredibly, a million people signed, making their names and identity numbers public; this sort of act typically led to detention. Even more surprising, the Muslim Brotherhood joined ElBaradei's effort, collecting millions more signatures. Something was shifting. People had truly had enough and were willing to take new risks in order to show it. Basem trained volunteers to talk people into signing the petition, and went out asking himself. He was willing to sacrifice his livelihood, the cohesion of his family, and even his father's health: all the things he most valued. He was not alone. What was the point of preserving order at home and across the nation if its individual human foundations were crumbling?

Then parliamentary elections were held in the fall of 2010. The tired and ineffectual secular opposition boycotted them, invoking a storied tradition. In modern Arab history, weaker parties had often used boycotts to level the playing field, scuttling agreements, elections, regional summits, and peace talks by staying away. But it was a weapon of last resort that worked only when used sparingly, when the group doing the boycotting had enough power to confer or deny legitimacy to the more powerful.

The Muslim Brotherhood decided to participate in the elections. The regime didn't even bother to disguise its fraud, simply locking voters out of polling stations in Brotherhood areas and awarding seats to regime loyalists. The government's caprice and violence in the parliamentary elections energized Basem and his new friends. They had bigger plans than elections and new rules. They thought they could force Mubarak to fire his despised interior minister Habib el-Adly, the man in charge of the riot police and state spies who watched and constrained the people's every move. Tunisians had unexpectedly revolted in December, putting a seasoned dictator on the run and jolting the entire Arab world. National Police Day was coming up on January 25, 2011, mere weeks after Tunisia's revolution. The youth would take to the streets, circumventing police blocks, and demand the interior minister's resignation on his own day of celebration. It was at one of these planning meetings, at the house of another activist's mother, that Basem Kamel met Moaz Abdelkarim, a young Muslim Brother who had cast his lot with this new wave of creative nationalist agitators.

Moaz was cut from different cloth than Basem. His family came from a noble pedigree of Islamists. Religion and politics were their oxygen. He had grown up around men and women who tried to live the words of the

Prophet Muhammad in their daily life, through Koranic study, charity work, and political resistance against a regime that never stopped tracking and persecuting them. Their faith was profoundly humanistic and also political. In his speaking, Moaz picked up the lulling cadences of the imams who shaped his prodigious sense of moral responsibility. On his own, he sharpened a borderline-sacrilegious sense of humor. Even as a teenager, Moaz had a potbelly and dressed like an old man, in the fashion of the Brotherhood: pleated pants, plaid shirts, furry sweaters. His hair arched skyward in a pomaded bouffant, and most of the time he wore a light beard. He ambled rather than walked, like someone with arthritic hips. When he laughed, which was often, he revealed a front tooth broken in half. As the years went by, he never found time to have it fixed, even though he could afford it. He was always late, even for meetings that he requested. Sometimes Moaz would phone a day or two after failing to show up to ask a friend if he was still waiting. Unless there was a street battle, Moaz seemed incapable of rushing. He would stop to tousle the hair of the street kids and tell them jokes. He had a slight streak of vanity too. His eyeglasses were the latest model Ray-Bans, and he posted pictures of his new shoes on Facebook. For all his jocular and bumbling exterior, however, Moaz was profoundly serious about his faith and his democratic principles.

Moaz's grandfather had agitated in the 1920s alongside Hassan al-Banna, the founder of the Society of the Muslim Brothers; three generations of his lineage had claimed allegiance to the secretive religious revolutionary group. The Abdelkarims' story was intertwined with Egypt's trajectory, like that of the Kamel family. But just as the Kamels were embedded in the Arab Republic of Egypt's proud tradition of secular nationalism, Moaz's family sprung from an equally proud tradition of radical religious dissidence. In modern times, Egypt has been the cradle of Arab political thought, giving the world Arab nationalism, the Muslim Brotherhood, and, later on, the extremist variant of Sunni fundamentalism known as *takfiri* jihad and the dictatorial innovation of the deep state. Moaz's family was part of the Islamist nucleus. The original Brothers worked in the Suez Canal city of Ismailia. The Canal Zone was the most strategic part of Egypt. It was a security priority for the British colonizers, but it also housed the country's best-paid, most urbanized workers because of the canal facilities. The British maltreatment of Egyptians intersected with a population that was especially well educated and organized, ripe conditions for the emerging Brotherhood. The austere religious activists who gathered under the Muslim Brotherhood banner in the 1920s and 1930s wanted to expel the British and vanquish the secular Egyptians who served the colonials. The Brothers also proselytized for their conservative religious views: they encouraged more separation of the genders, more women wearing head scarves in a country that was fast abandoning the tradition, and Koranic study as the center of everyone's education.

The founding Brothers made education their first battleground, correctly figuring that they could change society by changing children's minds. They also opened doors by spreading their message through charity. Islamic activists delivered food to the poor and paid school fees. Their clients in turn were receptive to the Brotherhood's political message, which at its simplest promised that a return to God and the injunctions of the Koran would be good for families and good for Egypt. Moaz's grandfather Hassan Mokhtar Hilal was a journalist and a typesetter, but in the years before World War II his main political activity was painting Brotherhood slogans on walls. A popular one declared: "God helps those who help themselves."

The Brotherhood, from its early years, vacillated between an almost bourgeois mission of communal self-improvement and a radical strain of violence. Some of its members, like Moaz's grandfather, engaged in intellectual polemics. Others concentrated on more physical action, training secret militias and assassination cells. In Canal Zone villages, Brotherhood vigilantes were known to beat collaborators and enemies. In 1948 the group's "secret apparatus" killed Egypt's prime minister. The promise of violence always hovered close to its religious rhetoric, and its insistence on an Islamic way of life left little room for the majority of Egyptians, who were Christian, agnostic, or more secular Muslims. The Kamels, for instance, were Muslims through and through; they apologized to no one for their piety, but their personal faith supported a belief in a secular, civil state as passionate as the Brothers' commitment to an exclusionary state of God.

When Gamal Abdel Nasser took over Egypt and exiled the king in

1952, he experimented with the Muslim Brotherhood as an ally. He gave the Brothers freedom to organize, and considered including them in his government. But Nasser's Free Officers and the Muslim Brotherhood were destined to clash. Both movements were authoritarian, and both claimed exclusive province over the truth. In 1953, thousands of Brothers protested outside the presidential palace. One of their leaders met in the palace with Nasser and agreed to give the president time to meet the Brotherhood's demands. He stepped out of the palace, raised one hand, and the crowd fell silent. "Let's go," he said, and the crowd dispersed instantly. In the telling most frequently repeated by members of the Muslim Brotherhood, Nasser was far more discomfited by the show of disciplined obedience than he had been by the protest.

Within months, he began to round up Muslim Brothers. A gunman tried to assassinate Nasser during a speech; the plot was pinned on the Brotherhood, and the group was banned, its leaders thrown in prison. It was never clear whether the Brothers had tried to kill Nasser or whether the president had staged the attempt to boost his own popularity and create a pretext to sideline the Brotherhood. Either way, Nasser ended open politics for a generation. Tens of thousands of Egyptians were detained, many of them Brotherhood sympathizers and many of them incidental victims, like Basem Kamel's father. Moaz's grandfather continued to write for Muslim Brotherhood newspapers until the risk grew too great and he fled Egypt, eventually settling in Kuwait in 1964. Much of the Muslim Brotherhood elite in that era took refuge in the Gulf, where they prospered economically and were allowed to organize against Nasser so long as they didn't challenge the local monarchs.

Israel's total victory over the Arab armies in 1967 discredited politicians and military leaders, prompting a region-wide depression and then introspection. Faith flourished in the aftermath. A religious awakening spread. The language of religion flowed into the ideological void left by the raw failure of Arab nationalism, and Muslim Brothers across the Arab world established themselves not only as credible community activists in their clinics and engineering offices but also as exponents of the next big idea. Islam became the new public square. Nasser's successor, Anwar Sadat, encouraged the Brotherhood as a counterweight to Nasser loyalists.

Moaz's grandfather returned to Egypt from his exile in 1974 with his daughter Mona Hassan Mokhtar Hilal. He had done well there writing for a Brotherhood magazine called *al-Mujtama* (*The Community*). He owned a villa in Imbaba, the same poor outlying neighborhood where the Kamel family had lived in the 1960s. A decade had ruined the place. It was barely livable, congested with with new arrivals. The Islamist elite was more upwardly mobile than its Arab nationalist counterparts. While the Kamel family had to flee Imbaba for a remote satellite community in the desert, Moaz's family was able to leap up several rungs on the status ladder. Moaz's grandfather built a spacious apartment building in central Cairo, in the elite upper-middle-class neighborhood of Mohandiseen, the Engineer's Quarter. Mohandiseen hugged the Nile, a quick drive to downtown just across the river. The neighborhood was laid out carefully with curlicue streets and tree-filled medians. His daughter finished university, worked briefly as an Arabic teacher, and then met a diligent young math teacher and Brother named Abdelkarim Abdelfattah Mohammed. The families quickly agreed on the match. Moaz's parents married in 1979. Both of them had grown up in Brotherhood families, and the secret society bound them as much as their faith. They moved immediately to Saudi Arabia, not out of economic desperation but as a financial investment, so that they could return to Egypt better equipped to secure their children's livelihoods.

Back in Egypt, things took a turn for the worse. For forty years, the Arab states had agreed that no country would make a separate peace with Israel; their only leverage came from standing together with the Palestinians. Sadat broke that understanding, and signed the Camp David Accords with Israel in 1978. President Jimmy Carter brokered the deal, which brought Egypt solidly into the fold as an American ally. From the moment he signed the agreement on the White House lawn, Sadat was marked. The Islamists that the president had let loose now turned against him. Alumni of one of the Brotherhood's more virulent strains plotted to kill the president, and in 1981 they succeeded. The crowded defendants' cage at the trial of Sadat's assassins contained the radicals who would go on to establish al-Qaeda and Islamic Jihad. Again, Islamists of all sorts were rounded up, jailed, and tortured. Moaz's grandfather was detained briefly. Under Sadat, the Brotherhood had been tolerated but never legalized, and Mubarak instructed his police to enforce the ban with renewed vigor. Once again the Islamist elite dispersed into exile, where it thrived in business and proselytization. The Brotherhood refined its message and expanded its web of business ventures.

Members of the Brotherhood honed a particular rhetorical style during their long discussions in the diaspora and inside Egyptian prisons. They nursed grudges against the Egyptian government and polished their idea of a more perfect Muslim society, led toward grace and vitality by a pious, driven, wheeling-and-dealing vanguard. They were free among themselves to argue about the responsibilities of a Muslim, about the kind of society they should build, about the Brotherhood's policies. No matter how spirited the arguments, however, once the group reached a decision, everyone had to support it unanimously. Every year after the hajj to Mecca, Muslim Brothers who had made their annual pilgrimage to the birthplace of Islam would then gather in nearby Jeddah and debate strategy. It was like a seasonal senate for the *umma*, the community of the faithful. Moaz's father, who taught math at university in Jeddah, met daily with his *usra*, or Brotherhood family. At the individual level, every member of the Brotherhood had an *usra* and a supervisor. The "family" studied Koran together, socialized, and acted as a support group. If a Brother needed help, he could turn to his *usra* as easily as to his blood relatives.

In 1984, in a momentous shift, the Muslim Brotherhood in Egypt decided to engage in democratic politics by running candidates for parliament for the first time. That same year, Moaz was born. The third of six siblings, he soon learned to depend on his own *usra*. When Moaz was still learning to read as a child in Jeddah, he would meet the children of other Muslim Brothers at the mosque after school. They played together and absorbed the stories of the Koran, building the bonds and values that were expected to define a Brother for life.

The Egypt to which Moaz's family returned in 1992 was at war. Fringe radicals from the Gamaa Islamiya, or Islamic Group, were fighting a full insurgency against Mubarak's "infidel" government. The Gamaa had tried to assassinate the interior minister (the immediate predecessor of the hated, but long-serving, Habib el-Adly) and routinely attacked government officials. In 1995 the group tried to kill Mubarak himself during a state visit to Addis Ababa, Ethiopia. These Islamists were the political descendants of Sadat's killers; most of them had passed through the Muslim Brotherhood but had since repudiated it as too moderate. The old neighborhood where the grandfathers of Moaz and Basem both had owned houses had now declared itself "the Islamic Republic of Imbaba," and fighters attacked any security that tried to enter.

Hosni Mubarak responded with force and guile. The military had always been dominant, but now the Egyptian president lavished resources on the police. State Security sent thousands of agents to infiltrate every single organization in the country, from prayer circles, to unions, to community groups that taught literacy. The state added hundreds of thousands of citizens to its payroll as informants. Every single residential doorman had to report to State Security about the comings and goings in his building. In every café, a state agent listened for subversion. Phone lines were tapped, and the apartments of Muslim Brothers were bugged. When a group of Brothers reserved a ballroom for an *itfar* meal to break the Ramadan fast, they found the booking mysteriously cancelled after State Security had visited the hotel.

Initially, many Egyptians welcomed the policing-on-steroids. The Islamic insurgency came to be seen as nihilistic even by Islamist sympathizers. It was poison for the tourism industry, especially after gunmen rampaged through the Temple of Hatshepsut in Luxor in 1997, killing sixty-two foreign tourists and Egyptians. Mubarak's police jailed radicals and dissidents of all stripes. As a warning to others, they sodomized detainees with bottles. Beatings and electric shock were a routine part of interrogation. The Islamist insurgency underscored Mubarak's greatest selling point: stability. Nobody wanted to live in a war-torn Egypt, and Mubarak promised through his longevity and his security forces to keep the country safe. Given a glimpse of the alternative by the jihadis in Imbaba, many Egyptians preferred the president's deal. By 1998, the insurgency was over, and Mubarak enjoyed a rare and final moment of popularity. Had he allowed fair and competitive elections at that point, he probably would have won. But he concluded that his state had been too lax, and he would never again permit an opening that might allow another challenge to his rule. He kept his new police force in place to balance out the military. That way, no single security branch could mount a coup.

Back home in Cairo, Moaz immersed himself in an Egypt apart: Brotherhood Egypt. He went to private Islamic schools run by members of the group. They were segregated by gender and were ideologically homogenous: only Brothers and fellow travelers sent their children. These young Brothers learned to see themselves as an elect group empowered by their morality, their community works, their political program, and the inviolable links connecting their *usra* to the *umma*; each Brotherhood "family" of a half dozen was connected in an unbreakable chain to the Islamic community, represented by an international confederation of Brothers under the supreme guide's ultimate authority.

The Brotherhood didn't have its own high schools, however, so as teenagers, Moaz and his confederates began their encounters with the rest of Egypt. Some found the world outside the Brotherhood bewildering or offensive; Moaz found it intoxicating. He loved arguing, persuading outsiders of the Brotherhood's views rather than discoursing comfortably with the converted. He found the presence of females pleasant rather than threatening. The world at large was a bigger stage than the Brotherhood. As a sixteen-year-old in a gargantuan public high school with nearly eight thousand students, Moaz discovered a knack for leadership and activism. He established a Muslim Brotherhood student group, which prayed together at lunchtime. He was elected vice president of the school-wide student union. It was the year 2000, and Palestinians had begun the second intifada. Anti-Israel sentiment often served as a proxy for opposition to Mubarak, who, after all, was one of the Israeli government's most important allies. Moaz organized solidarity teach-ins about the Palestinian cause. He shared copies of Muslim Brotherhood magazines smuggled into Egypt from the Gulf. This was exactly the sort of personal political initiative that Mubarak's regime was committed to rooting out.

The school principal stopped Moaz one day. "One of our friends wants to ask you some questions," he said.

"Who is our friend?" Moaz asked, perplexed.

"Come," the principal said.

They sat in his office, where a man named Khaled joined them. He was an intelligence officer from State Security Investigations, known colloquially as State Security or, in Arabic, Amn al-Dawla. The agency's local office shared a wall with the school. It was the most important arm of the deep state for policing Egyptians.

"I want to ask you," the smiling officer said, "who among you prays the most?"

The Brotherhood had coached Moaz for such an eventuality; he was to answer only "No" and "I don't know." With his natural affability, Moaz relaxed and threw himself with pleasure into the interrogation.

"I don't know," Moaz said.

"Why do you support the Palestinians?"

"Because we should participate in their struggle."

"What is your message to the youth?"

"We say they should improve themselves," Moaz replied. "They should behave with ethics. They should not harass girls from the nearby school."

The intelligence officer turned knowingly to the principal. "This is the thinking of the Muslim Brotherhood," he said. Then he turned back to Moaz. "What do you think of life in Egypt?"

"I don't know."

"Where is your father?"

"Saudi Arabia."

The State Security officer gave Moaz his phone number and instructed him to come by his office for tea.

"I will come when I have time," Moaz said, but he never did.

The small number of Egyptians who chose to pique the regime's interest, such as Moaz and his fellow Brothers, came to know well the intelligence officers assigned to them. They would refer to each of them as "my security guy." Official pressure only emboldened Moaz; he was acting not only on his own conviction and with the natural contrarian spirit of a teenager, but also he was doing the bidding of the grand organization of which he was part. He was doing God's work and Egypt's too. It was a righteous mix. He was every bit as politicized as Basem Kamel was muzzled. By the time the al-Aqsa intifada in Palestine was in full swing in late 2000, Moaz had been elected president of the student union. He assembled a display with photographs from his grandfather's magazine (the era of YouTube and Photoshop was still a few years away), which he laminated so it would be harder for officials to tear them up. He brought a Muslim Brother and a sheikh from Al-Azhar University, the most eminent institution of Sunni Islamic learning in the region, to address the student body. Moaz set an Israeli flag on fire in the school hallway. With his friends, he staged a play about an Islamic leader of the resistance against French colonialists a century earlier.

When Moaz's father returned from Saudi Arabia for a visit, security officers seized his passport at the airport. They summoned him for a not-so-friendly conversation about Moaz. "Tell him to quit the student union," they said. An eighteen-year-old's schoolyard protests were a matter of the highest concern for Mubarak's State Security. Moaz and his father met with the high school's head teacher, who laid out the options and then turned to Moaz.

"Choose," the teacher said.

"I came all the way from abroad, and I tell you to be responsible!" Moaz's father shouted.

"I made my choice because I think it is right," Moaz said, not budging.

"It is Moaz's choice," the teacher said.

Moaz's father kept trying to persuade him to quit the student union, but after the showdown at the school, he realized he couldn't force his son.

In the spring of his senior year, Moaz tasted tear gas and blood for the first time at a Cairo University protest in solidarity with the Palestinian intifada. He was clubbed by a police conscript and got stitches in his lip. His father wanted Moaz to concentrate on his education and told him to enroll in medical school or at least the hard sciences. Moaz wanted to study law, journalism, or political science.

"Politics leads to prison, and the media is *haram*," sinful, his father said. Moaz flunked all his science classes and tried to transfer to law school. Eventually father and son reached a compromise: Moaz enrolled in a private school of pharmacy. He was invited onto a state television program meant to fan anger about the American invasion of Afghanistan. "We should ask questions about life in our own country, not about the war in Afghanistan," Moaz said. He was ordered off the set immediately. Since the program was taped, the subversive comments made it only as far as his expanding State Security file.

He didn't reserve his defiance only for the regime. Moaz impishly mocked the Brotherhood's secretive paramilitary style. At one retreat for teenage members, a senior leader delivered a pointed lesson about obedience. After a long morning of lectures, he led his charges to a table of food. Everyone began to eat. Sternly, he stopped them. "Did I say the blessing?" he asked. "Did I give you permission to eat?" Sheepishly the young Brothers apologized.

"Now, all of you, to the pool, in your clothes!" the leader commanded. It was a cold day, and the pool was outside. All the young Brothers jumped in the water except for Moaz.

"Why are you dry?" the incredulous supervisor demanded.

"You only specified that we go 'to' the pool, which I did," Moaz said with his infectious smile. "You did not say 'in' the pool." Somehow, his reflexive subversion didn't get him tossed from the Brotherhood as he rose up its ranks.

As he made his way through pharmacy school, politics consumed far more of Moaz's attention than his studies did. He joined all the antiwar protests and took part in the antiwar conferences too. When his Brotherhood supervisor allowed it, he would march and fight the police, and sit for hours with the energetic youth activists from outside the Brotherhood. He assisted the presidential campaign of Ayman Nour. With other Brotherhood youth, he stood in solidarity protests with Kifaya.

In 2005 Moaz worked for three parliamentary candidates, including the inflammatory Salafi preacher Hazem Salah Abou Ismail, who lived a few blocks from Moaz. It struck Moaz as odd for the Brotherhood to back a cleric with such extreme views. Sheikh Hazem had made his name filing lawsuits against Egyptians he considered sacrilegious or unpatriotic, and he was forever touting esoteric conspiracies, such as his claim that the American manufacturer of the soft drink Pepsi was behind a Zionist plot, with the name *Pepsi* an acronym for "Pay every penny to save Israel." Moaz began to wonder whether his Brotherhood leaders were as reasonable as they claimed.

At the end of 2005, the most important organizers in the Brotherhood were arrested, including Khairat el-Shater, the millionaire fixer who effectively ran the organization, and Mohamed Morsi, an internal enforcer. A few thousand rank-and-file members were detained as well, and many of them were tortured and released. The whole operation seemed like a calculated oiling of the machinery, a way for State Security to signal to the Brotherhood just how much latitude it had. In the wake of the arrests, Moaz's supervisor told him to keep a low profile, but he ignored the instruction. He continued organizing with various leftists and Islamists. He was put on probation and ordered not to speak publicly as a Brother for a year. Moaz considered the penalty a suitable recognition of his zeal.

The supreme guide was allowed an office in a smelly first-floor walkup in a middle-class neighborhood on the Nile island of Manial. Visiting journalists and dignitaries had to run a gamut of State Security agents, ostentatiously lounging on plastic chairs out front, and then clamber over a pile of shoes on the landing. The leadership conferred around one end of a desk while the spokesman granted interviews a few feet away. Staffers noiselessly went about their work in the same room. The government made it clear that the Brotherhood operated at the state's pleasure. The Brotherhood's predicament aptly captured Mubarak's governing style: there was to be just enough freedom so that the people didn't rebel, and never enough so that they would be able to do so if they chose. Since 1981, Mubarak had told his people they were incapable of controlling themselves. They needed him to keep the peace. Millions had believed, and now they lived in an overcrowded, underfunded republic of perhaps ninety million people, with no discernible threat to the regime and yet no discernible dividend for such a massive communal sacrifice.

Moaz worked in a pharmacy and, during his days off, for the Brotherhood's Supreme Guidance Bureau in Manial. His primary task was to connect with other youth groups, which often meant long hours drinking soda pop in the cafés of Boursa, a pedestrian district behind the stock exchange. In 2008 State Security ransacked Moaz's family home at 34 Sudan Street in Mohandiseen, scattering clothes and papers all over the floor. Moaz's mother was apoplectic over the invasion of privacy. The family owned the entire six-story building, and Moaz agreed to move to an independent apartment so that his political work wouldn't incriminate the rest of his family.

In December 2008, Israel launched a three-week attack on Gaza known as Operation Cast Lead. On the tenth of Ramadan, at the beginning of September 2009, Moaz traveled to Gaza in a caravan meant to demonstrate solidarity. He couldn't escape the parallels between Palestinian life under occupation and Egyptian life under Mubarak, and even his own subjugation as a Muslim Brother to the supreme guide. "We cannot serve the organization at the expense of the organization's principles," Moaz told one of his traveling companions, a young Brotherhood webmaster named Abdelrahman Ayyash. This belief would come to define them both. Moaz lost count of the number of times he was detained. The Muslim Brotherhood leadership could often muster a quorum in Egypt's infamous Tora Prison, where all the most notorious criminals and political detainees served their time. Still, while the Brotherhood became practiced at resistance, the vast majority of Egyptians remained silent and uninvolved.

The Brotherhood mirrored the authoritarian regime that it hoped one day to replace. Mubarak squashed the faintest hint of legitimate challenge from the secular space, while the Brotherhood hewed to the limits established for it. Eventually, the Supreme Guidance Bureau believed it would rule Egypt. Time and God were on its side. Anticipating the day when it would be legalized, the Brotherhood published a draft political platform in 2007, with several revisions in the years that followed. It offered a glimpse of how the Brotherhood would govern if it had untrammeled power. It would prohibit women and Christians from holding the Egyptian presidency, and it would empower Muslim clerics to vet laws. These views terrified secular Egyptians and irritated young Brotherhood members, including Moaz. "I have a religion," he liked to say. "But a state cannot have a religion any more than a chair can have a religion."

Meanwhile, Mubarak, who turned eighty in 2008, disappeared for months at a time while undergoing medical treatment abroad, and was rumored to suffer from cancer. Generals expressed concern that Gamal would succeed his father in the presidency; they didn't like this young businessman who had surrounded himself with corrupt magnates and, moreover, never had served as a military officer. Interior minister Habib el-Adly controlled the police and State Security, and was beginning to be perceived as the most powerful man in Egypt. Fragmentation among the elite intimated a wider crack-up to come.

Younger Brothers like Moaz regarded the Brotherhood's wait-and-see pose with distaste. When workers organized the famous Mahalla strike of April 6, 2008, they wanted to join, but the Brotherhood leaders refused. "Those people are struggling for our rights," Moaz declared. "We should join them." Like the secular youth, the young Brothers were beginning to grasp the possibility that the regime was not invincible; that they could have a say in their nation's fate. Moaz was arrested again in March 2010 and was severely beaten. Afterward, he wrote a detailed account on his blog, which was titled "I Love the Brotherhood, O State Security!" He advised detainees to keep careful records of their interrogations and imprisonments. "We can take our rights," he wrote. "Once there is a revolution, all these officers will be the ones who go to prison." Each tremor in 2010 contributed to a cascade: ElBaradei's petition, the murder of Khaled Said, the violent rebuff of striking workers. Political energy was also flowing out of the soccer fan clubs known as "ultras." Like their counterparts around the soccer-loving world, the ultras often sought to rumble with police after matches. ElBaradei's activists and the Brothers presented millions of signatures from people willing to publish their dissent and risk official retaliation. But the regime ignored them completely.

Khaled Said's killing provided the catalyst to unify. When the news spread that police had publicly murdered this apolitical computer gamer, outraged Egyptians gathered in front of the Interior Ministry. No one organized the protest, and it drew people from across the spectrum. Basem once again defied his family, coming down with friends from ElBaradei's campaign. Moaz once again defied the orders of his superiors, alongside dozens of Muslim Brotherhood youth leaders. The veteran activists from

Kifaya and Ayman Nour's campaign showed up, along with youth groups from every political party. As usual, the police broke it up, but these youth had all seen each other on the street and realized that disparate strands were coming together. Afterward, Moaz and the other Brothers went to their leaders with a formal proposal to collaborate with all the other disenchanted Egyptians.

"We should work to topple Mubarak," Moaz insisted.

The leaders refused. "We must be careful now," they said.

The year ended with the wholesale fraud of the fall 2010 parliamentary elections. "Honorable citizens" materialized to attack voters with clubs and swords. Moaz filmed some of the worst abuses as part of a Brotherhood effort to document the fraud. The Brotherhood went from eighty-eight seats in parliament to zero. Mubarak's last election erased even the token representation previously achieved by the Brotherhood and the small faction of neutered but symbolically important secular opposition parties.

For more than a year, Moaz and his friends had chafed at the caution of crusty Brotherhood leaders and their refusal to boycott the sham elections. After the voting, the most dynamic among the Muslim Brotherhood youth joined young activists from secular movements at their marches and confrontations with police. Together they were lashed with canes, sprayed with tear gas, and beaten in paddy wagons and jail cells; this shared experience pointed in a direct line toward Tahrir. On Facebook they continued the conversations that began on the street and in detention. To their mutual surprise, they found an extensive common set of ideals centered on rights, economic justice, political reform, and a distinctly Egyptian freedom agenda: freedom of speech, freedom from police brutality, freedom of worship, and freedom from abject poverty. Longtime activists had already found new comrades through ElBaradei's campaign. Islamists such as Moaz found that they shared more with ElBaradei campaigners like Basem and with other secular activists than they did with their own rigid leadership. An agenda was gathering force, and, for now, it was transcending Egypt's old ideological divisions.

The dam broke all at once. Moaz and Basem, like all the rest of the agitators, expected very little on January 25, 2011. All they knew was that they were fed up and that plenty of Egyptians felt the same way. They had no idea how many others there were, or how committed, but they had caught hints at the meetings and demonstrations, at family gatherings and funerals, and in editorials, Facebook comments, tweets, and blog posts. Tunisians had risen up in December 2010 and within weeks had driven their dictator, President Zine el-Abidine Ben Ali, out of the country. If eleven million Tunisians could depose a regime, couldn't ninety million Egyptians do the same?

In what turned out to be its final days, Egypt's regime was smug and confident. Mubarak's state had grown so remote, so casually violent, that its mechanisms of perception no longer functioned. Anger was swelling, but the regime didn't notice anything out of the ordinary. It had no plans to punish the policemen who killed Khaled Said. It had no intention of placating the population with some token gesture simply because Arabs in a nearby country had overthrown their leader. Instead, it went on with the same tricks, dispatching dollar-a-day goons to beat demonstrators. On New Year's Day a bomb ripped through a church in Alexandria, killing twenty-three. The government had failed once again to protect a vulnerable minority. Young activists from all backgrounds took to the streets in solidarity with the Christians. Several protest leaders were arrested. The police blamed a Salafi named Sayed Bilal and tortured him to death. He turned out to have no connection to the bombing. Little demonstrations flared up around the country. The Journalists Syndicate had a tall building downtown used as a meeting space and conference hall; the syndicate's leadership allowed anti-regime protests on the front steps. Moaz was among a small group attacked by police there. When he returned home, his mother said nothing, but his father fumed. "This is not a smart investment," he told his son. "This is no way to lead a good life."

"If we can't change our life in 2011, then I will emigrate to Canada or find a new country," Moaz said. "If I don't speak against this regime, one day they will kill me, and nobody left will speak out."

Alexandria had now contributed a trinity of martyrs: first Khaled Said, the secular Muslim everyman; and then the Christians, for years the victims of state-sanctioned sectarian discrimination, blown up in their church; and finally Sayed Bilal, the pious Salafi, innocent of any offense but in thrall to a rigid and suspect faith. The state had targeted almost every kind of Egyptian. Now, in response to those crimes, a current of anger had united Egyptians across their many dividing lines in January 2011, after a decade or more of orchestrated cruelty.

Obtusely, the government elevated Police Day, scheduled for January 25, into an official national holiday. This was Mubarak's last insult. No institution was more universally detested in Egypt than the police. At a moment when the president needed to placate his enraged populace, he inflamed them. Youth of all backgrounds collaborated in the call for a national "Day of Rage," scheduled to coincide with the ludicrous new holiday: Muslim Brothers, Salafists, labor activists from the April 6 Movement, canvassers for ElBaradei, and the administrators of the Khaled Said Facebook page, which by now had 365,000 members.

It was during this final surge of planning that Moaz and Basem met, like so many other activists who until then had been agitating in lonesome obscurity. An underground cell convened at an apartment on the west bank of the Nile. It belonged to a middle-aged communist who had taken part in the Bread Riots of 1977, when angry Egyptians demonstrated against a government move to eliminate wheat subsidies. It was perhaps the last time before 2011 that a popular outcry had managed to unnerve the regime. Her son was a thirty-year-old secular lawyer named Zyad el-Elaimy, a bear of a man who had relished fighting the police since his days at university. Zyad had maintained close friendships with the Muslim Brotherhood leaders from his student union days, and he had become a top aide to ElBaradei. Now, using methods borrowed from his mother's days as an active communist, Zyad brought together the full array of activists, who had never before worked together in a coordinated fashion.

Basem and a few others represented ElBaradei's supporters. Moaz and two others came from the Brotherhood. There were independent leftists, Islamists, and labor activists. They removed their cell phone batteries and arrived at Zyad's mother's apartment one by one so as not to attract police attention. There was much to plan and little time to socialize.

Basem had met very few Muslim Brothers, and he was struck by Moaz's singularity of focus. Moaz at first mistook Basem for a foreigner, maybe an Algerian, because of his wan complexion and light eyes, and noticed that he was much older than the other activists. He found Basem temperate and professional, and effective at keeping his colleagues on task. The activists labored to keep their expectations low, but they wanted the January 25 protest to be big. At their most unrealistic, they hoped that they could force the resignation of the hated interior minister, responsible for so much incompetence and so many deaths over his thirteen years in power. Their first challenge was summoning a crowd large enough to combat the riot police, who were well versed at dispersing gatherings before they reached a critical mass. The question was whether there were enough angry Egyptians to confront the regime in a way that would shock Mubarak and his operators.

They hit on a simple plan. They would advertise twenty protest locations all over the city, at mosques and popular meeting places. Police would gather at those spots, which would serve as decoys. Meanwhile, Basem and Moaz's cell, which included dozens of the most seasoned activists and street demonstrators, the most charismatic chant leaders, and the toughest fighters, would meet at an unannounced and most unlikely location: El Hayiss Pastries, an industrial shop in a fringe working-class neighborhood, where the streets were too narrow for police trucks and water cannons, and where no demonstration had ever taken place previously. The ploy would work only if the denizens of the neighborhood joined the call to protest. If they did, then the organizers could muster a thousand people by the time they reached the main boulevard and drew the attention of the Central Security Forces. If the residents of Bulaq Dakrour ignored the chants of Basem, Moaz, and their friends, then January 25's Day of Rage would be just one more in a long line of protests that fizzled.

4.

THE REPUBLIC OF TAHRIR

The revolutionaries labored under twin fears as they converged on El Hayiss Pastries on the morning of January 25, 2011. The first was simply that they would fail, that the uprising they had announced with such fanfare would amount to nothing, and Egyptians would prove as docile as the regime said they were. The second was more vague and complex. They worried that if the public's anger were aroused, no one would be able to harness it for constructive ends. The fourteen activists who had planned the secret march out of Bulaq Dakrour represented some but not all of the activists laboring in Egypt. Basem had come to politics only recently, but others had been thinking about how to unseat Mubarak's regime for a decade or more. They included Islamists, labor activists, communists, socialists, and liberals. They weren't sure they could raise a revolution, but they were planning ahead just in case they succeeded.

This small group, almost alone among Egyptians, didn't consider politics a dirty word; they had formed a coalition with a goal of intimidating the regime and perhaps forcing the resignation of its top police official. They hoped they might prompt as many as ten thousand people to march to the city center, enough perhaps to demand Hosni Mubarak's attention. They had studied the politics of their own country and, even more assiduously, they had followed the lightning revolution in Tunisia, which had begun when a fruit peddler named Mohamed Bouazizi set himself on fire to protest the confiscation of his scales by a corrupt police officer.

Mubarak's minions were watching too, but they were unconcerned. "Egypt is a different case than Tunisia," an Egyptian cabinet member told the press. The regime was glib, but there was some truth to its claim. Tunisia was a tiny middle-class country. Egypt had ninety million inhabitants, most of them poor and many illiterate. Egypt's government had more people on its payroll than Tunisia had citizens. Perhaps Egypt's regime was blind to the threat against it, or perhaps it knew that deep foundations supported the tyrant at its head.

Basem was nervous. The organizers were afraid they'd be arrested, so they had gone into hiding for a week. On the last night, Basem called his sister. "Kiss your daughter Noor for me," he told her, a code that meant he would sneak into her guest room that night. Basem hadn't seen his own kids all week. In the morning, he followed the protocol they all had agreed on in their final meeting at Zyad's mother's flat. He removed the battery and SIM card from his cell phone to make himself hard to track, and then took a series of taxis and minibuses toward Bulaq Dakrour. He finally found his way to the potholed lane, hidden beneath a cloverleaf intersection, that led into the dense flank of the neighborhood. It was an area that until this day had never attracted the notice of authorities or activists. The smell of roasting butter and caramelized sugar wafted from the bakery. Trays of baklava lined the glass counters, which opened to a little tiled plaza about the size of a garage. There were no police in sight. By twos and threes, the activists drifted into the plaza, until they numbered a few dozen. Zyad arrived and pulled a bullhorn from his bag.

If Moaz represented the typical Muslim Brother and Basem the freshly politicized citizen, Zyad represented the small but boisterous clan of career leftists. In 1977 Zyad's communist mother had faced off with riot police in the Egyptian Bread Riots. His lawyer father channeled his dissent into articulate writings. Unlike most of the activists whose families pressured them to avoid politics, Zyad's family pushed him into a life of civic engagement. He studied law and led the leftist contingent on the student council. He discovered during the 2003 anti–Iraq War protests that the toughest demonstrators and the best organizers were communists, revolutionary socialists, and Islamists. He was surrounded by baying law students that year when a pair of cops lit into him, breaking his arm. Zyad wore the cast with pride. The dissident lawyers, secular and Islamist, became his closest friends. He read Marx and Lenin, and in addition to practicing law, he established a charity to tutor children in his neighborhood. The more that Zyad thought about the inequities of Mubarak's law, the less appeal he found in doctrinaire communism. The dictatorship of the proletariat was just another dictatorship, and he became convinced that Egyptians needed to be freed from oppression as well as from poverty. He drifted toward the pragmatic center, pursuing any tactic that might work against the regime. When ElBaradei returned to Egypt, Zyad quickly became one of his most important organizers and aides. In the planning for January 25, he was the center of a group of activists from across the ideological spectrum whom he trusted and considered effective.

"Bread! Freedom! Social justice!" they chanted. (It rhymes in Arabic.) And: *"Al-shaab yurid isqat al-nidham."* "The people demand the fall of the regime." These were unprecedented, seditious calls; saying out loud that you wanted the fall of the regime on the morning of January 25 could quickly lead to prison. A few onlookers joined, and gradually more materialized. Within an hour, still no police had appeared, but to the pleasure of Basem, Moaz, and Zyad, about five hundred people were chanting in front of the pastry shop. At a signal from Zyad, the organizers spread up the congested lane while others took their place along the perimeter to maintain the march's cohesion and energy. *"Inzil! Inzil!"* they chanted, waving at the apartments around them. "Come down! Come down!" To their surprise, people did. They came out of their houses or up from the side streets, and they joined the march. All who saw knew it was subversion. By joining this march, they were joining a revolt.

"Come down! Come down!" they chanted, and the march swelled in size. By the time it poured out of Bulaq Dakrour and into the fancier neighborhood of Dokki, the shuddering, angry, focused mass was no longer connected directly to the fourteen men and women who had catalyzed it.

These enraged Egyptians filled the main boulevards of Giza, the half of Cairo that lay on the west bank of the Nile. In harmony, the soccer hooligans, the unemployed, the college graduates, and the activists finally met the riot police who were still puffed up with a bully's confidence. In sixty years, they hadn't met a crowd that they couldn't dispatch easily with clubs, tear gas, and occasional assistance from paid thugs armed with guns, swords, and knives. The riot police formed neat, straight lines, blocking the avenues and bridges. Their black uniforms made them look tall, and their Plexiglas shields shimmered in the sun. Behind them, drivers eagerly revved armored paddy wagons and water cannons. From a distance, the defenses had a serene beauty, like a sentry wall snaking across the streetscape. The rulers of Egypt believed that they ruled not simply because they had power but also because they were just. The army and police conscripts reflected this misplaced moral confidence. Those who disagreed simply didn't know better, the regime believed, and they were destined to fail in any challenge to the state; the people's weakness and stupidity fed each other in a vicious circle. The state couldn't imagine a serious challenge because the state didn't believe there were any errors or defects in its ways.

The police were ready for these protesters, expecting to apply the usual deep state formula and be done in a few hours. What the conscripts couldn't see, and what their masters in the regime had yet to recognize, was the lengths to which Egyptians' frustration had soared. Moaz was not alone in his conviction that if the country didn't change now, he would have to emigrate. Basem was not the only petit bourgeois citizen to conclude reluctantly that Egypt's politics were the cause of Egypt's misery. The ultras were not the only teenagers to recognize from previous fights that one didn't need sophisticated equipment to fight back. An entire generation of electrified citizens had nothing to lose.

The serpent of marching people met the line of riot police. An extravaganza of violence followed. But history didn't repeat itself. On this day, when the police hit people, the people hit back. They were fearless and also prepared. They covered their faces with scarves soaked in vinegar to dampen the effect of the tear gas, and they tossed smoking canisters back at the police. The police fired water cannons and brandished truncheons. Protesters answered with stones. They broke through the police cordon and spray painted the windshields of the paddy wagons and cannons so that the drivers couldn't see. Each time the police repulsed the marchers, they regrouped and surged again. Egyptians watched electrified on the pan-Arabic satellite news network Al Jazeera, since state television ignored the spectacle. As the fight continued, tens of thousands joined. The demonstrators broke through line after line of cops, making their way closer to Tahrir Square. They fought one final climactic battle at the last choke point before Tahrir: the antique two-lane Qasr el-Nil bridge, guarded by a pair of enormous granite lions left from the royal era. On the bridge, the riot police drove their trucks into the crowd, running people over. In vain, conscripts fired tear gas point-blank while others swung their sticks wildly. A group of demonstrators dropped in neat lines to the ground mid-melee to pray. The police sacrilegiously trained the water cannon on them. The demonstrators rose and kneeled, completing the full prayer. When they were done, they rushed the police and cleared them off the bridge, almost as an afterthought. This was the moment that Egypt's dictators had feared since 1952. The math was not on the side of Mubarak or his generals. If one million people convinced of their righteousness stand against your police, the only way to stop them is to kill and kill and kill until everyone dies or goes home. Not every dictator is that merciless.

During the peak of the fighting, Basem's father commanded one of his sons to go downtown, find Basem, and bring him home.

"No," his brother replied, turning the television to a satellite channel broadcasting the battle for the Qasr el-Nil bridge live. "You must pray for him and be proud of him."

The march filled Tahrir Square, and the police stayed away. All at once, Tahrir Square was the freest public space Egypt had known in a half century, maybe more. Dissidents, critics, and kids chanted and chatted, angry and euphoric. They had occupied Tahrir. Basem, Moaz, Zyad, and the rest of the fourteen youth activists conferred with one another and sought advice from elders who'd come to the square once the police had surrendered control. They talked to activists, lawyers, politicians, intellectuals. They had not expected to get this far, and instantly they understood that, without care, their victory would evaporate. By midnight, they had settled on a plan. They would escalate, calling for a massive nationwide "Friday of Rage" on January 28.

"The wall of fear has been broken," they told one another, equally proud and in awe of themselves and their fellow citizens. The wall of fear would quickly become a cliché, but it was no less true for that. The police had crumbled before common folk armed only with fury; in a single day, Egyptians had learned that it was possible to fight the regime and win. This lesson could not be untaught. Like a child who realizes that his father is an unbalanced, raving drunk, Egyptians would never again cower the same way before their state.

The revolutionaries who for so long had labored as lonely pariahs suddenly counted legions of new friends. Almost every group in Egypt that wasn't part of the state joined the groundswell for the Friday of Rage. The Muslim Brotherhood had sat out the January 25 protest despite requests from Moaz and other youth members. Now it smelled opportunity and followed out of self-interest. Basem, Moaz, and their youth cell were planning a march from the Mostafa Mahmoud Mosque in Mohandiseen. This time, though, they were just one of hundreds of groups joining a national day of revolt. The Muslim Brotherhood was dispatching organizers to mosques all over the country. Middle-class kids invited friends on Facebook to join them in upscale neighborhoods, while in poorer quarters, people spread the call by word of mouth. The regime was frightened enough that, before dawn on January 28, it arrested as many known dissidents as it could, including dozens of senior Muslim Brothers. It was a sign of their disconnect from reality that the police thought the Brotherhood was leading the uprising. The inchoate revolutionary movement was led by no one, but its vanguard consisted of independent youth and small new factions operating without support from Egypt's tired old politicians.

Early in the morning on January 28, Zyad's mother fried the spicy cured beef called *basterma* with eggs for her son's team. She passed out sweaters so they wouldn't get cold during a long day of marching and fighting with police. Before noon prayers, they strolled to the mosque, just a few blocks from Moaz's house. The plaza was packed. People, mostly teenagers and folks in their twenties, had filled the fast-food chain restaurants near the mosque and then flocked there at the last minute. Basem was afraid as he approached. "What if no one shows up?" he asked himself. Then he heard a roar: tens of thousands of voices chanting in unison, spoiling for a fight. The small demonstration on January 25, with its symbolic victory over the police and reconquest of a public space, had triggered an avalanche. The police, it turned out, were too busy to block the way to Friday prayers. There were about two million Egyptians on the Interior Ministry payroll, but it seemed that their number wouldn't suffice to control the country's streets on the Friday of Rage. Rowdy crowds had assembled at dozens of Cairo mosques and all over the nation. Normally, the regime could move police from the provinces to deal with disturbances in Cairo or Alexandria, but on the Friday of Rage, it appeared that every population center in Egypt was in revolt.

At the conclusion of prayers, the march from Mostafa Mahmoud Mosque pushed toward Tahrir with the inevitability of a tectonic shift. A concatenation of hundreds of thunderous marches rippled across Egypt. Basem, Moaz, Zyad, and their coconspirators were swept along, bobbing in the crowd. This time the battles with the police were quick and methodical. Each time riot police tried to block the march, the crowd ripped them away like weeds. Protests had engulfed Alexandria. The port city of Suez was burning. Fighting convulsed the factory and farm towns of the Nile Delta. Early in the afternoon, the outnumbered police simply gave up, leaving the streets without armed custodians for the first time since 1952. Just like that, Egypt belonged to its people. Triumphant mobs set neighborhood police stations aflame. In Tahrir, maybe a half million celebrated. This ill-groomed traffic circle, mottled with scruffy tufts of grass and flanked by concrete slab buildings and the gaping hole of a suspended construction site, would be the capital of liberated Egypt. When the military deployed that evening, it kept to the edges of the square.

Armed camps ringed Tahrir. Army tanks and armored personnel carriers sealed the busiest entrance points. Soldiers checked IDs and sent foreigners, activists, and similarly suspicious people to security agents. Inside the square, plainclothes police milled about, filming everybody with their mobile phones. They affected intimidating stares, but now they were figures of impotence, with their clenched jaws and oversized leather jackets. The people in the square no longer feared arrests and beatings. The army's gun turrets weren't pointed at the crowds in Tahrir, although it would only take a minute to swivel them into place.

The denizens of the square debated endlessly whether the military would attack. Basem spent every day there, leaving only to change clothes or sleep for a few hours in nearby apartments lent by supporters of the uprising. Moaz was coordinating a pharmacy stocked with first aid supplies, and worked as a medic at one of several field clinics established around the square. He never slept more than three hours straight, and at times was semidelirious. One night he asked me to meet him at the field hospital located in an arcade just off the square; fruitlessly, I searched for him among the bustle of doctors, citizen-journalists, and protesters waiting hours at a time to use the bathroom. Finally, I found Moaz beside a clump of blankets and bandages, curled up in a ball, asleep with his glasses on.

The Muslim Brotherhood was now providing crucial personnel and know-how. The Brothers could smuggle medicine and food into the square. The Brotherhood could summon round-the-clock shifts of security guards and doctors. It assigned members to stay in the square overnight, ready to fight during the hours when the protester population was at its smallest and most vulnerable. Many of the original protesters considered the Brotherhood opportunistic, joining Tahrir only once it looked like it might succeed, but they welcomed the bodies and the help it provided. By now everyone in the square was ready to fight, but the protesters were at a loss to predict how the regime would strike.

On Wednesday, February 2, they found out. Camel drivers wearing traditional galabiyas led a parade of thugs and hired hands into Tahrir. Police snipers hid among hundreds of civilians in muscle shirts. Tourists had fled because of the uprising, so the workers at the pyramids had nothing to do. The regime wanted to empty the square but wanted to disguise its involvement. So it hired its usual operatives, and brought in the workers from the pyramids to give the assault a populist flavor. The assault's absurd appearance belied its lethality. The day's violence would go down in history as the Battle of the Camel.

From the roofs above Tahrir, men threw rocks the size of fists onto the heads of protesters below. Demonstrators and thugs fought hand to hand at the entrances to the square. Activists quickly smashed the pavement to make projectiles and threw them at their attackers. Police snipers returned fire methodically, shooting and killing demonstrators from an overpass. Dead and gravely wounded protesters piled up in the field hospitals around Tahrir, with new casualties carried in every minute. Moaz held one fighter as he died. A charismatic Che Guevara look-alike came to him bleeding where rocks had struck his temples. Moaz put three stitches in each side of the boy's head with no anesthetic. The young man smiled the whole time. It was Moaz's first encounter with Mina Daniel, a Coptic Christian who later in the year, after another fateful encounter with government security forces, would become an icon of the revolution.

Women and men fought shoulder to shoulder. Revolutionaries snuck across lines to flush thugs from the rooftops. They outflanked the police snipers on the overpass. Twelve hours after it had begun, the Battle of the Camel was over. At least twenty-six demonstrators were dead and hundreds more seriously wounded. By defeating the Camel brigade, the revolt had scored a pivotal victory. The square reached its apogee; the euphoric golden period that Egyptians affectionately called "the Republic of Tahrir." Volunteers guarded the spur streets. Garbage brigades picked up litter, while street kids distributed donated sandwiches and cookies. The ass-grabbing, sexual harassment, and rape that were everyday hazards for women in downtown Cairo subsided to almost zero. People who had reflexively shushed one another in public now couldn't stop talking. They talked and talked, offering their names for publication and their cell phone numbers to stay in touch. People lined up patiently at the Omar Makram Mosque, which along with the field hospital offered the only two public bathrooms open to the hundreds of thousands in Tahrir. Christians and secular Muslims joined hands to protect those who were praying. To me, it felt like these frank people in Tahrir Square were redeeming the whole world's age of defeat along with Egypt's era of fear.

The youth in the square welcomed anyone who entered with the requisite humility. One of the most striking denizens of Tahrir was an old diplomat named Mohamed Fathy Rifaah al-Tahtawi. He was a luminary of the establishment, the ruling class embodied. A descendant of one of the most important Islamic scholars of the nineteenth century, al-Tahtawi had served as deputy foreign minister and later as the spokesman for Al-Azhar, the preeminent seat of Islamic study. He was also a well-traveled intellectual who knew the world and saw that Egypt's place in it had slipped. For decades he said nothing and pleased his masters well. But when he saw the youth congregate in Tahrir Square, he felt ashamed and seized his moment. On national television, al-Tahtawi resigned his post at Al-Azhar and decamped to Tahrir. There he made no speeches but asked many questions.

When I met him, he led me to a quiet back alley. This man who had spent his entire professional life on fine upholstery and leather sofas brushed off the filthy curb with his bare hand, sat down, and said, "This will be my office now." His demeanor said as much as his words. "Our children understood what we had forgotten," the ambassador told me. "Now it is our turn to follow them. They might save the country that we have ruined."

He wasn't the only mother, father, grandmother, or grandfather to enter Tahrir, head tilted in apology. They came and asked forgiveness for a lifetime of moral cowardice and for their final failed attempts at authoritarianism in the home, when they tried to prohibit their young from joining the revolution. Those parents, even more than their children, made a journey of stunning proportions out of the walled gardens of fear in which they had lived their entire lives.

Scenes of euphoria and newfound faith played out everywhere in the square. Men and women circulated in yellow construction helmets, ready to withstand barrages of rocks. Security details ran drills in the middle of the night and staffed a jail in a subway stairwell. Anonymous donors sent in sandwiches, water, cookies, and *koshari*, the traditional Egyptian poor man's dish of rice, lentils, noodles, and onions. An unemployed teacher working as part of a formal security detail told me that his best qualification as a fighter was that "I have nothing to lose."

Ayman Abouzaid, a cardiology resident, had joined the civilian protesters who were sleeping on the tanks beside the museum, to prevent them from intruding farther into the square. Each night, soldiers fired shots in the air and sometimes revved their tank engines. Ayman and the other men would cluster closer, daring the drivers to run them over. A light drizzle was falling, and the sun had set. Ayman wore a white medical jacket smeared with dirt. His glasses were dirty, and a bloodstained bandage was wrapped around his forehead. He had been in the square for ten days straight. "We will leave in only two situations," he said. "When Hosni Mubarak and the National Democratic Party are judged and executed. Or we all have to be dead."

The revolutionary youth made their headquarters in a green tent on a traffic median at the southern end of Tahrir, where Abdelkader Hamza Street led toward the Omar Makram Mosque and the American Embassy. Activists passed through the tent around the clock. Sometimes a few would curl up and nap along the edge while others sat cross-legged, smoking inside the nylon hothouse as they drafted communiqués and plotted negotiating positions to present to the public and the generals. The Islamists dressed like old men, no matter their age, in pleated pants, Oxford dress shirts, loose sweaters, and leather shoes, usually in matching earth tones. The women wore loose cloaks, or *abaya*s, and head scarves in muted grays or browns. The leftists tended to wear brighter colors and tighter clothes. When they expected a fight, everyone wore jeans, hoodies, and sneakers.

Basem was preoccupied with sustaining turnout at the square. He believed that Tahrir itself was the best recruitment tool for the revolution. He was older than most of his confederates, and he was determined to woo people from his generation. His goal was to draw as many skeptics as possible to the Republic of Tahrir, so that they would return to tell their families and neighbors that the revolution was not as dark and destructive as it was being portrayed on state television.

"Once people come here to see us and go back to the community, it changes," a younger friend said to Basem outside the tent.

"Today," Basem said, "I was afraid I would find the square empty."

It was raining hard enough that the ink in my notebook ran. A child no more than ten passed out free chocolate-and-cream cookies.

"Already the youth have accomplished more than we had asked for," Basem said. "Nobody can control the square."

The fourteen youth leaders who had worked together on January 25 weren't trying to control the square, but they were trying to lead it; they understood that a people power movement needed an agenda and spokespeople to harness its potential. However, they also understood that the spontaneity and diversity that gave Tahrir its potency could easily prevent it from cohering behind any single leader or idea.

Even at Tahrir's pinnacle, the seeds of future divisions had already taken root. A bitter divide had sprung up between the Egyptians in the square and those outside: the revolutionaries versus the Hizb al-Kanaba, or "sofa party," who preferred to sit at home on their couches watching government television. State newspapers published unsourced accounts of cars with diplomatic license plates cruising through the square, with mysterious figures handing out cash from the windows. State television announcers delivered fabricated reports that the people in Tahrir Square were, in fact, being paid by European governments and Israel as part of a plot against the Egyptian nation. The perks of being a protester supposedly included free meals from Hardee's, Kentucky Fried Chicken, and Pizza Hut, restaurants too expensive for most Egyptians. Outside Tahrir, I heard these baseless rumors repeated as fact by countless Egyptians, from the wealthy and well-read to the poor and cloistered. Inside Tahrir, in actuality, the fast-food restaurants had been shuttered since the first day of the revolt, and the protesters were living in primitive, overcrowded conditions. Such slander led to classic Egyptian humor. Protesters in Tahrir who hadn't showered in days shared bowls of *koshari*. When choosing between measly portions, they'd say, "Is this Kentucky or Hardee's?" A pair of Muslim Brothers who had slept on the dirt median for a week turned out their pockets. "I can't find my euros or shekels anywhere!" one said, laughing at his own joke.

Yet the government had successfully driven a wedge between the minority in the square and the majority at home. The people in Tahrir controlled no platform by which to address the wider public. They couldn't get a moment's airtime on state television; even regime-approved guests who mentioned Tahrir in anything but noxious terms were evicted from the studio. International media aired sympathetic reports about the revolutionaries, so Egyptians with satellite dishes could learn about the goals of Tahrir on Al Jazeera. The elite and the open-minded were more likely to seek out and believe foreign media (whether from the Arab world, like Al Jazeera, or the West, like the BBC or CNN). The majority, however, watched the monotonous false reports on state television or read the propaganda published in the most widely circulated newspapers, also run by the government. I heard some activists debate whether they should storm the state television headquarters a few hundred yards north of Tahrir in the squat fortress-like Maspero Building, its curved façade hulking like an alien bunker above the Nile. They dismissed the notion as impossible; there were dozens of army tanks surrounding the complex. They also thought it would be futile to take Maspero even if they could, since the government had alternate broadcasting venues. But that thinking signaled a failure of verve and imagination. Had the revolutionary youth taken over state television on January 28, they might have been running the country now. Instead, they fought a war of attrition for public opinion, using the platforms of family dinner tables, Twitter, and Facebook against the state's vast broadcast and print conglomerates. The revolutionaries had no way to make their case to the masses of their peers. To some extent, they gave up from the start, figuring that the constituents of the sofa party had never made a difference in the past and wouldn't in the future. Contempt for the majority, poured into the revolution's foundation, would weaken it in later stages.

There also were divisions within the revolution, which crept into conversations despite the effort to present a united front. Already some revolutionaries looked askance at their fellow activists who went on television or drafted talking points and demands. Some reflexively opposed any authority, and some were committed anarchists who subscribed to the theory that the best path to progress was to obliterate all institutions of control, inside and outside the state. Tahrir's de facto organizers had quickly coalesced into a coherent team, communicating and plotting on an almost hourly basis, but they had yet to formally announce an organization. When Basem and his companions published statements, some demonstrators immediately condemned them as power hungry, a label that stuck to all those who engaged in the first forays into politics. Anarchists went further, viewing any attempt to lead, organize, or represent as an unacceptable grab for glory.

There were other disagreements of substance inside the square, whose denizens could be roughly broken down into reactionaries, reformists, and revolutionaries. Tahrir's conservative faction objected only to Mubarak; they genuinely loved the army and brooked little criticism of the state. Most typical of this group were the Nasserists, who desired a different type of authoritarian to replace Mubarak. Then there were the veteran activists who had been considering system change even before Tahrir. They had researched, detailed proposals. Among them were reformers such as Basem, who were hardly ideological. They had a centrist vision of a nationalist Egypt, its system overhauled and reformed but still recognizable: essentially the same state, but with nicer police, less corruption, and respect for the laws as written. Labor activists and leftists, meanwhile, demanded the full explosion of Egypt's system and all the state's institutions of repression, including the security services and extending to the framework of its capitalist economy. Some among this category hoped for a revolution so complete that it would dwarf France's and Russia's in the history books.

Then there were the Islamists. Because of their late entry and the suspicion they aroused, many of them kept quiet in Tahrir, but there were plenty of conservative, older Muslim Brothers and Salafis who shared none of Moaz's progressive open-mindedness. They were old-school organization men, and their vision was of a regimented Egypt where governance flowed directly from the Koran. These were vast, perhaps unbridgeable differences in belief. Crowds united in their call for Mubarak's head found little other common ground.

———————

The exuberance in Tahrir was astounding but, at the same time, seemed fragile compared with the vast indifferent expanse outside, where Egypt went about its business as leaden as ever. For all the chastened parents who embraced their children's revolution, an equal number did not change. At a checkpoint just a few minutes' walk from Tahrir, a police officer in his dress uniform cornered me. "Why are you reporting from Tahrir?" he scoffed. "For every whiner there, you will find a hundred Egyptians out here who oppose them. You should be reporting from here, from Egypt!" At the fancy cafés on the island of Zamalek, rich kids groused over four-dollar coffees that, with Tahrir occupied, traffic was worse than ever. In poor neighborhoods, people worried about their livelihoods and "the wheel of production," mouthing a line heard often on state television. According to the ruling party, it wasn't Mubarak's twenty-nine-year tenure that had hobbled the economy and imperiled tourism, it was the last few days of demonstrations in Tahrir and the other squares. Even at El Hayiss Pastries, where the revolution began, the manager was contemptuous; I couldn't tell whether he had completely internalized government propaganda or if he was just parroting the required lines while he waited to see how it all turned out. "These people in Tahrir Square represent only a minority of Egyptians," he said, leaning over a pan of sweets, speaking in a dull monotone. "We are the majority. We live here. We talk to the people. No to America, no to Israel, no to Iran." His passionless manifesto delivered, he fell silent.

The nation's still-confident masters were counting on the fear they had fostered for decades. As Mubarak clung stubbornly to his office, I sat poolside with a group of retired generals at the Gezira Club, a leafy bastion of privilege on the island of Zamalek. There in the middle of Cairo, the richest and most established families escaped the traffic and congestion. Kids roamed through five playgrounds. There was ample green space to explore on horseback or on foot, and several swimming pools, including a serene one from which children were banned. The retired officers relaxed in polos and sweatpants, sheltering from the midday sun beneath umbrellas before heading to the tennis courts. At first none of them wanted to talk to me, but I had been in Tahrir every day, and they had not, so after a while their curiosity got the better of them.

"We thought the revolution would be started by the hungry people," said the most friendly among them, a retired air force general named Hisham. "We didn't think it would start from these well-educated, well-fed young guys." Hisham thought there was a graceful way out: dump Mubarak and preserve the regime. He feared that the people in power weren't wise enough to leave unless forced. "I know Mubarak. He is a stubborn man," Hisham said. "The regime probably won't give up unless Egypt is burning."

A retired police general named Tarek began grilling me. "Who are the people out there? How many are Muslim Brothers?" he asked. I told him my impression that the Brothers made up about a third of the committed activists, and that political neophytes filled the big daytime crowds in Tahrir.

"You are wrong," he said, laughing. "The Brothers are behind this." In his world, a man could know with certainty only as much as he was allowed to see in files. Possession of dossiers was the primary avenue to power in Mubarak's system.

"You don't have access to enough files to understand the situation," he told me. "Maybe your editor does, but not you."

He was quite sure that everybody in Egypt loved and trusted the police, the events of the past weeks notwithstanding. I asked him what other policemen thought, but he answered all my questions with questions.

Hisham, the air force veteran, chuckled at my efforts to crack the police officer's façade. "They have been trained to get information, not to give it," he observed. He was taking my side, trying to probe his friend. Hisham pointed out to Tarek that Egyptians had tired of secret police meddling in their lives. The air force general's empathy for the revolutionaries further exasperated his brother from the police. Finally, Tarek broke his irritable silence. "I think you are CIA," he said to me, and then excused himself to pray. He returned later, tennis racket in hand; he wanted one last go at me.

"You have information from inside the square," he said. "Who are the leaders? Who controls the majority: ElBaradei or the Brotherhood?"

Tired of his boorish manners, I tried to get a rise out of him.

"How will the police regain public trust when they are so hated?" I asked.

"People still trust the police," he said.

"Do you understand that Egyptians hate the police?" I goaded him.

"The majority of people love the police," General Tarek sputtered, his face flushed. "They will respect the police because they need the police."

As an assessment of popular sentiment, Tarek's pronouncement was delusional. But as a threat, it was prescient.

The army brass had refrained from turning Tahrir into Tiananmen Square, or Hama, or Halabja, although it was willing to let others attack. The military wasn't going to back Mubarak, but it wasn't going to join the revolution, either, like its counterpart in Tunisia. "The army and the people are one hand!" shouted the people in Tahrir, surrounded by immobile tanks. It was as much a supplication as a statement. A few days after the Battle of the Camel, General Hassan Ruweini, the army officer in charge of Cairo, made an ominous tour of the square. He clambered over the barricades beside the Egyptian Museum with a small detail of meaty bodyguards. This was a listening tour, Egyptian army–style: first Ruweini wanted to hear from the protesters, and then he wanted them to shut up and listen to him. "It's time for life to go back to normal," he said. "You can express yourselves without interfering with others." He told the protesters to clear the burned cars, corrugated metal sheets, and requisitioned construction material that kept Ruweini's tanks out of Tahrir. He wanted the youth to go home.

The crowd surged, summoned by shrill whistles and the low, thunderous banging of clubs on metal. Ruweini ranted and tugged at a barricade. His soldiers quickly pushed it over. Young men reassembled it in a few seconds, but the general was already inside their cordon. A cry rose: "We will die here!" The general pushed through. Army snipers watched from the museum roof. One of General Ruweini's bodyguards placed his beefy hand on a demonstrator's face and shoved it aside. General Ruweini clasped another man's head in one hand, pulled him close, and gently slapped his cheek. The gesture was paternal, intimate, and carried a whiff of menace. "The military will remain neutral," Ruweini said firmly, with the strain of a man not used to explaining his orders, much less needing to persuade anyone. "We will not use force against you. But we need to get things back to normal."

"We won't go until he goes!" the crowd chanted in response, referring to President Mubarak. Demonstrators refused to let General Ruweini move deeper into the square, linking arms in a human chain to block his way. For the next hour, the general zigzagged among the rebels.

"You keep bandaging up people's heads to make it look like they've been wounded," he snapped at a doctor. "Why?"

The volunteer protested: the bandages on people's heads were soaked with real blood. Ruweini laughed as he yanked at the gauze on a patient's face.

"See, this man's not even wounded," the general said. "His bandage is just for show."

The wounded man winced and his head lurched. The bandage was tightly affixed to the bloody wound underneath. Ruweini, not in the least contrite, pulled a little more and then gave up. Still smiling, the general departed. His performance had unnerved the crowd, which was perhaps its purpose. Some in Tahrir trusted the army, but others were wary; the military had controlled Egypt since 1952, and was the backbone of a repressive regime. Why should soldiers feel any solidarity with the revolutionaries?

Lots of young people were talking in Tahrir, but no one was speaking for the youth. Basem's group understood that in order to exercise leverage, the revolution required leaders and institutions. The foot soldiers of January 25 liked the idea of the world's first leaderless revolution, but they wouldn't get far without structure. In the first days, the revolt had been able to escape police because it was an organic mass; there was no single brain trust to decapitate. Once the revolution had become a train, however, someone needed to steer it. Otherwise, who would tell the generals and the sofa party what the people wanted? Who would try to translate people power into the real thing? Unfortunately, even the revolutionary public in Tahrir Square had internalized state propaganda, which since 1952 had belittled all politics as inimical to the pure ideal of the nation. Anyone who wanted to represent Tahrir to the wider public, or, God forbid, negotiate with the regime, was attacked immediately as a vain egomaniac or a reactionary agent. Despite these dangers, or perhaps because of them, the core group that had set forth from El Hayiss Pastries to Tahrir decided to organize a secretariat for the square.

Already they had been meeting every day, usually three or four times, in the green Coleman tent, or in borrowed apartments on the outskirts of Tahrir. Normally, secular Egyptian political groups detested the Muslim Brotherhood and vice versa, but there was profound trust among these young men and women despite their varied political backgrounds. On Monday, February 7, fourteen young organizers and a few of their intimates crammed together in a small room just out of earshot of Tahrir's din. Several of the leaders had just been released from detention by government security forces. One of the independents, Abdelrahman Fares, had been held over the weekend and then released blindfolded; one of the soldiers detaining him held a gun to his head and whispered, "Your life is worth less than one bullet." Although people in the square chanted regularly, "The army and the people are one hand!" Fares reminded his colleagues, "The army is not our ally."

The same week, several ElBaradei activists were arrested on their way back to the square from dinner. Earlier, on the very Monday that the Tahrir organizers made their union official, Moaz had been arrested crossing into the square. He affected infinite patience and told his police guard a stream of jokes. "Maybe I will stay here forever," he said. "Maybe I will die in your office." The officer questioned Moaz about what was happening in the square. It had been the same with all the other young people who had been detained. Who was in charge? How many Brothers? Who was paying them? "I am a simple pharmacist," Moaz repeated. Finally, the cop changed the subject. "How much money do you have on you?" Moaz emptied his pockets. For three hundred Egyptian pounds, or about fifty dollars, the officer let him go. Moaz made it to the meeting of the core activists just in time.

That Monday night, the fourteen men and women who had converged on El Hayiss Pastries and labored together for a week and a half in Tahrir voted to band together officially. They called themselves the Revolutionary Youth Coalition. "We don't run the square," Basem said. "But we must try to keep it focused and organized." The name came easily. No jargon, no melodrama, no invocation of January 25. Just a straightforward explanation of who they were: young, radical, collaborative. For the sake of their dream of change, and the millions who were shaking the old order, they wanted to keep their power and extend it. Separately, each revolutionary organization could pursue its own special causes, but when the groups spoke in unison, they would speak under the banner of the Revolutionary Youth Coalition. They would operate by consensus. The coalition would have heft because its demands would represent the most critical desires of every important group. Theirs would be the agenda that united socialist workers, bourgeois liberals, and pious Islamists.

There were only two Islamist seats on the fourteen-member council, but like everyone else, the Islamists had veto power. They wielded special influence because of the Brotherhood's resources. Basem mistrusted the Brotherhood as an organization even though he was personally fond of some of his Islamist colleagues. "You're nice people, but your fundamentalist radical ideology is bad for Egypt," he told Moaz. For now, though, Basem and Moaz had more in common than in discord. Moaz and the other Islamist youths were running a rebellion within a rebellion. In addition to their resistance against the regime, they were defying their own autocratic bosses inside the Brotherhood by joining forces with Basem, Zyad, and the rest.

The youth of the revolution now had a name. They had a method. And they had an agenda: no negotiations until there was democracy in Egypt. The Revolutionary Youth Coalition was the first institution born of the Tahrir Revolution, and it was meant to enshrine all the values and best practices of revolutionary youth. As a collective, its founders hoped they could surpass their reach as a pastiche of motivated but narrow organizations. The crowds in Tahrir were winning, and the Revolutionary Youth Coalition was going to be the vehicle through which the crowds would transcend themselves, maturing from mob to movement. The regime was terrified. Mubarak was tottering, and so was the entire deep state that had controlled Egyptian life in every conceivable way for sixty years. These young activists were as pragmatic as they were bold. They wanted to build a new society, not simply rip the head off the old one. To do it, they'd need an organization that was nimble and representative. They'd need to be able to stake out political positions quickly, and then back those positions on the street with muscle and crowds. The coalition included five groups: the youth branch of a liberal party called the

Democratic Front; a left-wing group with ties to labor called the Youth Movement for Justice and Freedom; the proworker April 6 Movement; ElBaradei's supporters; and the Muslim Brotherhood Youth. There were also four independents, including Sally Moore, the only woman on the leadership committee, a Coptic Christian psychiatrist with an Irish father and an Egyptian mother.

Mubarak's prime minister sent emissaries to the square. He invited the youth leaders to meet him. But if Mubarak stayed in power, the revolutionary leaders believed, all of them would be executed or end up in prison for life. Some people in the square said there was no harm in talking to Mubarak's ministers, but the members of the new Revolutionary Youth Coalition voted unanimously that they should talk to the government only after Mubarak had stepped down.

One seat on the Revolutionary Youth Coalition was reserved for Wael Ghonim, the young Google executive who had managed the We Are All Khaled Said Facebook page, and who had been arrested at the start of the Tahrir uprising. Wael Ghonim was a successful boy-next-door, the kind of character who made middle-class Egyptians feel safe. He had spent his life trying to avoid politics and controversy. When someone like Wael Ghonim turned to revolution, it was safe to say that the regime had lost a natural constituency. The night the coalition was formed, Ghonim was released from prison. Immediately, he appeared on a television show, condemning the regime. When confronted with photographs of people who had died in Tahrir while he was in detention, Ghonim began to weep. "I want to tell every mother and father who lost a son that it's not our fault," Ghonim said through his tears. "It's the fault of everyone who held on to power and clung to it." His endorsement of Tahrir swayed countless fence-sitters to visit the square for the first time, filling it with unprecedented numbers.

The coalition had other public relations weapons, such as Sally Moore, with her flowing dark hair and tightly groomed, arched eyebrows. She did a lot of television. In English, she cut a perfect figure of modernized, globalized safe revolution. In Arabic, she reassured liberal Egyptians that Tahrir Square welcomed unveiled women, Christians, and the sort of Cairenes who like to drink a Sakara beer at the Dokki Jazz Club. The

men and women from the April 6 and Justice and Freedom Movements
had credibility among workers and leftists. And the Muslim Brotherhood
Youth, with their scruffy facial hair, potbellies, and rhythmic speaking ca-
dence, resonated with Islamist youth. These activists believed they knew
what Egypt needed, even if most of the people in the square didn't. Tahrir's foot soldiers spoke vaguely of freedom, Islamic values, and the utopia
of Egypt without Mubarak.

The coalition leaders wanted an entirely new kind of society, and they
were down in the weeds with specifics from the very beginning. "The
January 25 Revolution has cancelled the old social contract between the
people and the regime," the Youth Coalition wrote in its first manifesto.
The Revolutionary Youth Coalition had a plan to remake Egypt. The
1971 constitution was to be suspended. New laws would guarantee freedom to organize political parties and independent labor unions. The state
of emergency would be cancelled. No more military trials for civilians.
In the future, there would be separation of powers, a weaker president,
and a stronger parliament. Independent technocrats would govern Egypt
until a new constitution could be carefully drafted. Once a credible new
body had been created to oversee fair elections, the people would choose
new representatives. The secret police would be disbanded and the old
ruling party banned. This was a specific and comprehensive political
blueprint, and the Revolutionary Youth Coalition trotted it out at every
conceivable opportunity.

To some, it made them seem like nerds at a time when chanting
"Mubarak is a fag!" could spark enthusiasm in the square. To others, it
made the coalition leaders seem like little Mubaraks. "No one speaks for
me!" several activists said. But the Revolutionary Youth Coalition was one
of the uprising's best hopes. The size and bravery of the crowds elevated
the people into a credible threat against the established power. Yet politics, and politics alone, could channel the gushing stream of anger into a
force concentrated enough to erode old formations and sculpt new ones.

One of the main news sources for Tahrir and its supporters was a Facebook
page called RSD, an Arabic acronym for Monitoring News Network,

with a logo suspiciously reminiscent of the BBC's. An old acquaintance of mine, Abdelrahman Ayyash, was editing the surprisingly thorough news coverage there. RSD precisely reflected the revolution: powered by a geyser of raw energy, it harnessed the spirited work of unpolished but talented budding journalists. Its core staff came from the Muslim Brotherhood, although at first the site claimed it was independent. RSD covered the politics and the social life of the square, which were being ignored by the entire state-run Egyptian media; a half million people were following the RSD page within a week. Ayyash and the other editors worked from wherever they could sit, on laptops with cellular connections to the internet. The site's work was uneven; untrained webmasters frequently posted and then retracted unconfirmed rumors of attacks or political developments. The operation was quintessential Tahrir: Build what you need from scratch and perfect it later.

Ayyash, too, was an exemplar of the revolution. He didn't aspire to political leadership like the men and women who had founded the Revolutionary Youth Coalition; he was a back-end operative. He came from a Brotherhood family, and at fifteen he had been hired by the organization's strongman and chief financier, Khairat el-Shater, to put together the group's English-language website. Ayyash was now twenty and studying engineering, but his real calling was building websites, generating ideas, and building networks of people. He would have been a natural among the entrepreneurs of Silicon Valley. In revolutionary Egypt, he was a kind of Zelig, seemingly involved in every major event and able to blend in everywhere. He had crossed into Gaza with Moaz in 2009. He had collaborated with Basem in 2010 to collect signatures for ElBaradei's petition. He appeared to know every activist and politician, and every player on the Islamist scene.

When I first met Ayyash years earlier, he was working for the Brotherhood under an alias, blogging against the regime, and in his spare time compiling humorous articles for a website about Islamophobia. He had a sharp gaze and furrowed his forehead when he concentrated. He had fantastic powers to recall names, faces, and dates. He also had a prodigious appetite; at Hardee's, he liked to garnish his burger with a hot dog. He had first been arrested in 2007 for his critical writings on the internet,

and he had periodically seen his interrogator since then. Once, the police threatened to arrest Ayyash's father to make Ayyash stop blogging.
Ayyash was detained the first week of the revolution, but this time his
familiar police contact released him quickly, begging Ayyash to return to
his young friends and calm them down. An assistant to the prime minister had phoned Ayyash in search of any young activist willing to meet
with the government. Ayyash refused but invited the aide for a tour of
Tahrir Square so that he could tell the prime minister just how formi-
dable the state's revolutionary enemies were.

Now, sitting cross-legged on the floor of the field hospital while Moaz
slept a few feet away on the dispensary floor, Ayyash was feverishly editing stories, video clips, and newsfeeds. Much of it was critical of the
Brotherhood, his own group. He was aghast that the Brotherhood officials had met with the regime while revolutionaries were still holding
the square and refusing to negotiate. He suspected that the Brotherhood
might sell out the revolution to carve its own path to power. He believed
that the Brotherhood was brittle, incapable of tolerating pluralism within
its own narrow and homogenous ranks. "How will they ever be able to
accept pluralism in the rest of the world?" Ayyash asked rhetorically. For
him, the revolution was opening the door to question not just the regime
and the government, but also the organization that had provided the
framework of his days and thoughts since adolescence. He would no
longer limit the targets of his critical thinking.

Egyptians now occupied squares all over the country; in Suez, they
had taken over the entire city and installed a "people's governor." In
Cairo, the crowds burst out of Tahrir and took over the street in front of
parliament a few blocks away. Others surged north of Tahrir to the state
media headquarters at Maspero. "Our mere presence here is threatening,"
said the labor activist and blogger Alaa Abdel Fattah. He was encouraging demonstrators to escalate strategically every few days. But he was also
spreading the word that even when Mubarak was gone, Egypt's problems would persist. State oppression, a fact of Egyptian life for centuries,
wouldn't disappear along with one sagging, elderly president. There was
an intricate system behind Mubarak. General Tarek, the policeman I had
met at the club, might have been arrogant, but he was wise to the resil-

ience of the rule of the gun. Mubarak might go, but his regime would not surrender quietly.

On Thursday, February 10, 2011, the Supreme Council of the Armed Forces, or SCAF, issued "Communiqué Number One," which endorsed the "legitimate" demands of the protesters. Supposedly, the military wouldn't be running the country, but there was a uniformed general explaining how the country would be run, with nary a word about Mubarak. The transitional order taking shape was going to wear khakis. No one had heeded the highfalutin proposals from the Revolutionary Youth Coalition for a temporary presidential council that would include four civilian dissidents and Islamists, and one token general. At that moment, no one realized that a quiet coup had transpired; it no longer mattered what Mubarak was going to do. The military had stepped out from the curtain behind which it had been running most of Egypt's affairs since 1952. Uniformed men had openly taken control of the political realm.

Mubarak appeared on television for a final address. The people in Tahrir expected a resignation, but the president spoke from a place of deep denial, as if he would rule for some time to come. The father of the nation did not understand that his children had cast him off. People in Tahrir brandished shoes at the television screen.

"He wants blood!" someone screamed.

"*Khawwal!*" chanted others. "Faggot!"

"He thinks he can win people over with his emotions, but it's over," Basem said.

Moaz was already worried about the military's machinations. He was looking ahead to the next step, after Mubarak's coming departure. "We've had enough of military rule, but people still trust them," Moaz said. "They know only orders. We should have guarantees the military won't turn into another Mubarak."

The speech turned out to be the end for Mubarak. The next day, another Friday, more people came to Tahrir than ever before. The press of bodies was so dense that it was nearly impossible to move. The air was crisp and cool. Demonstrators exuded confidence. Some had been there for eighteen days; others had come for the first time. But they were sure that, sooner or later, Mubarak would be gone. I ran into Ayman Abouzaid, the young cardiologist. He had traded his dirty doctor's coat for a preppy white canvas jacket. He was stepping lightly in his blue suede shoes. He trusted nobody, not the "little Mubaraks" on the Revolutionary Youth Coalition, or any of the elderly politicians suddenly proposing reforms on television. "If Hosni Mubarak disappears," Ayman said, "the problem will remain: the deformation of a society."

The young revolutionaries by the green tent were smiling but nervous. They anticipated countless burdens. Zyad smoked continuously, rendering the air inside the tent unbreathable. It wasn't that cold, but Sally wore the fur-lined hood of her trench coat erect over her head. It flew like a banner of concern. Moaz had hardly slept, shuttling between the hospital, the green tent, and Brotherhood offices outside Tahrir. Ayyash worked out of a car in the morning and out of various apartments in the afternoon; one of his tasks was to prepare work-arounds in case authorities cut the internet again. Basem kept his orange scarf knotted tightly around his throat and spent much of the day editing statements and political strategy memos.

Without warning, Egypt's spy chief, Omar Suleiman, appeared on television. In his low, guttural voice, he announced Mubarak's resignation. The president was gone; the SCAF was in charge. A rumbling rose from all of Cairo. Inside the square, it was deafening, enveloping all senses. People seemed struck dumb, shouting whatever came to mind.

"Enough!"

"Good-bye and Godspeed!"

"Fuck his mother!"

Some of the soldiers in the cordon around Tahrir were grinning. Celebrants hugged them, and a few of the soldiers hugged back. Three men wept and thanked God, using newspapers as prayer mats. "This is the beginning of freedom," a young man said. "Message to the world from Egypt: We can change the world. We hate Israel."

His friends murmured in assent, "God is great."

Fireworks were popping. Thousands were singing "Biladi," the national anthem. The rumor spread that the Israeli Embassy had shut down, prompting more cheers. This was the revolution rolled into one ball in all its contradictions, with its hatred for injustice, powerlessness,

Mubarak, and Israel; and its love of God, dignity, country, and Great Egypt's army. Millions still thronged the square at midnight. Party boats skittered across the Nile, decked in neon and blasting music. Despite the chill, boys had stripped to their underwear and were swimming beneath the Qasr el-Nil bridge.

For the youth leaders, the moment provided a transitory respite from the already stomach-turning anxiety about what would come next. Standing beside the tent, Zyad lifted me off the ground in a bear hug. "Tomorrow belongs to us!" he said. Sally's hood was off. "We won!" she exclaimed, beaming. She embraced Moaz and other Islamists, whom she had considered political enemies a few years earlier. "I've been hugging people who normally wouldn't even touch a woman," she said.

Moaz was smiling so widely it made my face hurt; I realized that I too was grinning like a fool. "It's our country now," he said, squeezing me tightly. "People all over the world now are going to respect us because we are Egyptian. I think these days will not be repeated in history."

Ayyash cried as the news set in, and said the prayer of thanks usually given once a year at the Eid al-Adha. Then he bounced through the crowd like a teenager in a mosh pit. "I don't know what to do with myself," he said. "For the first time in my life, I am free."

Mubarak was gone. The military junta was issuing a flurry of decrees. The Revolutionary Youth Coalition was already planning a return protest, but the people in the square seemed ready to celebrate and move on, as if Mubarak's leaving had been the sum goal of the entire uprising. All the lofty words about dignity and fear had been forgotten in the whirl over Egypt's change of CEO. For the first time since the uprising, a soldier I had seen several times before blocked me from entering Tahrir. "Today is for Egyptians, not foreigners," he said. "Go out." The January 25 Revolution had most decidedly not vanquished xenophobia. I walked around and entered from a back street.

The coalition wanted to keep momentum on the revolution's side. It would be harder now that the battles would unfold on the less dramatic stage of governance, constitution writing, and elections—areas where their willingness to die would provide less of an advantage than it had in the street fights. But the revolutionaries hoped to summon a million or more people to the square every Friday until the nation's laws reflected the precepts of the Republic of Tahrir. Sally was drafting a strategy for a meeting between the revolutionary youth and Egypt's new rulers, the still-anonymous generals on the Supreme Council of the Armed Forces. Moaz was plotting a frontal challenge to keep the Muslim Brotherhood out of politics. Basem was fantasizing about a new political party.

Heedless of these political machinations, cheerful men and women lined the square from north to south, armed with brooms, dustpans, and plastic bags. Crews of volunteers mopped the street with squeegees. Others tried to fit paving stones back into place where the sidewalks had been torn asunder during the Battle of the Camel, as if the consequences of the eighteen days could be so swiftly assimilated. The youth of Tahrir were saying with this gesture, "We're all good kids, we didn't come to make a mess, and we're going to leave the place neater than we found it." Their extreme politeness, deference, and timidity were out of sync with their revolutionary aspirations. The youth weren't responsible for the trashing of the square; that was the fault of the police and the thugs who attacked them. It would have been more fitting for the aggressors to be forced back to sweep the square in atonement. The revolutionary cleanup suggested a naïve and premature thirst for closure. It would prove far easier to sweep away the debris in the square, and even Mubarak himself, than to topple just one pillar of the regime's edifice of control.

5.

SEEDS OF DISCONTENT

Mubarak had fled to his villa on the Red Sea, but no one had touched the guts of the regime: its secret police. Every time the Revolutionary Youth Coalition gathered in public, the same old informants and agents appeared, filming and taking notes. At one meeting, several leaders of the group had their phones stolen. One of the coalition members found a bullet hole in his car mirror. Moaz saw his old minder from State Security tailing him. These were unreconstructed regime techniques; surveillance and intimidation rolled into one. The Revolutionary Youth Coalition had made police reform a top priority. "The revolution is not complete," Moaz said. "The police must be judged."

Even though the police force still retained its former power and capacity for violence, the revolutionary leaders spoke fearlessly about their plan to gut and rebuild it. All at once, restrictions had been lifted on Egyptian media, so every night the talk shows hosted a raucous, open public debate. Revolutionaries and dissidents who had been banned from television studios were invited on night after night to describe their plans and enumerate the sins of the old regime. Moaz appeared one night in February on a popular program called *Coffee*, where he outlined the revolutionary agenda for police reform. The revolutionaries wanted a civilian placed in charge of the Ministry of the Interior, something that had never happened in Egyptian history. A police general had always controlled the ministry, just as a military general had always held the post of defense minister. In order to restore trust and reform the police, this independent civilian would suspend and investigate every police official suspected of crimes, from the minister down to the lowliest patrolmen. Those who broke the law or tortured or killed Egyptians would be convicted and imprisoned. A "truth commission" would handle the stories of the rest, who might have dabbled in minor corruption but couldn't be held responsible for the odious regime that had employed them. Other countries had reversed a culture of torture and impunity in their police forces. It wasn't impossible, but to do it required something that Egypt did not yet have: a zealous, powerful government premised on the rule of law, not fear.

Mistrust of the police burned deep in Moaz's heart. As a Muslim Brother, he had suffered from the security state's caprice his entire life, unlike many of the secular revolutionaries, who had grasped only recently the negative side of the state's authority. The police apparatus could strangle everything, Moaz believed, but he also knew that many Egyptians—perhaps most Egyptians—didn't share his inborn skepticism. The Egyptian everyman didn't object in principle to an all-powerful secret police force. They just wanted it to work better. Moaz sensed he was fighting against public opinion at a great disadvantage. On his way home from the studio, a large vehicle suddenly shot out of a dark alley, rammed Moaz's car, and then sped off. It couldn't have been an accident. He took it as a message from State Security.

———————

A month after the revolution in Tahrir, mini-revolutions had seized workplaces all over the country. Inside the Maspero Building, the headquarters of state television, once-docile journalists went on strike in the lobby. "The people want the fall of the minister!" they chanted, clutching posters with slogans such as "Free speech." On the mezzanine floor, the army had set up a machine-gun nest inside the international press center. A soldier scanned the Nile-front corniche while middle-aged functionaries processed journalist credentials. "We're still trying to figure out who's in charge," the headman said. "Everyone wants to make their own revolution, and every boss is another Mubarak. We'll find the way."

In addition to the usual student demonstrations, university professors marched across campus demanding the right to select their own deans.

Traffic police wanted higher wages. Everything felt up for grabs, from the loftiest to the most base. Those who cared for politics fought over what sort of liberties should be inscribed in the new constitution. Those more preoccupied with the sudden hiatus of state authority took advantage prosaically. Street vendors hawked their wares on previously forbidden sidewalks. Drivers flouted the few remaining traffic rules. Farmers erected outbuildings and walls along Nile tributaries where construction was banned; they figured inspectors would be preoccupied during this revolutionary moment.

Possibilities shimmered everywhere, and so did risks. The police had not returned to work since the January clashes. Criminals took note. Carjackings, once rare, threatened the entire busy ring road around Cairo. One taxi driver with whom I often traveled began to carry a retractable metal club beneath his seat. Before driving on lonely roads, he slipped a switchblade into his sleeve. A month after the revolution, he bought a gun as well. He fantasized about robbing a bank truck and retiring. In a single week, two well-known politicians were mugged in downtown Cairo, and another had his car stolen at gunpoint. Some people saw the lawlessness as a consequence of the revolt and blamed Tahrir for leaving Egypt exposed. The Revolutionary Youth Coalition saw it as blackmail. The police still accepted their government salaries but refused to do their jobs; eventually Egyptians would need them badly enough that they'd be willing to forgive previous crimes and give up on their revolution.

Police presided over all aspects of daily life, not just criminal justice. Egyptians registered to vote at their local police branch. They filed affidavits there for almost any bureaucratic necessity, from obtaining a passport or driver's license to reporting health code violations. State Security was the division that monitored and controlled everything else. It determined the hiring and firing of anyone in a politically sensitive job, which included everything from corporate middle management to medical department heads. It hired the millions of informants and thugs who reported on their neighbors and coworkers, on the local gangs, even on proregime politicians. State Security had infiltrated drug rings so deeply that it was impossible to tell whether they were spying on the dealers or running the deals themselves.

Revolutionaries were scrambling, the police were in hiding, and the military junta was making a passable show of comforting the nation. One general on the SCAF, Mohsen el-Fengary, had delivered a moving tribute to the martyrs of January 25, saluting them for "sacrificing their souls for the freedom and security of this country." His words struck the right tone, and as a result, few paid attention to what was actually happening. Only a few high-profile officials had been arrested: most prominently the steel tycoon Ahmed Ezz and interior minister Habib el-Adly. Superficially, it might have appeared like the start of accountability, but, in fact, the only major figures in detention were those whose power and financial interests conflicted with those of the military, which not only controlled its own security and intelligence branches but also ran a vast financial empire involved in everything from highway and resort construction to olive oil and ovens.

Egyptians had noticed that despite the theatrics, the secret police were still at work. In early March, impatient to reap something tangible from the revolution, activists gathered in front of the State Security headquarters in Alexandria. Inside, agents hurriedly shredded evidence of their vast clandestine apparatus. The anger of the youth outside outweighed the power of the snipers and the guards. They breached the perimeter and broadcasted incriminating footage of destroyed documents. Within hours, crowds overran every other major secret police headquarters in the country. On March 5 they penetrated the heart of the deep state itself: the State Security headquarters in Nasr City, Cairo. Inside, activists found piles of burned records, bags of shredded documents, and more reams diligently assembled and awaiting destruction. Zyad and Ayyash looked in vain for their files, but Moaz found transcripts of his telephone conversations with other Islamist activists. They were sure that they had taken the security establishment by surprise; otherwise State Security would have hidden its archives more carefully. "This is the most important thing we have done," Moaz declared.

Soldiers formed a cordon to make sure that the vigilantes didn't walk off with state secrets. The military was willing to allow its rivals in the secret police to be humiliated, but it didn't want the actual evidence of the deep state to emerge in public. State Security officers were arrested in front of the television cameras and then released discreetly. The scenes from state police bunkers were tweeted and livecast on Bambuser, an online personal broadcasting service, with citizen journalists narrating their triumph, no longer dependent on state media. This was the iconic scene of popular agency, like the people of Romania overrunning the palace and lynching dictator Nicolae Ceauşescu. The police had mishandled the Egyptian people, and, finally, the Egyptian people had struck back and won.

Even at the moment of triumph, however, Moaz and the other activists weren't fooled. They had achieved something pivotal by putting State Security on the defensive, but they hadn't seized the deep state's secret archives. Wise to the risks, State Security had hidden or destroyed its most important records. Activists had found almost no documents about torture or about State Security's network of secret prisons. And where were the dossiers on prominent politicians, plutocrats, and Muslim Brothers who had lived under the State Security microscope? Where was all the dirt collected as blackmail reserves against regime supporters who might one day need to be kept in line? None of the mountain of papers found by the activists concerned Egypt's real security issues: jihadists, the Sinai, the Israeli border, and armed domestic insurgents. It seemed that all the interesting security files had already been moved or destroyed.

The military had stood by while people stormed State Security. It hadn't choreographed the assault but had allowed and contained it. Some popular anger had been sublimated, as in the days of the marches for Palestine. Meanwhile, one of the military's most threatening bureaucratic rivals had conveniently been dealt a critical blow. Military police made sure to confiscate most of the secret police files seized by demonstrators. It wasn't as if the government had become more civil toward its citizens. The police and its old central security forces had fled the streets, but the military had replaced them. Now soldiers in camouflage uniforms beat and interrogated civilians with the same arbitrary vigor. Egypt still labored under a dictatorship, one with a greater concentration of power and even less transparency than Mubarak's. The Supreme Council of the Armed Forces never had published a list of its members. No one knew who was running the country and how.

———

Man doesn't kill by the blade alone. When a regime wants an entire people to submit, it cannot put them all in prison. It must bore their spirit to death, and among the best weapons for this purpose are rules and regulations. Egypt's generals knew the power of paper. Bureaucrats to a man, the SCAF generals hadn't smelled combat since 1973, except on the lucrative battlefield of contracting. They were going to contest power, and they were going to do it where it counted: in the small print, where they would aim to write themselves into a legal and permanent position of power. Why settle for informal power when you could be Egypt's legal guardian forever? People noticed sometimes if you shot them in the street, but they almost never read the terms and conditions published in the government's official gazette.

In spite of everything, many Egyptians believed in the law, the sanctity of their constitution, and the ideal of a government in which independent courts policed the separation of powers. Playing to this sentiment, and perhaps believing in it to some degree, the junta appointed a panel of scholars to draft a legal path forward. In a few days, the panel came up with a package of constitutional amendments. Few members of the general public paid attention to the details. The amendments seemed to spell a legal path forward to freedom and a less dictatorial system. The next president would be limited to two terms. There were some rules about how to run for president, which seemed more open than the old rigged system. Best of all, the newly liberated people of Egypt would get to vote on the amendments.

But the small print enraged the revolutionaries and even the more cautious liberals such as ElBaradei. The amendments were full of restrictions that seemed designed to disqualify liberals with their international lifestyles and history of exile; for example, presidential candidates couldn't be married to foreigners or have a parent who was a citizen of a foreign country. These articles clearly targeted ElBaradei, whose wife was widely if incorrectly believed to have a foreign passport. Even worse, there was no timeline for a transfer to civilian rule. In the Egyptian media, SCAF members said they'd like to hand over power within six months, but they made no promises or formal commitment to any specific process or date by which generals would surrender power to civilians.

Such obtuseness could come only by design. The amendments were superficial and sloppy, drafted by a panel chosen by an opaque junta and dominated by the Muslim Brotherhood. The Brothers supported the generals' plan because it provided an advantage to those who already had a political network: themselves. All those who were suspicious of military rule coalesced against the whole idea: the young revolutionaries and the disparate society of pluralists, liberals, and secularists. They believed the military should hand over power to civilians: any civilians, or even a presidential council that would include three or four luminaries along with a uniformed representative of the military. Then a newly legitimate presidency could design a process to draft a deliberate, revolutionary constitution for Egypt that would have popular input and legal foundations.

The list of amendments was finalized on February 26. The Egyptian people would have a chance to vote on them only a few weeks later, on March 18. Only two groups actually wanted the referendum to pass: the SCAF and the Muslim Brotherhood. They were the only two groups in Egypt that contributed to the text of the transitional constitution and that had the money and the organization to run nationwide election campaigns. The general public, maybe influenced by the cheery coverage in state media, applauded what seemed like a road map away from Mubarak's times to something better. The offended revolutionaries scrambled to explain exactly why they opposed the amendments. They couldn't even communicate with one another, distracted as they were by their different projects and ideological communities. How would they figure out how to talk to the public? Their opposition was to military rule, and in a brilliant act of political theater, the military junta was presenting itself as the champion of popular democracy. The people would get to vote, present their voice, in perhaps the first election in Egypt's history that wouldn't be a fraud. Could the revolutionaries oppose this popular referendum without seeming petty and petulant?

In a nod to the newfangled methods of January 25, the Supreme Council of the Armed Forces opened a Facebook page, where it posted its decrees. The junta was experimenting to see how much attention it had to pay to the unremitting daily protests. Twice the generals invited representatives of the Revolutionary Youth Coalition to meet. Moaz and the others reeled off their demands: Fire the prime minister, reform the police, end the state of emergency, hand authority to a civilian, and initiate economic reforms. The bemused generals listened politely and then ignored them. Soldiers beat up some protesters, but the SCAF apologized on Facebook. The small demonstrations intensified; to appease them, the government froze Mubarak's assets.

Prime Minister Ahmed Shafik was dispatched to nighttime television to mollify public sentiment. Shafik was an air force general and a Mubarak man through and through. Like most of the old guard, he was still learning the conventions of these new, post–January 25 politics, in which it was no longer acceptable to show open contempt for citizens. In his appearance, a red-faced Shafik insulted the "garbage" in Tahrir. He didn't want to talk about putting his old boss Mubarak on trial; he wanted to order people off the streets and back to work. He seemed incredulous that a revolutionary novelist had equal billing on the talk show and was daring to ask him questions. Finally, the bewildered old general exploded.

"I fought in wars!" he screeched, his irritation driving him to nonsense. "I killed and was killed!"

The SCAF decided to fire Shafik even before he went off the air. They replaced him with an avuncular professor of traffic engineering named Essam Sharaf, who had been featured on the Revolutionary Youth Coalition's list of acceptable candidates. Basem, Moaz, and the others took this as a sign of their strength; the junta had jettisoned one of its own loyalists for a man promoted by the revolutionary youth. But just a few days later, the military sent a countervailing signal, breaking up the small sit-in that had persisted in Tahrir. Soldiers burned tents and rounded up activists. They subjected the women they detained to "virginity tests," probing their vaginas with their fingers. Supposedly this would determine whether their prisoners were already sexually active, so that they couldn't later falsely accuse their captors of rape. One of the detainees was Ramy Essam, a singer who had become famous as the balladeer of Tahrir; he had become a symbol of the revolutionary youth and he performed his anti-regime songs at nearly every major protest. He was beaten across every stretch of his face and back.

Egyptian media took the side of the military, refusing to publish the detainees' accounts of torture and molestation after they were released. An unknown general named Abdel Fattah el-Sisi made his public debut defending the "virginity tests" as a distasteful necessity. A small group of human rights activists ramped up a campaign against the rampant use of military trials for civilians. But the military had succeeded in convincing much of the public to swallow any account offered by its rulers.

The SCAF had begun a long experiment by first preying on those rebels who were the most marginal, and therefore the most vulnerable: artists, feminists, supporters of gay rights. These revolutionaries were viewed with distaste even by some of the more conventional activists. The military was going to find out whether there would be any uproar over their treatment. If it could finger-rape female demonstrators and scar a visible musician with impunity, then it could move on to bigger objectives.

A sort of disorienting drunkenness had swept the revolutionary organizers; they were not sure what to do next. One week a dozen activists would appear on television repeating the same talking points; they would overexpose themselves, appearing self-promotional and undisciplined. The next week, in an effort to appear less eager, they would disappear, failing to address key developments about the referendum or condemn the beating and arrest of civilians. They scheduled press conferences but forgot to invite any journalists. The Revolutionary Youth Coalition agreed that, for now, it needed to maintain the street pressure. Sally was organizing revolutionary visits all over the country, a caravan that would link Tahrir to the cities and towns that endowed the uprising with its national character. Activists from all over Egypt had made the eighteen days possible; Sally knew that a true revolution required their continued involvement.

The supporters of Mohamed ElBaradei who were now on the coalition also wanted a political tool that could pressure the military and articulate a change agenda for Egypt. They believed "the doctor," as they affectionately called him, could lead an enduring movement, but they waited in vain for ElBaradei to take action. "It's time for us to form a political party," Basem told ElBaradei. "The people need your leadership." But El-Baradei hesitated. He kept postponing a decision, frustrating the acolytes who had welcomed him back to Egypt so effusively. Alone among them, Basem had a clear direction. Yes, there were infinite possible courses of action, but Basem had learned from his life that he preferred to choose one. Now he wanted to make an impact in politics. ElBaradei's ideas had galvanized him in the first place, and he cared more for them than for the man. He would work to establish the strongest political party that embodied ElBaradei's principles, with or without ElBaradei as the leader.

The referendum was looming, and ElBaradei refused to take a position for or against it. Finally, the secular activists on the coalition decided to move on their own, but they differed on their priorities. One faction, including Sally and most of the veteran street fighters, wanted to preserve the tactics of Tahrir, opposing the referendum and spreading a revolutionary agenda through amorphous grassroots ventures. The other faction, led by Basem and Zyad, was convinced that only a viable political organization could exert any real influence. Anything else was a half measure. They wanted to build a national political party with a concrete social democratic agenda.

Long after it might make a difference, the revolutionaries finally decided to make a public stand against the constitutional referendum that the military was foisting upon Egypt at knifepoint. Just four days before the March 19 vote, the Revolutionary Youth Coalition called a press conference in a borrowed lounge at *Al Masry Al Youm*, one of Egypt's few credible independent newspapers. Nobody in the building seemed to know about it. Finally, someone directed the press corps to the newspaper's kitchen, where a grumpy attendant brewed tea and reporters took their smoke breaks. The Revolutionary Youth Coalition leaders arrived an hour behind schedule; by then it was hard to see through the cigarette fumes.

"We are late, as usual," Basem said.

Indeed. With days to go before Egyptians were to vote, the revolution was finally ready to tell people why they should vote "no." Even if they had concocted a brilliant rationale, there was no time left to explain it to anybody. What they had to say made sense, but it was hard to imagine it catching on as a national slogan: "Constitution first." That was their message. First, a fully representative assembly should write a blueprint for Egypt's new government. Then the people should vote on their new constitution. Then, with the duties and separation of powers of the new government clearly established, Egypt could elect a new president and parliament. It made sense, but it was a complicated idea, hard to market. The Muslim Brotherhood was telling voters that a vote against the constitutional amendments was a vote against God. The military was telling people that a "no" was a vote against stability and progress. Meanwhile, the trusting revolutionary youth were eager to make their case but would respect anyone who disagreed. It was a clear mismatch, which they were sure to lose.

The members of the Revolutionary Youth Coalition unanimously opposed the referendum. Such unity was rare. Naïvely, many of them thought that their common sense of purpose would translate into an immediate effect on the public's perception.

Basem wasn't so confident. "I am worried," he said. "The army is not good. Things are not good. The old regime and the Islamic movements are all united against us."

That night, the revolutionary youth leaders refused to meet with US Secretary of State Hillary Clinton. They didn't want to be seen conversing with a symbol of American power. So Clinton's aides assembled a random assortment of second-tier activists, who told Clinton that they didn't believe in political parties. From then on, Clinton had the mistaken impression that the revolutionary youth leaders of Tahrir had stayed clear of politics, when the truth was that most of them had dived into politics wholeheartedly; they just weren't necessarily any good at it.

The Revolutionary Youth Coalition wanted to burnish its nationalist credentials and perhaps feared that it would be portrayed as a tool of the imperialists if it met with Clinton. In style, however, it was displaying the same kind of dumb nationalist chauvinism that was the stock-in-trade of the military and the old regime. The revolution was all about dialogue and combining principles with action. Yet reality presented complicated choices about how to craft a political campaign message, influence senior leaders, and negotiate deals with military officers and rich power brokers.

What had worked during the eighteen days in Tahrir might not be the best approach now.

On the eve of the vote, a few delegates from the Revolutionary Youth Coalition traveled to the provincial delta city of Mansoura to rally against the constitutional referendum. Mansoura was an Islamist stronghold, and the revolutionaries wanted to make a point of establishing beach-heads beyond the two major cities of Cairo and Alexandria. I met Ayyash outside the rally; Mansoura was his hometown. It only took a moment to sense how greatly the promilitary, pro–Muslim Brotherhood forces out-numbered the hapless liberals and revolutionaries. I could barely discern any of the white revolutionary banners in the sea of yellow Brotherhood signs that read simply, "Yes for the constitutional amendments." Many in attendance planned to vote for the amendments but had come to the rally to see what the revolutionaries and liberals had to offer. They weren't impressed.

The secular leftists who opposed the Brotherhood had emulated the Islamist tent revival style for their rally. They had set up plastic chairs beneath an awning at a major intersection. Pop music and prayers blared from the system so loudly that it hurt my ears and rendered words un-intelligible. First, they appealed to emotion. The father of a boy killed in Tahrir hugged a picture of his son, bringing many in the audience to tears. Speeches extolled the martyrs of January 25. Then the rally orga-nizers tried to galvanize the audience to action. Zyad, perhaps the only speaker under the age of fifty, said that voting "no" was a way to continue the revolution. One speaker called those who wouldn't vote his way "trai-tors." Overall, the speakers sounded shrill, intolerant, and incoherent, and they went on for three hours. In private, I had heard revolutionaries make plausible arguments for why the new amendments would doom Egypt's transition to democracy by handing too much power to the army and the Muslim Brotherhood, but no one made that case clearly in pub-lic. The audience was tiny, maybe a thousand, and afterward I couldn't find a single person whose mind had been changed.

Basem and Zyad had been busy with their plans to set up a new political party. They treated the "no" campaign and the Revolutionary Youth Coalition almost as necessary distractions. Instead of thinking about their primary enemy—the military junta that controlled Egypt and its transition—they were scheming about how to compete with their biggest future political rival, the Muslim Brotherhood. Political liberty and free elections were by no means guaranteed while Egypt suffered military rule, but the liberal revolutionaries had already jumped ahead to the electoral contests of the future. They had decided not to wait for ElBaradei and had collected a core group of a few hundred intellectuals and businessmen who shared a commitment to classical liberalism and progressive economics. Their basic idea was European-style social democracy: civil liberties and a free market but with enough government intervention to protect the poor. The Friday night before the referendum, about five hundred of them gathered in a conference room on the fourth floor of the Journalists Syndicate. Smoke stifled the room as they fought over the new party's name.

"Tomorrow!" someone suggested.

"That's already taken."

"How about Egypt Tomorrow?"

"The Road!"

"The Free!"

"The Path!"

"The Square!"

The proposals were listed on a whiteboard. From the stage, the party's presumptive leadership refereed the debate. Sally and Zyad sat beside Dr. Mohamed Aboul-Ghar, the famous gynecologist and dissident whose chants had fallen flat the night before at the Mansoura rally. Tonight he held the central place of honor. Most of the Tahrir activists sat in the room, with the exception of youth from Islamist backgrounds and the April 6 Movement activists, who tended to be more socially and economically conservative. Finally, a more precise if far less evocative name won the day: Egyptian Social Democratic Party. The outcome presaged what would become a persistent problem with branding the revolution and reform.

"This name—it's what you get with the democratic process," Sally said. "I would have preferred El Tarik, 'the Road,' or El Masri, 'the Egyptian.' "

"We are beginning something now," Zyad said, as if to fend off any premature sense of achievement. "We must start working."

These might have been the first and perhaps even the best of the secular activists to establish a political party after Mubarak. Yet it was already apparent that they would be one faction among many in a bickering, fragmented space. Notably absent was Amr Hamzawy, a good-looking young academic who had recently returned from a career abroad to teach at the American University of Cairo and Cairo University. He had spoken charismatically at the rally in Mansoura the night before. The public seemed to like him. Hamzawy found that the social democrats in the making didn't have clear answers to his questions about how to promote a genuinely liberal Egypt unyoked from military rule, so he had decided to start a one-man party of his own. Naguib Sawiris, a Christian billionaire, was also bankrolling his own more probusiness party.

Afterward, the younger founders repaired to a downtown beer garden. Basem stayed only a few minutes, while Zyad had one ear in the conversation and one on his phone. He was talking to activists in the provinces, trying to make sure that he had contacts at every major polling station.

"I think we will lose tomorrow," he said. "But we have gathered many people to vote no. And we will build on this for the parliamentary campaign."

It was easy to see why the revolutionaries and their liberal allies were likely to fail. Yet, in some ways, the coming referendum felt like a birth. No matter who won, the referendum was a sort of victory for the revolution; a democratic process at work after a half century of paralysis. It set forth a map that was imperfect, flawed, with devils sewn into every detail; but, as bad as it was, it was a map to somewhere. And even if the generals displayed contempt for the people of Egypt, they still had been forced to respect the people's sovereignty and to seek their approval by ballot. Undeniably, that was something good.

Saturday dawned crisp and warm, a perfect spring day. Even the outgunned liberals and their doomed "no" campaign couldn't help themselves, grinning foolishly as they gathered in front of the Kasr el-Dobara Evangelical Church a block south of Tahrir Square. Once again they looked like a wedding party. On this day, everyone in Egypt did. The venom and rancor of the campaign dissolved briefly in the ritual of the vote, the first vote that would actually be counted. Yesterday everyone had traded toxic recriminations. The "yes" voters were undermining the revolution, in bed with the military and the *felool*, the remnants of the old regime. The "no" voters were trying to turn the country into a chaotic, perpetual Tahrir. Amending the constitution would pave the way for a military dictatorship or the ascendance of Islamic fundamentalists. Or perhaps amending the constitution was the only way to enshrine the revolution into rule of law. Today, however, for a few hours, everyone in Egypt was a democrat, expressing a free will, ready to respect the outcome no matter who won. This was the first tangible achievement of the January 25 revolution.

The streets were empty of traffic; this debut Election Day was a holiday. The founders of the newly christened Egyptian Social Democratic Party and some of their revolutionary friends had agreed to meet at nine in the morning to walk together to the polling station. They gathered an hour late. Zyad wore a tennis shirt and slacks. Professor Amr Hamzawy had turned up the collar of his polo shirt, like a frat boy, and it mirrored his wild hair. A who's who of liberal Egypt strolled down Qasr el-Ayni Street, past the parliament entrance and the cabinet of ministers—the seat of government and the site of so much past and future strife. *"Sabah al-demokratia,"* they greeted one another. "Morning of democracy." At a primary school, already hundreds of Cairenes were in line to vote.

Many of the people in line were still afraid to give their names. Almost all of them said that the big thrill of the day was voting without knowing in advance how the election was going to turn out. The governor of Cairo province arrived with a ten-man entourage, in the arrogant style of the disbanded ruling party, of which he had been a senior member. His motorcade double-parked in front of the polling station. Wearing sunglasses, he strode past the line of voters without a word of greeting. This man certainly didn't betray any recognition that the revolution had changed anything, even regarding the aesthetic requirements of power. He behaved as if he still owned Cairo. The people, however, were done with this sort of display.

"Wait in line like everyone else!" some shouted.

"Barra! Barra!" shouted others. "Get out!"

"Even the prime minister is waiting in line!" someone hollered. "Why are you better?"

George Ishak, a retired teacher, human rights activist, and founder of Kifaya, knew the governor from years of personal run-ins. He approached, shaking with rage. "I thought we were done with these old games," he said.

Ignoring it all, the governor walked into the voting room, took a look, chatted briefly with the judge in charge, and exited. Only then, in the courtyard, did he deign to speak to anyone.

"I am making an inspection to ensure everything is as it should be," the governor said.

A woman shouted, "He at least could talk to the people!"

The governor stared straight ahead. The chants of the crowd synchronized and swelled. "Get out! Get out!" they roared. The governor slipped into his car, and thunderous applause rang out as the motorcade pulled away.

On the Nile island of Manial, voters booed when the supreme guide of the Muslim Brotherhood went to the front of the line, even though he was entitled to do so because he was older than sixty. Ahmed Shafik, the general and recently humiliated prime minister, was seen driving himself to a polling station, wearing a tracksuit. Mohamed ElBaradei went to a polling station in Moqattam with a group of supporters but was attacked by thugs who smashed his car windows.

Unlike his liberal friends, Moaz voted for the amendments. He was loath to vote the same way as the Brotherhood, but he wanted power out of the military's hands as quickly as possible. "Power is like an apple for the military," he said. "Even if it does not suit them well, it is sweet. I am afraid of the military's power. We should make as short as possible the time that the military sits in the president's chair."

The results overwhelmingly favored the generals, with 77 percent approving the amendments. Turnout was higher than in any election in Mubarak's time, which comforted the revolutionaries. But their showing did not. The "no" side won 40 percent of the vote in Cairo and a third in

Alexandria. Everywhere else, it had been completely overwhelmed. The vote had demonstrated the inability of secular and liberal forces to unify and organize. It had also shown the potency of the military and the Islamists, especially when they were collaborating. They had used the state media to campaign for the referendum, and the Islamists had employed shameless libel, spreading rumors that a "no" vote would erase existing references to Islam from the constitution.

The amendments would be the original sin of the transition. A dictatorship by committee had taken over from Mubarak, and, with a popular vote, it now had gained the stamp of legitimacy. The devil *was* in the details. By fiat, with no consultation and little thought, the generals had published a vague constitutional road map that contained the recipe for disasters for years to come. The constitutional declaration haphazardly banned some candidates based on whether their relatives had obtained second passports. It didn't set forth a balance of powers among the parliament, the president, and the assembly that would write the next constitution, setting the stage for confusion, power grabs, and a hyper-empowered bureaucracy. It didn't establish a timetable for the transition. Any lawyer who read the document saw these perils. To underscore the referendum's real significance, immediately after winning, the SCAF published the revised constitution that would henceforth govern Egypt. Its text was significantly different from that of the amendments subjected to the vote. But now the generals were confident that they could act capriciously in their own interest, and most Egyptians would still hail them as saviors of the nation.

The other kingmakers, the Muslim Brothers, were adjusting to the sunlight after decades of operating in secret. Nominally, Supreme Guide Mohamed Badie since 2010 had run the group with a small cabinet called the Guidance Council. A larger body called the *Shura*, or Consultative Council, elected by the membership, gave input on important matters. In practice, however, the supreme guide, a retired physical education professor, wasn't considered the most important man in the group; that honor was reserved for Khairat el-Shater, a self-made millionaire with thriving enterprises in technology, textiles, and construction. He was the

Brotherhood's financial wizard. He'd been sent to prison in 2007 by a military tribunal, but from his cell he had continued to run the Brotherhood's finances and his business empire. He had just been released by the SCAF a few weeks before the referendum, in March.

Ayyash arranged a meeting with el-Shater; he had good contacts with him because el-Shater had established the Brotherhood's online presence, in which Ayyash had been pivotal. The day after the referendum, I entered a quiet apartment bloc overlooking the palm-lined square beside the Belal Mosque in Nasr City. El-Shater sat on a gilded Louis XIV sofa, talking with two men. He was a bear of a man, with a huge head and body, wearing a navy blazer with gold buttons. His reading glasses sat crooked on his nose. He looked like a yacht captain or a tennis club owner. El-Shater's aides had set up a fax machine and a laptop on a small table. Two weeks out of prison, el-Shater had back-to-back meetings, all day, every day. He spoke directly about the Brotherhood's plans.

"We believe the problems facing Egypt are far bigger than us and our quest for power," he said. The Brotherhood knew that it was the most important political factor in Egypt other than the military, and he had no doubt that eventually it would dominate. He saw no hurry: Egypt should handle its transition carefully and establish sound rules for political life, and once the military had been gracefully steered out of power, the Brotherhood could clobber its competitors. He was well aware that his organization had a horrible reputation among secular Egyptians. The Brotherhood, he said, had to tread carefully; political life had opened up, but for decades the government had terrified the public with its anti-Brotherhood propaganda. The Islamists would have to win trust. He sounded all the right notes to reassure those who feared the Brotherhood: "We must cooperate with all Egyptian people, all religions, men and women, all political parties," el-Shater said. He wanted to persuade skeptical Egyptians and Westerners that the Brotherhood didn't want to grab power. The group, he promised, would contest only one-third of the seats in parliament, even though it was certainly organized enough to win more. And to reassure Egyptians afraid that a Brotherhood juggernaut might impose religious rule, el-Shater assured me and later on everyone else he met that the Brotherhood wouldn't run a candidate for president.

"We know people fear us, and we have to work to make a better image among them," he said. "There was a lot of cooperation between us to topple the regime. People came together on demands, not on ideologies. After the revolution, we need to convince people to stay in the same spirit."

He thought that the Brotherhood could lead a unified coalition to contest the parliamentary elections, which would include everyone who resisted the old regime. Such unity, of course, had never been achieved before. Even before Tahrir, in the fall of 2010, when most political opposition parties had called for a boycott of the parliamentary ballot, the Brotherhood had refused to join. El-Shater didn't seem to understand how much the liberals hated the Islamists, and how much the revolutionary Islamist youth mistrusted the Brotherhood leadership, himself included. He used some inclusive rhetoric when he talked about secular political parties, although there was no evidence as to whether he meant it. When it came to his internal critics, el-Shater sounded as authoritarian as Mubarak. Young Muslim Brothers, including Ayyash and Moaz, had publicly criticized the Brotherhood's decision to enter directly into politics. They thought the Brotherhood should concentrate on its charities and religious outreach, leaving its members free to form an assortment of different political parties that would be fully independent of the supreme guide. El-Shater dismissed the breakaway Islamists as inexperienced and impatient. "I spent twelve years in prison under Mubarak's reign," he said. "The youth don't realize how hard we've had it. They can talk about change, but the Brotherhood as an organization will decide what it wants."

Ayyash hedged his bets. He froze his active membership in the Brotherhood, but he agreed to work for el-Shater as a consultant for the Brotherhood's websites. His mentor in the Brotherhood had always entertained Ayyash's critical thinking but had advised him to "hold fast to the group with your dog teeth." Now Ayyash had grown to loathe the authoritarian leaders of the group and their backward policies against women, Christians, and secular Egyptians. He also feared the organization: he had seen the Brotherhood slander former members who broke with it. Yet so deeply ingrained was the society of Muslim Brothers in his life that he could not imagine rejecting the group fully. All his friends and coworkers bore the stamp of the Brotherhood, whether their membership was active, dormant, or lapsed. Even his mentor's son Mohammed had quit in disgust.

"I won't leave the idea of the Muslim Brotherhood," Ayyash told Mohammed over orzo soup one afternoon. "I will leave the organization of the Muslim Brotherhood."

"It's become a dictatorship," his friend said, shaking his head angrily.

"I will leave the country if the Muslim Brotherhood is ruling!" Ayyash agreed. "Maybe in ten years' time, they will be ready."

Moaz and the top leaders of the Muslim Brotherhood's youth wing, who had worked for the revolution since the beginning, made a clearer break. They told their supervisors that they could not support the transformation of the Brotherhood into a political party, which they believed would erase all its moral authority. They planned to establish their own political party, which among other things would clearly endorse a secular state.

"Why don't you join our new Freedom and Justice Party?" his supervisor asked him. "You can be a founding member."

"It is a huge mistake for the Brotherhood to become a political party," Moaz said. "I cannot support it. We will go ahead with our own plan."

"If you do this, you risk expulsion from the Brotherhood," the supervisor warned him.

"The Brotherhood's rules are not from God or the Prophet. If these rules don't fit our time, why not change them?" Moaz replied. "I will never leave the Brotherhood. I hope it does not leave me."

There were other schisms in the party too. A senior member of the Guidance Bureau, a popular doctor and lifelong Brother named Abdel Moneim Aboul Fotouh, had declared that he would run for president. He had immediately been kicked out of the group, and the leaders had announced that any Brother who worked for Aboul Fotouh's presidential bid could be stripped of his membership. The disaffected Muslim Brotherhood youth met at a hotel in Zamalek, in defiance of Khairat el-Shater's direct orders. It was understood that anyone who attended the conference would be in trouble. Moaz and the other independent liberal

Islamist youth felt ready to test their appeal. If they could draw enough of the dynamic youth activists to their conference, they could decisively break with the Brotherhood and galvanize their own movement.

Hundreds of elite Muslim Brotherhood youth showed up, among them the children of senior Brotherhood leaders who had been groomed for important futures in the group. Two Islamist lawyers who had gone to school with Zyad, Islam Lutfi and Mohammed al-Qasas, were selected to lead a new party, which they would call al-Tayyar al-Masry: the Egyptian Current. Their idea had a beautiful simplicity: As individuals, they would bring Brotherhood values to their party: discipline, focus, hard work, good morals, and a dedication to helping others. But as a group, al-Tayyar al-Masry was to be the opposite of the Brotherhood in every possible way. Egypt was for everybody, they believed, and not just for devout Muslims. Al-Tayyar was premised on a commitment to a secular, inclusive state. Beyond that, the party's members would choose, through transparent internal votes, every single policy position. In this party, no leader would tell the rank and file what to think. The members would have full control, and the leaders would serve them.

Moaz loved this bottom-up philosophy, but he cared less about the idea than whether it would work. If al-Tayyar could attract members and money, it could spread its message. From the start, the party's democratic idealism interfered with recruiting. People flocked by the hundreds to the party's early interest meetings in the spring and summer; they were drawn by the pedigree of al-Tayyar's founders. Once in the door, however, prospective members were confused to find the party a work in progress.

"I came here because I don't like what's going on in the Brotherhood, and I like the youth. But I want to hear an ideology. What is your program?" a potential recruit asked quizzically at an interest meeting I attended.

"That'll be for you to decide," the recruiter explained. "We won't be a dictatorship. Once we have a critical mass of members, we will convene a convention, and the members will decide the party's program."

In the abstract, it was a magnificently democratic notion, but in practice, it confused people who were seeking an idea to rally behind, not a project to shoulder. As the months wore on, al-Tayyar's membership lingered in the low thousands.

However, the Brotherhood still took its young critics seriously. It moved first against the official leaders, expelling Islam Lutfi right away and initiating hearings against the others. Moaz they hoped to persuade to recant; he thought just as eagerly that he could get the Brotherhood leaders to see things his way. He was summoned to a disciplinary hearing. His supervisor asked him to respond to charges of disobedience and doctrinal heresy. Moaz spent nine hours explaining his view that he was, in fact, staying true to the Brotherhood's actual mission, based on its founding texts, and that it was the policies of the group's current leadership that were deviant. Naïvely, perhaps, Moaz thought he had a chance to change the minds of his inquisitors. He had never stopped calling his supervisor every day. He had never hidden any of his thoughts or plans. In May, when the long-banned Brotherhood opened a gleaming new hilltop headquarters on Cairo's edge, Moaz came to congratulate el-Shater and the rest of the leaders. It was a surreal scene, with an Islamic pop band singing and old state security agents and politicians politely shaking hands with Brothers fresh out of prison. Moaz wandered through the party like an estranged cousin. Technically, this was still his group and family; he had yet to be formally expelled. But he left alone. A few blocks down the hill, he got a flat tire. He jacked up his car, unscrewed the wheel, and, without help from anyone, rolled it to a repair shop, all the while bathed in the percussive beats of the Brotherhood's music.

By July, Ayyash had withdrawn from all his Brotherhood projects. The second leader of al-Tayyar al-Masry was formally kicked out of the Brotherhood, and Moaz realized that he would suffer the same fate sooner or later. Moaz's hearings went on for weeks. He brought a lawyer and rallied support among young Brothers on Facebook. Already he had stopped meeting with his *usra*, and his supervisor no longer spoke to him every day. When the decision came, it sent Moaz into depression. The secular activists on the Revolutionary Youth Coalition had never known the feeling of identifying so completely with a vast and powerful organization. They asked Moaz with genuine wonder how it felt after a lifetime to no longer be a Brother. "It's like a split in a big family," he said quietly. "Like I am no longer welcome at my father's table."

The Brotherhood juggernaut crashed forward, with simple, compelling slogans such as "Elections first." A huge number of Egyptians trusted that the Muslim Brotherhood was, at a minimum, competent and moral. Its members were religious, and the organization had been providing health care, education, and religious instruction since 1928. It was a record no other group in Egypt could match. The Brotherhood leaders believed that they should force elections on the quickest possible timetable for two reasons: it would maximize the Brotherhood's advantage over other political forces, which were still getting organized, and it would allow a civilian government to take office before the military and the old regime had time to regroup and cancel the whole democratic experiment. Gone was the caution of Khairat el-Shater in the spring, when he was concerned about mollifying the Brotherhood's critics. Now the Brotherhood was claiming that it represented 90 percent of the population, and that Egypt was "by nature an Islamic state." Once elections were held, the Brotherhood would consider itself entitled to do whatever it wanted, with the blessing of the majority. The group's awesome organizational muscle was on display in every province. While the revolutionaries scrambled to establish tiny political parties, and young activists convened teach-ins and tweet meetups, the Brotherhood was campaigning for political office. Parliamentary and presidential elections hadn't been scheduled yet, but the Brotherhood rallied its base of millions for an inevitable contest.

Mohamed Morsi, a rocket engineer and el-Shater loyalist, was running the Brotherhood's newly established political arm, named the Freedom and Justice Party. The name was confusingly similar to that of the much smaller revolutionary group called the Youth Movement for Justice and Freedom. Morsi barnstormed Egypt. His rallies drew thousands of spectators to a well-calibrated mix of inspiration, political talking points, and patronage. I attended one of these Brotherhood events in the corn-growing delta town of Shibin el-Kom. Brotherhood businessmen sold food and household goods at a discount. Clerics were on hand to talk about the Koran, and agronomists to explain the Brotherhood's plan to streamline farmers' cooperatives. There was a protected area for children to play. Morsi gave a feisty speech packed with policy specifics and with market-tested suggestions for his supporters. He repeated a simple summary of the Brotherhood's platform, and he asked every member to approach seven voters a day. In what would later become his signature cry, Morsi issued a warning against the military, which had begun to act like it was in charge.

"The people made this revolution! The military is only temporarily protecting it!" he shouted. "The only legitimacy in this country today comes from the people!"

At the end of July, a few weeks later, just before Ramadan, the Brotherhood and its Salafi allies scheduled a pan-Islamist demonstration in Tahrir. The military gave its blessing. The SCAF and the Brotherhood shared a common interest in strong-arming secular liberals. It turned out to be the most crowded protest since the revolution: maybe a million people, some of them carrying the black flag of jihad or the green flag of Saudi Arabia, chanting, "The people want God's law!" The show of unity and religious extremism unnerved liberal revolutionaries, who called it "Kandahar Friday," after the Taliban stronghold in southern Afghanistan. A half year after Mubarak's fall, the momentum lay not with revolutionary idealists but with a clandestine organization run in absolute secret by a group of bearded men.

6.

STUCK IN THE SQUARE

Tensions were flaring within the Revolutionary Youth Coalition. Its obsession with the process of democracy often distracted its leaders from the goal of transforming Egypt into a more democratic place. The commitment to pluralism and transparency made the revolutionaries at times seem much too reasonable for the dirty fight at hand. The Islamist members felt marginalized, and there had been a lot of anger over the decision of Zyad and the other ElBaradei supporters to form a political party. Many of the revolutionaries, secular as well as Islamic, felt it was premature to enter such a deformed political process, especially one that was designed and controlled by the military. In the contest of stability against chaos, stability seemed always to have the advantage. The generals in power had set the terms of the narrative, employing the dominant machinery of the state bureaucracy and media. The revolutionaries were afraid to criticize the military in public and had produced no real, visible leaders. There was talk of disbanding the coalition, even though it was the only trustworthy group that could speak for Tahrir. Its Thursday-night meetings at the Café Balad bookstore, on Mohamed Mahmoud Street beside the Cilantro coffee shop, felt less and less like a font of possibility and more like drudge work. Maintaining manpower and focus was a problem. Some of the major strategists among the revolutionaries were struggling to make ends meet. Alaa Abdel Fattah, the blogger and labor activist, and one of the smartest thinkers among the revolutionaries, had to take a computer programming job in South Africa to earn a living.

At the end of March, the SCAF had proposed a law that would criminalize all protests. There was just enough backlash from young people in the squares and from the new political leaders to make it shelve the idea, at least for the moment. Weekly protests drew only a few hundred hard-core activists, who groused that the coalition, and the founders of political parties such as the Social Democrats and al-Tayyar, were "stealing the revolution." People preoccupied with politics would talk instead of fight, the thinking went, and the old regime would win.

On the last Friday in May, the Revolutionary Youth Coalition organized its first million-man march in Tahrir without any help from the Islamists. The coalition was determined to prove that it could assemble a crowd even without Muslim Brothers, but it won only a Pyrrhic victory, filling the crowd but exposing its divisions. Speakers screamed from five competing platforms. There were dozens of different messages. The only thing everyone agreed on was that Mubarak should go on trial. Moaz was proud that hundreds of Brotherhood youth had attended, heeding the call of the breakaway al-Tayyar al-Masry faction rather than the command of the supreme guide.

Despite its tiny number of recruits, al-Tayyar had managed security for the protest, which was called "the Friday of the Second Revolution." Basem saw danger in the incoherence. "Everyone still wants to have his own stage," he said. "We have to make dialogue between all of us to decide on what we need." Basem wanted the law to come first: a bill of rights that would protect the Egyptian people from any surge by powerful forces: the Islamists, the military, the old regime. The old energy was gone. Basem, Moaz, and the rest of the Revolutionary Youth Coalition hoped they could reinvigorate the same people who had filled Tahrir from January 25 to February 11. This time around, though, the protest felt like a party, with ice-cream cones, cotton candy, and garbage underfoot. Even the songs lacked punch. The anthem of the eighteen days was a guttural ballad directed at Mubarak by the folk singer Ramy Essam, entitled "Leave!" Now Ramy sang new words to the same tune: "Civil state! Civil state!" It didn't rouse the crowd.

For the first time, the liberals in the revolution, people such as Basem and Zyad, imagined that they might have more in common with the military than with the civilian Islamists. Liberals were asking for a delay in the elections: they wanted more time to prepare so that they could compete fairly with the Islamists, and they wanted to enshrine protections in the constitution for a civil, not religious, state *before* the Muslim Brotherhood gained a foothold in government. Uncomfortably for Basem, many of the young activists revealed a disturbingly uncritical love for the military.

A small minority understood that the transition was fixed in favor of the army and the old elite, and that even the slightest reform faced an uphill battle. But the more dreamy masses thought they already had reached the promised land, and had simply to choose their preferred way. Egypt was in ferment, with everyone dreaming of an ideal constitution and convinced that, in a few short months, a relatively painless transition would be over. A sterling new ideal would be established for the Arab world by the trailblazing Egyptians. Libya and Syria were rising up against their dictators, which many Egyptians interpreted as proof that a revolutionary Egypt was leading the Arab world again. It felt like things were changing. Even the SCAF generals were on Facebook. Egypt seemed dynamic, influential, important. Revolutionaries were barraged with invitations to travel abroad and lecture about their experiences. Free trips were on offer around the Middle East, Europe, and the United States. Moaz joined a caravan of volunteers to deliver medical supplies to Benghazi, where the Libyans welcomed them as inspirational brothers in revolution. Basem was headed to Holland to meet with Social Democrats from around the world. Moaz was planning a trip to Germany for a conference about nuclear energy. Zyad was invited to a film festival in Germany and a junket in Italy. Muslim Brothers were being dispatched around the world to refresh old ties and construct new ones. Ayyash's mentor had meetings in Japan, Europe, and the Maghreb region of North Africa.

It was a time for dreamers. Some of Egypt's great minds were imagining a constitution of remarkable simplicity, brief and enduring, that could inspire the entire Arab world with its recipe for freedom, rights, responsibilities, and—at long last—accountable governance. Some of Egypt's bravest citizens were putting their bodies on the line to force power into the hands of the people. And some of Egypt's smartest bureaucrats were scheming to keep everything the way it had been. In this contest, the bureaucrats had an advantage: they were veterans, with experience running the machinery of state and managing its millions of minions. And, Tahrir notwithstanding, they were still in control.

The deep state seeped to the surface on June 28, in a rare display of its surviving powers. Families of some January 25 martyrs staged a commemoration, which was broken up by hecklers. Many believed they were provocateurs sent by State Security. The families went to Tahrir, where, to everyone's shock, they met the riot police, unseen since January 28. With batons whirling and shields raised, the uniformed men charged elderly men and women who were already grieving children killed six months earlier. Tear gas wafted over downtown, and dozens were wounded. Fighting raged for a day. A policeman removed his shirt and danced through the melee, twirling two swords. He was clearly taunting the victims, but no one could make sense of the whole affair. Why had the riot police returned suddenly? Who was in charge? Was this part of the deep state's comeback? Or was it a feint in some power struggle between the army and the police, a message to the SCAF that it would have to bring its Interior Ministry colleagues aboard?

The Revolutionary Youth Coalition had to respond to the riot police's attack but had no idea how. Its leaders were all the more confounded because many people had applauded the police; at least, they said, the government was restoring order. Prime Minister Essam Sharaf invited the Revolutionary Youth Coalition to his house for dinner and asked what he should do. Moaz, Zyad, and Sally joined a delegation of seven, and they offered the prime minister a blueprint: He had to stop military trials for civilians, get the Mubarak trial started immediately, and pay compensation to the families of the January 25 martyrs. He had to fire the leaders of the police and purge the lower ranks, and get rid of all the Mubarak-era holdovers in his cabinet. If the military junta blocked any of these moves, he could simply resign, his honor intact.

The leaders of the Revolutionary Youth Coalition knew they had to regain the initiative, and they understood that they weren't going to get anywhere through a sympathetic but weak prime minister. Only one thing had worked for them in the past: big crowds in the street. Even though they recognized that this had fast become a limited, even counterproductive, tactic, it was to Tahrir that they turned again. July 8 would be the "Friday of Determination," and if they wanted it to be big, they'd need a simple agenda. For hours they argued in a tiny, smoky borrowed office downtown.

Most of the leaders around the table were men who talked out of turn and rarely took their eyes off their smartphones. Sally chaired the discussion, struggling to keep it moving. She desperately wanted a plan that would bring the disparate revolutionary groups back into harmony: a massive protest on July 8, followed by a serious conference to unite everyone around a lowest-common-denominator demand for justice and a transition to civilian rule.

"What will our titles be?" someone asked.

"Which party gets to host the conference?" added someone else.

Zyad was scrolling through Facebook on his BlackBerry. He had decided he most definitely would run for parliament, and he was already figuring out a campaign team. He looked up only when he couldn't find a lighter. He was clearly annoyed by the petty interests of his colleagues, although he himself was barely paying attention to the crisis at hand.

"We need an agenda," he said.

"We need to sound like we're all on the same page," Sally said. "We should talk in public only if it's about things we've agreed on."

"If it gets out that we're having problems working together, it will look like the revolutionary forces are fighting with each other," Zyad said. "Let's concentrate on making this Friday go well, and afterward we can think about the long term."

The revolution's internal bickering had long been public knowledge; most of the personal feuds spilled quickly onto Facebook and the pages of liberal newspapers and websites. The state exacerbated the divisions by establishing a barrage of ersatz youth fronts that confused the public and irritated the revolutionaries. The fake groups had unknown numbers and intentionally similar names, like the Revolution Coalition, the Union of Revolutionary Youth, the Front for Youth of the Revolution, and so on. Revolutionaries also suffered from continuing slander in the state media. Activists were still depicted as drug users, foreign agents, sexually promiscuous, or gay. Anti-Christian sentiment and xenophobia were rising; I had been arrested one afternoon downtown by passing citizens convinced that I was an Israeli spy. Sally was constantly under suspicion because of her mixed parentage. During Tahrir, she had spoken on television as Sally Moore, the Irish-Egyptian. Now she was Sally Toma, Egyptian, and she avoided speaking English in public.

Although its leaders seemed to focus on the coalition less and less by the week, its success mattered to all the youth groups. Tahrir Square, where the coalition had been formed, was the one place where they all came together, the one place that was home for Islamist and secular revolutionaries alike. The coalition's loyalty to revolution was unquestionable. In practice, however, the revolutionary leaders behaved like teenage boyfriends with noble intentions and truncated attention spans. Sally was the one who stitched together the group, ushering the meetings along, emailing around the minutes, wringing consensus out of their brains. "You are like little boys," Sally complained. "Every six hours, we accomplish five minutes of productivity."

After many hours of meetings, the coalition finally settled on a protest agenda, and it drafted a public apology entitled "Revolution First."

"We apologize to the Egyptian Revolution, the revolution's martyrs, and the Egyptian people for engaging in debate between Constitution First and Elections First that divided the political scene in Egypt, when we should have paid attention to the security issue," their statement read. "We support a sit-in at Tahrir Square, but only if there is a consensus among the political groups and parties."

The solution was elegant, if facile: Forget about the ideological divisions and political mess and focus on something everybody wanted to see: Hosni Mubarak on trial. The Brotherhood agreed to join the revolutionaries for one day in Tahrir, but for its own interests; the organization wanted to make sure the military didn't postpone the elections that the Brotherhood intended to win. Sure, the whole point of a revolution was to install a new kind of government and to reinvent the relationship between ruler and subject. But that was complicated. Hanging Mubarak would be simple.

An angry crowd filled Tahrir on July 8. The mood veered between jubilant and bloodthirsty. Orderly Muslim Brothers milled about the square,
but in unison at sunset, they all filed out. The square remained half full,
and Basem glared darkly at the retreating Brothers. "The Islamists are no
longer interested in revolutionary unity, but we will keep trying," he said.
People were in the square because they didn't have any idea what else to
do. Lost, without a sense of purpose, thousands simply lay down to sleep
that night in Tahrir. The next morning, they were still there. They declared a popular occupation of the square and swore to stay put until the
government relented to their revolutionary demands. They numbered
just a few thousand, but they were enough to close Cairo's central square
to traffic. They erected tents with hand-lettered signs and swore to stay
put until their demands were met. Tahrir looked like a squatters' camp.
No one wanted to look like a coward, so the leaders of the Revolutionary Youth Coalition got their own tents too. At a crucial moment, not a
single one of them was willing to voice the opinion that a summertime
Tahrir sit-in was a bad idea.

Almost instantly, the little remaining public sympathy for the revolution dissipated. The revolutionaries were snarling city traffic. To make
matters worse, they had blockaded the Mogamma, an imposing hive of
government offices that dominated the southern end of Tahrir, where citizens went for most of their paperwork. The revolutionaries were trying
to attract attention but instead irritated fellow citizens who were no less
victims of the Egyptian state than the people in the square. Zyad knew
from the start that the revolutionaries were wasting precious goodwill,
but he was powerless to convince the Tahrir hard-liners to go home. The
pragmatists from the Revolutionary Youth Coalition had little influence
over the activists occupying the square, who sank deeper into a state of
revolutionary fervor and paranoia about threats from the deep state. It
never crossed their minds that the SCAF would bottle up the revolutionaries in Tahrir and ignore them, leaving the activists themselves to alien-
ate the Egyptian public without any help from the authorities.

Basem Kamel and the Social Democratic Party were trying to do the complicated thing, building their organization in an office a few blocks away from Tahrir on Mahmoud Bassiouni Street. The Social Democrats had wealthy backers, a Machiavellian alliance with Naguib Sawiris's *felool*-packed party, and air-conditioning. Basem didn't hide the fact that he was having fun. He was on his party's presumptive list of candidates for parliament. He regretted that he had hardly seen his family in the last year and a half, but he was sure that his work now would reap real dividends. Everyone agreed that the revolution's paramount task was to communicate with the "street" and the provinces. Few, however, were eager to bounce over the crappy roads of the delta or Upper Egypt for six-hour trips. Basem was more willing, and thus had spent much of the last month establishing Social Democratic Party branches in far-flung cities. The party had fifty thousand members already and had absorbed a raft of energetic volunteers who had worked for Mohamed ElBaradei. Organizationally, they were leagues ahead of al-Tayyar and the other revolutionary groups but completely outmatched by the legacy movements such as the Muslim Brotherhood and the establishment Wafd Party, which was the boisterous home of liberal politics in the 1920s but had long devolved into playing the role of the regime's loyal opposition.

In Cairo, many people had tired of the revolution, complaining about the Tahrir sit-in and cheering when the military talked tough. General el-Fengary, the same SCAF member who had eulogized the revolution's martyrs, issued a threat in July: "No one can take away the authority that the revolution has bestowed upon the army," the general said. "We will not budge in the face of threats. We will punish those who try to harm the public interest." In the provinces, things weren't much better. Near the Mediterranean coast, Basem had established an active chapter of the Social Democratic Party in the town of Kafr el-Sheikh. They held their first public meeting on the same day as General el-Fengary's threat. Even though they were the first non-Islamist party to seek recruits, they drew at best 150 people. The café outside was more crowded. The local chapter head explained it to me simply: people were looking for cues from local notables. New parties like the Social Democrats would have trouble signing up members unless they first attracted the rich, the big employers, and the famous local fixers and power brokers. Another party activist I knew well complained that urbane liberals didn't know how to connect with poor people on the stump. Basem was an exception. He spoke engagingly, warming up the crowd with a joke about how they were using an old ruling party clubhouse for their prodemocracy gathering. He ended on a rousing note about equal citizenship for Egyptians of all classes and religions. Families lined up to take their pictures with him. Basem presented well as a candidate. But while his party was leagues ahead of the other new revolutionary movements, it was nowhere near ready for prime time.

Still wearing his blazer and dress shirt, Basem drove across the country and straight back to Tahrir after the meeting. He felt that the Revolutionary Youth Coalition had to do something to try to gain control of the square, ending the sit-in before Egypt turned against the very idea of revolution. That night, a few minutes after three o'clock, the coalition finished a meeting. "Tomorrow we will keep the Mogamma open," Zyad announced. This meant persuading the more radical protesters to clear the way to the bureaucratic building, and clearing by force those who wouldn't agree. This was the kind of tough choice that politics demanded—and that the consensus-hungry revolutionaries had mostly avoided until now. The coalition painted its political demands on a twenty-foot-tall wood-and-canvas obelisk erected on the Mogamma lawn: trials for the old regime, an end to military trials for civilians, police purges to fight corruption, a stronger prime minister, and a cabinet reshuffling. The revolutionaries in the square had so lost their bearings that someone had felt it necessary to write down the core values of the uprising as a list called the "Tahrir Code" on the other side of the monument. In a sign of how low discourse had sunk, the "spirit of the square" instructed demonstrators, "Don't call other people traitor or spy."

While Basem continued the groundwork for his party's national political campaign, the theater of protest in Tahrir had frozen the rest of the revolutionaries' work. Moaz's Egyptian Current Party had cancelled its membership drive. "We have put everything on hold while we're in Tahrir," said Abdelrahman Fares, Moaz's friend and fellow al-Tayyar al-Masry Party founder. "Everyone keeps asking about party activities. We have no activities while we're here." Gone for now was the sense of urgency.

The Revolutionary Youth Coalition leaders usually gathered beside the statue of Omar Makram, a descendant of the Prophet Muhammad who had led resistance against France's invasion of Egypt in 1798 under General Napoléon Bonaparte. Omar Makram had helped elevate Muhammad Ali, Egypt's first modernizing king, to the throne; he symbolized the nationalist partnership between secular and religious Egyptians, united in resistance. It was a symbol that the coalition should have adopted but, sadly, never did.

"I think we need to stop the sit-in," Zyad said one afternoon after waking from a midday nap in the statue's shade. "I think it is hurting us. There are some people who won't leave. There's a lot of silly kids." He knew that each day fewer and fewer people in the square listened to him. Every bit of credibility that he and Basem and others acquired with Egyptians outside Tahrir seemed to deplete an equal amount of credibility inside the square.

The revolution was collapsing upon itself in a vortex of paranoia and self-importance. Talk of violence percolated among the few thousand left in Tahrir. A father whose son had gone missing in January swore to me that he would kill the sons of the government officials responsible. Discussion circles mulled over whether the revolution would achieve more if vigilantes began murdering police officers. Alaa Abdel Fattah, the blogger and labor activist who had returned from South Africa, tried to confront the idea head-on. "Our best protection is that we are unarmed. We only defend ourselves," he said. "If we take up arms, it becomes a civil war." Quietly, though, some protesters began saving money for guns.

Finally, Tahrir's interminable sit-in burst its seams. The dwindling number of protesters couldn't stand it anymore, enraged by the lack of justice for the martyrs and the utter indifference of Egypt to their rage. They would do something bold, and people would pay attention: they would march on the Ministry of Defense in the city's Abbasiya section. From within their bubble, the demonstrators thought this move would clarify matters, convincing the public that the military was aggressive and the revolutionaries were innocent victims. However, the military was still popular with most Egyptians, and it was currently the only functional Egyptian institution. Marching on its headquarters would look to most

Egyptians like a gratuitous provocation, an attack on a national symbol. To make matters worse, the neighborhood was rabidly pro-regime. There were few roads in and out. If fighting broke out, people could easily get trapped. It was a risky idea on many levels, but the hard-core revolutionaries, like Sally, felt they had to go along with it. Once again, instead of walking away from a bad idea that percolated up from the grassroots, the Revolutionary Youth Coalition played along.

On the day of the march, the situation quickly soured. The people of Abbasiya welcomed the marchers with bottles, rocks, sticks, and knives, while residents, thugs, and security men chased them without restraint or mercy. They pursued the protesters into the Noor Mosque even as the imam shouted over the speakers for peace. They beat them in the streets, they beat them in the alleys, they pelted them with Molotov cocktails. The military police stood by, protecting the thugs but not the demonstrators. It took nearly twenty-four hours for those in the march to fight their way back to Tahrir. At least three hundred were wounded. The SCAF had shown its ugliest face so far, gambling on the public's distaste for the revolutionaries and deploying plainclothes henchmen to attack unarmed demonstrators. The utopian stage of Revolutionary Tahrir, for all intents and purposes, was over.

Ramadan offered a chance to regroup. For Muslim families, the month was a time for togetherness, reflection, and camaraderie. Every evening, families would gather for *iftar* to break their dawn-to-dusk fast. They would often gather with friends for a second meal, the *suhoor*, a few hours after midnight. The revolutionaries, considering the whole of Egypt their family, hoped that they could stage *iftar*s everywhere to talk and break bread with their countrymen. In reality, such a gesture required more money and organization than they had, but they did what they could. After the violence during the ill-considered march to the Defense Ministry, they understood that their relationship with the Egyptian people needed repair. "We realized we weren't doing a good job explaining ourselves," Sally said when I ran into her downtown. The Revolutionary Youth Coalition organized street *iftar*s or conferences anywhere it had

a toehold: Mahalla, Kafr el-Sheikh, popular quarters of Cairo and Alexandria. The revolutionaries wanted to explain to the people what had
happened since January 25. They wanted to explain that the revolution
was not over, that the old system was still in place, and that the military
weren't saviors but were, in fact, worse in many ways than Mubarak. They
wanted to explain that the failing economy, lost security, and other disasters befalling Egypt were the responsibility of the nation's rulers. So far
the only problem for which the thousands in Tahrir were solely at fault
was the gnarled traffic downtown.

What a mismatch. Just as in the run-up to the constitutional referendum, the youth had waited too long to concentrate on their message.
Only now had it dawned on them that the public image of their campaign was integral to its success; that the revolution needed a bigger public. So some dozens, maybe hundreds, of articulate young revolutionaries
were ready to talk to Egypt at large. They wanted to wrestle the narrative
away from the mendacious machinery of Maspero's official media.

The state understood the power of narrative focus, singling out a
handful of activists for special vilification. Generals ranted on television
about Asmaa Mahfouz, a telegenic and articulate young woman who was
at best a bit player in revolutionary circles. They accused her of anchoring
a plot against the nation, of taking orders from abroad, and of slandering
the military and other symbols of Egyptian unity. SCAF understood that
the facts didn't matter. The generals wanted to deter other activists by
persecuting a single target, and they calculated the effect would be all the
more chilling if they harassed people like Asmaa and Alaa Abdel Fattah,
who weren't instrumental in hard power gambits such as political parties
and community groups. Asmaa was arrested for tweeting disrespectfully
about Field Marshal Mohammed Hussein Tantawi, and then released on
bail.

It was not an accident that when the Free Officers staged their coup
in 1952, the state media building was one of their first targets. It's an old
formula for taking over a state: secure the barracks, arrest the president,
and take over the official media. If that's in hand, all else will follow. The
revolutionaries hadn't taken Maspero during the original uprising, and in
the six months since January 25 the generals had freely and strategically

written their own story of the revolution. In the SCAF narrative, artfully peddled on every channel of state television and in every newspaper, the generals were revolutionary patriots who rescued Egypt from Mubarak's predatory circle. The dirty and entitled kids in Tahrir had no vision and no constructive aims. They had jammed a stick in the nation's wheel of production and had rendered Cairo unlivable. Traffic, crime, garbage piles: all could be traced to the slothful ethos of the demonstrators.

While Mubarak still held on to the presidency, regime lackeys alleged that foreign diplomats were handing cash to demonstrators from their limousines. What else but a foreign conspiracy could explain all these new activists? That fantastical claim had blossomed over the summer with state media reports that the CIA, the Mossad, and perhaps others too had paid and trained the revolutionaries. The military was success-fully pushing the line that American money and meddling were entirely to blame for an artificial wave of protests, but that the military itself was immune to any untoward influence from Washington, despite $40 billion in assistance during more than three decades of tight collaboration with the United States and Israel on security matters.

Just before Ramadan, the SCAF granted the revolutionaries their most heartfelt wish: it would put the old tyrant on trial, at last. Hosni Mubarak and his interior minister, Habib el-Adly, the two most hated men in Egypt, appeared in court on August 3, two days into Ramadan. For many Egyptians, Mubarak was the symbol of what went wrong, and the great travesty of the revolution was that he had yet to face justice. The revolutionaries, however, understood by now that Mubarak was but one in a den of vipers, and that his trial was a necessary but insufficient condition for system change in Egypt. The courts and the SCAF had delayed the trial as long as possible, but they had understood from the protests of July that a great many Egyptians were on the verge of exploding over this one matter; in fact, it appeared to be the only remaining issue that could unify the full spectrum of people power. So in quick succession, like a theater director bringing a performance to its dramatic climax, the SCAF cleared Tahrir and announced that justice would be served. Hosni Mubarak was wheeled into a courtroom in his hospital bed and placed in the cage where all Egyptian defendants are tried. The arrogant Pha-

raoh lay there picking his nose. He was flanked by his sons Gamal and
Alaa, and his long-serving interior minister el-Adly. These venal courtiers
flashed with anger at their jailers and behaved as if all Egyptians were still
their subjects.

This was the spectacle the people had desired. The outcome felt almost immaterial. The fallen tyrant had been humiliated, forced to face
the law like any Egyptian. So what if he was living in comfort? So what
if his trial, before a civilian judge, seemed rigged to give him light treatment, while, since the revolution, thousands upon thousands of Egyptians had been summarily sentenced to years in prison by military courts,
usually without regard for procedure or evidence, and with no protections for the accused? That was the kind of detail that kept legal activists
busy for days on end. It didn't enter the grand narrative: that was the Supreme Council's production. Now the SCAF had the headline it wanted:
"Mubarak On Trial, Revolution Wins." Satisfied, many Egyptians turned
off their televisions on August 3. With Mubarak on trial, they could stop
worrying and learn to love the SCAF.

The Revolutionary Youth Coalition met again with the prime minister. They complained about voter registration rolls, which were still
crammed with dead people. They raised their concerns with old regime
holdovers still in the cabinet, with military trials, and with the lack of a
concrete timetable for a handover to civilian power. Every night during
Ramadan the activists would collect at their favorite cafés along Boursa.
There were tensions. One night, some unknown belligerents picked fights
in a way that felt staged, like a State Security provocation.

Moaz and the other Islamists on the Revolutionary Youth Coalition
had fought off a move to expand the group. There were many new activists who weren't represented, and many of the most important independents, including Sally, had joined political parties. Even though Sally was
conflicted about whether to support more staid electoral politics or more
radical street action, it was difficult to present herself as an independent
when she was a founding member of the Egyptian Social Democratic
Party. The other original independents were in similar positions, all of
them having joined organized movements or parties. Moaz liked the idea
of a more inclusive coalition, but he feared the swamping of the Islamist

voices, especially now that the official Brotherhood had no relationship with the revolutionary youth. "The coalition is like the critical mass in the nuclear bomb," Moaz said. "The balance is what produces the good work." Between the *iftar*s and the meetings and the plans and the disrupted sleep schedules of Ramadan, the helmsmen of the revolution appeared to be everywhere and nowhere all at once. The SCAF might be stumbling along with a blunt strategy, but it had a great machine in its hands. The revolutionaries, for the moment, were scattered. Everyone seemed to need a break at a time when no one could afford to lose focus.

———

The revolutionary youth disagreed on most everything beyond their common contempt for Mubarak. The most driven of the secular activists rose from the left and retained an unhealthy regard for the most doctrinaire readings of Marx, Lenin, and Mao. In the view of this hypervigilant rank and file, anyone who aspired to lead or run for elections was a poseur. They were waiting for a worker's revolution that would wipe away the entire structure of the old regime. "We can negotiate with them after they're all dead," one such activist told me glibly. He was saving up for a gun, although he didn't know how to shoot. This doctrinaire thinking seemed dangerously naïve and out of step with the historical moment. It was one thing to argue that Egypt's well-behaved revolutionaries needed to assert more radical demands. It was another altogether to explain Egypt through Lenin's analysis of imperialism as the highest stage of capitalism. These rigid leftists mattered because they formed one of the most dedicated phalanxes of labor organizers and street fighters. They showed up for the long, earnest political meetings, for the protests, for the workers' strikes, and they didn't flee when the police came. Their voices counted disproportionately to their size, and their ideological purity won them a lot of credibility. They were the secular answer to the fervent, young Muslim Brothers.

Now they had the Revolutionary Youth Coalition in their sights. They found repugnant the very notion that someone would purport to lead the youth or the revolution. They oozed with disdain for the coalition's bourgeois style. Many of the angriest critics operated under the banner of the Revolutionary Socialists, so named long before January 25. Writers and organizers such as Hossam el-Hamalawy and Kamal Khalil never stopped agitating for a full-on workers' uprising. Meanwhile Sally, Zyad, Basem, Moaz, and the rest of the coalition members were pushing for change and reform through any path they could see. They took a radical line on what Egypt needed, but they were willing to meet with most people in power to communicate their demands. They had stopped meeting with the SCAF after it became clear to them that the SCAF wasn't interested in consulting outsiders, only in dictating to them. But they met with ministers, influential notables, friends of the army, and, in late September, Egypt's top spy, Murad Muwafi.

For these hardheaded revolutionary pragmatists, it wasn't such a hard decision. Muwafi controlled the General Intelligence Directorate, which for decades under Mubarak controlled most of Egypt; he had taken over during the revolution, but he was an old regime holdover, with copious assets and files in his hands. The Revolutionary Youth Coalition took a vote whether to accept the invitation to meet with the intelligence chief, and agreed overwhelmingly. Who better to hear the youth's demands for the continually deferred overhaul of the intelligence and security apparatus that strangled Egyptian life? Probably Muwafi wouldn't do what the youth asked, but at least he had the power to fix things if he could be swayed. The only dissenters after two days of arguments were the Youth Movement for Justice and Freedom, perhaps the most leftist and secular of groups in the coalition. "We need to have political relationships with the authorities of the state," Moaz said. "We don't have to always resort to a million-man march to have our voices heard."

So, on September 22, delegates from the coalition found themselves in a secret briefing room with Muwafi. In keeping with regime tradition, Muwafi wanted the entire meeting off the record. The youth refused. In Mubarak's time, opposition activists and politicians had always met discreetly with intelligence operatives, and were all tarnished by the suspicion that they had cut some kind of deal with the regime. The Revolutionary Youth Coalition leaders believed that such contacts would shed their stigma if discussed openly. They thought it should be normal business for political activists to meet with government officials, including the powerful intelligence chief, without sacrificing their reputation. So the revolutionaries announced their rendezvous with Muwafi in advance and planned a detailed public briefing afterward. It was a huge break with tradition, but it did them no favors.

They talked for nearly four hours. Muwafi tried to argue that Egypt faced so many major threats from nefarious entities, such as the jihadis in the Sinai, that it was hard to deal with mundane security matters. In response, Moaz and the others ripped into Muwafi. They ticked off all the problems with the security forces, of which Muwafi's intelligence service was the most important: abuses of power and popular trust, thugs and bandits rampaging in poor areas all over the country, civilians shunted into military courts, police refusing to do their jobs, military police disappearing mysteriously at key moments. "What are you waiting for to stop these people?" Moaz asked the intelligence chief. "Use the law and the authority of the state. Stop military trials immediately. Police have to return to the streets and do their job well."

In the strident halls of youth opinion, the revolutionaries who met with Muwafi immediately were pilloried as sellouts who chased any opportunity to cuddle with power. They were suspected of trying to engineer a secret agreement with Egyptian intelligence in exchange for seats in parliament. Reporters phoned Moaz, who had been designated the coalition's spokesman on this question, perhaps because his Brotherhood background afforded him extra credibility.

"People are attacking the coalition as if we sat with the Mossad!" he complained a few days after the meeting with Muwafi as he fielded calls from derisive Egyptian journalists on his cell phone at a café in Boursa. He looked more stressed than I'd ever seen him. The brouhaha over this relatively inconsequential conversation with an intelligence official was drowning out the most important revolutionary project afoot.

Moaz, along with Sally and a few dozen of the most idealistic activists yet, had just unveiled a parliamentary slate called the "Revolution Continues." They were determined to resuscitate the spirit of the square in a unified, nonpartisan political campaign that would be dedicated to the original aspirations of the revolution: better economic conditions for the poor, less corruption, and an end to torture. But no one, it seemed, wanted to talk about this underfunded revolutionary campaign. Many small, poor parties joined the Revolution Continues, but even stalwarts such as Basem and Zyad preferred the advantages of an alliance richer and more powerful than the revolutionary firmament from which they had sprung. The Revolution Continues campaign received threats continually. Thugs often disrupted its public gatherings, swinging sticks and fists. The revolutionary youth were nervous, because thugs usually had the blessing of the police or intelligence. They were worried enough that they didn't publicize the identity of the six people leading the elections campaign. "It would be very easy for someone to kidnap or kill those six," Moaz pointed out. He was trying to focus on the elections, but the accusations swirling after the intelligence meeting had distracted and depressed him. Tonight there was no laughing and joking. "That's a filthy habit," he snapped when sweetened tobacco smoke from my waterpipe blew his way.

The coalition had refused to sit with generals from the SCAF since April 8, when military police attacked a demonstration in Tahrir and arrested a group of dissenting soldiers who had joined the revolutionaries. This, too, disturbed Moaz. It shouldn't matter whom you talk to, he reasoned; what should matter is what you say. "Even if we are in a war, we must have political communication channels," he said. "You want to boycott Israel? Fine. But SCAF is part of our state. Boycotting the SCAF won't harm the SCAF, but it will hurt the Egyptian people."

In early September 2011, the SCAF faxed a censorship directive to all the Egyptian media. No one could write about the military or the SCAF without prior permission. This was a tighter restriction than Mubarak had ever imposed. The state of emergency was set to expire that month, for the first time since 1967, but the generals announced that they would extend it another year because of "circumstances." Finally, they published the full new election law, which gave the old ruling party an enormous advantage. An arcane system split the parliament between party seats and "independent" seats, which members of any political parties were barred from contesting. These were the seats that always went to powerful, corrupt families with local patronage networks; who had always been stalwarts of the regime in all but official party membership. The new law appeared designed to maximize their performance.

State television aired long specials about Field Marshal Moham- med Hussein Tantawi visiting factories, extolling Great Mother Egypt. Prosecutors advanced an investigation of "illegal nongovernment orga- nizations" accused of taking foreign money. In a December raid, po- lice arrested forty-three NGO workers, including sixteen Americans, from organizations that had been operating openly in Egypt for years. The targets included some of the most important Egyptian monitoring groups, along with the US-based Freedom House, National Democratic Institute, and International Republican Institute, all apparently selected because they documented the SCAF's abuses of power. These organiza- tions were continuing the work they had done under previous regimes: counting, tracking, and defending the detained; verifying torture; advo- cating at home and abroad against criminal governance; and organizing counterweights to the state in realms from election monitoring to film- making. The junta appeared willing to try an absolute power grab, testing to find out how much the public would squirm. Perhaps the SCAF could take a level of authority that had eluded even Mubarak and give Egypt the tough paternal love that Tantawi and his generals thought it deserved.

One could imagine Egypt gathered like an extended family in its mansion the day after the patriarch's death. Everyone scheming, chaos coursing below the surface, but open conflict still just over the horizon. In September the SCAF was focused on the established quantities: in private meetings, generals sought understandings with leaders from the Muslim Brotherhood and from all the known liberal parties. Bolder forces were beginning to assert themselves: on the left, new labor, tired of impossibly low wages and the sycophantic leadership of their state- selected unions; and on the right, the Salafi Islamists, charismatic theo- crats with dreams of a literal faith imposed on a wayward society.

Workers on strike all over the country had prosaic concerns. They were lucky to be employed but were forced to support families on $100 or $200 a month. They didn't disparage the revolutionary youth and their preoccupation with deracinating the *nidham*, or the system, but they wanted a "Revolution of the Hungry," not a political one. "The workers aren't afraid of being dragged before military courts," Kamal Khalil told me. He led the Workers Democratic Party and all along had argued that without mass strikes, Egypt's oppressive martial system would remain intact. "If the strikes are strong, the military won't be able to stop them."

Teachers across the country were on strike, threatening not to begin the school year. They wanted an end to the feudal system that paid them $100 a month and encouraged them to supplement their income by withholding instruction in the classroom and charging extra for it in private after-school tutorials. In Mahalla, where years before Tahrir Square the textile workers had scaled the wall of fear, independent unions now demanded regime change. Outside the defunct parliament, hundreds of striking bus drivers demanded better wages, showing every passerby the pay stubs in their hands that chronicled their subsistence. Even more than the habitual Tahrir protesters, these workers were aware that the SCAF had formally criminalized all strikes and demonstrations with a rarely enforced March 2011 decree. The workers knew that they, more than the students and the political activists, faced the risk of arrest or loss of livelihood. They wanted more money, and they also wanted more dignity, symbolized by their demand for uniforms. A young driver showed me his monthly haul: $60, significantly lower than the average Egyptian monthly income of $270. A veteran nearly twice his age teased him: "Work another nineteen years like me, and you'll get up to a hundred twenty dollars." "Wages and prices are out of balance in Egypt," said Adel Mahmoud, a driver with a missing front tooth and a soft, diffident voice. "We're just demanding our bread."

The Salafis, meanwhile, were agitating for a "Revolution of God." They spoke in more urgent, aggressive tones than either the secular workers or the faithful Muslim Brothers. A special level of repression had been reserved for Egypt's Salafis under the old regime, and not without reason: their ranks had spawned an international elite of jihadi extremists. Fanatical Egyptian Salafis had murdered President Anwar Sadat; they had helped found and lead al-Qaeda; they had led an overt war against the Egyptian state in the 1990s; and they had surfaced in violent plots and movements around the world. Unleashed into politics by the Tahrir

Revolution's clean slate, Salafi preachers and leaders careered into the political arena with the wind of millions of animated, passionate, and maximalist followers at their backs. If Egypt was in the throes of a family succession, the Muslim Brotherhood would have been the patient elder son who had served his apprenticeship and was sure that if he was willing to wait and show respect, he would succeed the father. The Salafi movement was the youngest sibling: perhaps a little more sharp and clever than the older brothers, and definitely at the peak of his physical vigor. In the hotheaded tradition of youth, he interpreted the world in absolutes and was willing to use force in service of his ardent ideals.

Their presidential contender was Sheikh Hazem Salah Abou Ismail, who preached on television and every Saturday night at his neighborhood mosque in Dokki, the West Cairo neighborhood. He drew thousands of young male followers so inspired by his words that they identified themselves as Hazemoon, partisans of Hazem, which had an added ring because it also meant "the determined ones." To the alarm of the Muslim Brotherhood and Egyptian liberals alike, the man's candidacy was viable; there were scenarios in which this antediluvian cleric could succeed Mubarak. Sheikh Hazem was the kind of guy who could be found on YouTube decrying modern women gone wild or suggesting that if Egyptians saved their change and planted crops in the desert, their beggared nation could become economically self-sufficient in a couple of years.

Hazem Salah was fat, with a beatific smile and a ragged Salafi beard, and he said all the kinds of things that drove liberals into an anticlerical frenzy and made incremental Islamists like the Muslim Brothers terrified that they would lose all the most fervent religious youth to irresponsible fundamentalist clerics. He drove his followers to ecstasy. His central slogan declared simply, "By sharia, we shall live with dignity." Sharia, the Islamic law, meant something different to every individual Muslim; the call to sharia was vague, allowing some observers to think that Hazem Salah was appealing to widely shared Islamic values and others to believe he was calling for the restoration of the caliphate, the leader of the faithful who had presided over the Islamic empire in its early centuries. His followers had adapted the revolutionary chant to call for Islamic law rather than system change. Unlike most political figures, there was nothing mealymouthed about Hazem Salah. He wanted Egypt's social mores restored to those of the seventh century, but he also spoke forcefully against the military's abuse of power, and constantly demanded the lifting of the state of emergency. In September many secular liberals were saying that a period of semiauthoritarian transition under military rule would be better than a democracy that brought Islamists to untrammeled power. Hazem Salah, by contrast, unequivocally condemned state torture, detentions, and military trials of civilians.

He walked into his weekly confab in Dokki at the end of September after nightfall, holding a yellow wildflower in his hand. The men mobbed and kissed him. He walked slowly to the front of the mosque, sat by the *minbar*, or pulpit, and spoke without a break for nearly three hours. There was a crisis, he said, and no time for the faithful to stop to wait for clarity. It was a time for action, a decisive time. He made his case quietly, and his audience strained for every word. In every speech and at every meeting, Hazem Salah invoked a state of religious emergency. There was no message with which to better rally the youth. "We are the most humiliated of nations, but Islam has raised us high," he said. He scorned those afraid to take sides, or those like President Barack Obama, "who have completely submitted to the Jews and the Zionist lobby."

"Don't wait for an order," he warned. "This time is crucial. Wash well, pray well. Every man must prepare himself to raise the flag of reform." The ranks of the Hazemoon were growing more quickly than any other political current.

The parallel ferment among the workers and the Salafis discomfited not only the military wardens but also their would-be replacements in the revolutionary mainstream. The Brotherhood and the liberals both wanted to supplant the old order yet retain much of its machinery. Real revolutionaries, however, were baying for blood, and they sought a much more anarchic reinvention of Egypt, with little concern for procedural niceties like the law.

Worry had only grown among the revolutionaries. The government had set a date for elections: November 28, two months away. Time was wind-

ing down, and none of the revolutionaries seemed prepared. Field Marshal Tantawi had released what looked like a campaign video of himself
strolling about downtown Cairo. The *felool* had emerged from behind
the curtain, announcing new political parties composed of former leaders
from Mubarak's ruling National Democratic Party. The old bosses were
running for their old seats in parliament. The Salafis and the Muslim
Brothers were spreading the message that the secular parties would spit
on custom and force humiliating, godless, libertine lifestyles on the conservative folk of Egypt.

Nasser Abdel Hamid, a Revolutionary Youth Coalition leader from
Mahalla, received a spate of threats after attracting thousands to a campaign rally there. Sally wouldn't even consider running: her dual na-
tionality would make her a target for xenophobic attacks. Moaz was
despondent. Two months before the election, there was no revolutionary platform to speak of, no unified group of candidates who had real
constituencies and who could honestly be described as representing both
Islamist and secular Egyptians. "It's a disaster," he said as he tried to organize the parliamentary campaign from a table at the Costa Café. "How
do they organize campaigns in the US?"

Perhaps eager to forestall new protests, the generals announced a series of minimal but important concessions. Parliament would convene in
January on an accelerated timetable rather than later in the spring. Members of political parties would be allowed to stand for independent seats,
vastly curtailing the advantage of the ex–regime figures. Emergency rule
would be suspended during elections, but not ended. Military trials for
civilians would be curtailed. In exchange, the generals convinced a host
of established party leaders to sign a document endorsing the SCAF's
good faith.

But as soon as the signatures were published, the politicians realized
that they looked like fools. At a moment of power, civilian politicians had
forced the SCAF to compromise. As if they regretted backing the junta
into a corner, the same leaders had then signed a meaningless document
that made them sound like toady courtiers. The SCAF said it would continue military trials "for those matters covered by military law," which
in Egypt could mean anything; and it had refused to implement the

"treason law" that would ban former National Democratic Party officials from running for office for a period of five years. Within hours, at least two party leaders rescinded their signatures, but it was too late: the document was all over Facebook, and everyone knew that its significance was only symbolic.

The symbolism was this: the old men who led Egypt's political parties, even its revolutionary parties, didn't have the balls to stand up to the SCAF generals on an entirely ceremonial matter when they found themselves face-to-face in the same room, pressured by a coot in uniform blabbing about the national interest. At best, the political leadership looked like amateurs. "It's like the guy who throws the bones to the dogs," Moaz scoffed. "They will get all busy with the bones and forget that behind these bones is a lot of meat. The bones are the elections. The meat is the power to control the state."

At its most elemental, state control was exerted town by town, neighborhood by neighborhood, by local bosses whose power had survived across generations and regimes. They usually controlled the police, the criminals, and the major businesses in their sphere. For some time, word had circulated in Upper Egypt that the old regime henchmen had emerged from hiding. An activist from the hamlet of Nag Hammadi told me that the area's old dynasty had officially registered a new political vehicle, the Horreya, or Freedom, Party. According to the activist, the top families in Nag Hammadi made their money from construction and gunrunning, and for decades had maintained a lock on the local parliament seats and the police chief's office. Tahrir Square had some say over Egypt's narrative, but not over its machinery, which remained the supreme power in the rural communities where two-thirds of the population lived.

Moataz Mahmoud, the head of the Horreya Party, wanted as much press as possible for his *feloul* revival. He was handing out free plane tickets to anyone who wanted to fly to Luxor and drive another hour to Nag Hammadi, where he was holding a national rally. He had money and an office that hummed with efficiency. The party's chief of staff was a retired police general. Most of the staff and candidates already had careers in parliament, the police, or the military. Revolutionaries were calling for the revival of an old "treason law," which they thought could be used to bar senior members of the old ruling party from running for election. The Horreya Party took this as a clarion call. What about *their* rights as *felool*? They called their event "Beware the Righteous Anger of the *Said*," the colloquial name for Upper Egypt. Even though the treason law was a theoretical prospect, the entitled stalwarts of the old regime were beginning to fear for their survival. If they couldn't get a sliver of parliament, they would become even more vulnerable. They feared for the fortunes they had amassed through patronage; for the illegal enterprises that continued to enrich them; for the fiefdoms they controlled in the provinces, free from any state oversight; and for their own liberty, which in a just society would be imperiled by inevitable, and deserved, trials and prison terms.

Moataz Mahmoud was a rich man, accustomed to power and deference but also to maneuvering and manipulation. It took more than submission to obtain power in the olden days, especially in the competition for loot and local authority in Upper Egypt. He was struggling to adapt now, although he was a cynical opportunist. He had a support base among the tribes and the families that depended on him for their livelihoods, and he had a natural web of allies around the country from his class. They were trying to figure out how to play it: quiet strong-arming behind the scenes, or overt nastiness? Buy votes and pressure judges, or march down Main Street with machine guns—as Moataz Mahmoud's friend Hisham el-Sheini had recently done in Nag Hammadi? These Horreya men all came from old feudal families. For centuries, they had owned all the land. The poor, not long ago, had literally been their vassals. Today the legal relationship had been liberalized, but the web of control was not all that different. They controlled the local industry and the local police. They had more to lose from a revolution than anybody. Even a half-assed junta like the SCAF could destroy their way of life.

Their style was evolving, but the deep strategy remained the same: mobilize the privileged by appealing to their fears. Moataz Mahmoud wore a trim gray suit, a white shirt, and no tie. When he spoke, he sounded very old-school: 2005 with whiffs of 1955. "We need a national ideology," he said. "Ours is to resist the constructive chaos mentioned by Condoleezza Rice. We want to stop the American plan to divide the Middle East and to divide Egypt into pieces like Iraq." Like many conspiracy-obsessed people in the region, he had seized on Rice's offhand comment from 2005, which he continued to believe revealed America's secret long-term plans. He went on about the dangers of American domination and the Islamists who were scheming to take power in Egypt and turn it into a hellish version of seventh-century Arabia, when Islam was first revealed to the Prophet Mohammed. "We are in a state of chaos!" he cried. "There will be a civil war when the Islamists try to impose sharia law. And now they want to strip the tribes of their power and ban us from politics."

A bald and threatening power play was afoot. The young activist Asmaa Mahfouz had proclaimed her support for the treason law that week. She was a popular figure on YouTube and among young revolutionaries because she was a veiled believer totally committed to the principles of a secular state, and she was a compelling orator. By no means, however, was she a figure of major influence. Like the Mubarak propaganda machine, however, the Horreya Party wanted a villain, and Asmaa Mahfouz became the galvanizing scapegoat. "When Asmaa Mahfouz comes out and says that families in Upper Egypt should not be allowed to run for office, people get emotional, they get angry. They want to block the roads. I will try to calm them down," Moataz Mahmoud said. It didn't matter that Asmaa had said no such thing; she could be blamed, and then Moataz Mahmoud could make a show of unleashing and then restraining his offended followers.

Moataz Mahmoud's father had served nearly a decade in parliament. His brother had taken over the seat in 2010. Now it was Moataz's turn. The seat, he believed, was a hereditary right, along with the family's ceramic factory and its landholdings in the city of Qena and Nag Hammadi. If they were allowed to run, he promised, the *felool* would get a third of the vote easily. I flew to Luxor the next morning with a group of Horreya Party members. All year long, people had wondered what the old regime was up to. Now one of its appendages was reemerging. The police and intelligence remained behind a curtain, along with some of the more powerful plutocrats, but these ruling party clans represented an elite whose feudal power predated the Egyptian republic and whose influence would last far longer than Mubarak's or the National Democratic Party's.

At the EgyptAir gate for the Luxor flight, it became quickly apparent who was on their way to take part in Beware the Righteous Anger of the *Said*. The Horreya Party delegates were louder than anyone else, smoked in the no-smoking areas, and wore bright tribal vests embroidered with gold thread. The flight was short, and a party employee steered us to a waiting minibus with a Persian carpet on the floor. Two twentysomething cousins from Marsa Matrouh, a coastal town between Alexandria and the Libyan border, squashed their cigarettes into the ornate pile. They spoke to each other in a staccato dialect that was unintelligible to the other Egyptians on the bus. I quickly felt like I had stumbled into a private meeting of a sinister fraternity. Their tribal name was Sanousi, and they wore sparkling white robes and impressive deep-green brocade vests. They smoked cigarette after cigarette, and then sang an ode of praise to recently martyred Libyan dictator Mu'ammar al-Qaddhafi, a distant relative in the Sanousi clan. A popular revolt had driven al-Qaddhafi from power, and eventually his own citizens hunted him down in a ditch and killed him. His tribal kin mourned the fallen dictator. They kept rhythm with a peculiar kind of finger clicking, accomplished by feverishly striking their middle fingers against their thumbs. A middle-aged Cairene in professional dress grimaced at the tribesmen. Her name was Iman el-Bawwab, and she clearly did not relish having these crude men as her political bedfellows.

"They talk about isolating us," AbdelShafik Sanousi said. "We are not a contagious disease."

Atallah Hassan Atallah, the other cousin from Marsa Matrouh, leaned back in his minibus seat. "Our religion says we can marry four women," he said, smiling lewdly.

"The Koran limits that freedom," Iman corrected. "You can marry four only if you have the resources to take proper care of four."

Atallah began to curse her in the Marsa Matrouh dialect, and the tribesmen laughed together. Iman and the other Cairenes on the minibus recoiled at the rudeness.

A few minutes later, Atallah leaned over to me. "You know what I was calling her?" he asked me.

"I can guess," I said.

"I called her a cunt!" he said, and burst into laughter all over again.

It wouldn't be fair to say that this behavior represented the entire ethos of the old ruling class, but it would be dishonest to ignore the integral part it played. The lords of the old regime didn't merely tolerate abusive bullies; they depended on them as enforcers. I was suddenly in the equivalent of a private back room where the old ruling class was behaving at ease, and it was ugly. As the sun set, we pulled up to a great tent erected next to Hisham el-Sheini's estate, among the irrigated fields. Several thousand tribal notables sat in the rows of chairs. Moataz Mahmoud, clean shaven in a suit, greeted the newcomers. El-Sheini, with a walrus mustache and bald head, roamed in his flowing white galabiya, extending hospitality and kisses in every direction like a jolly chimney sweep from *Mary Poppins.*

Hisham el-Sheini was aghast at the elections, which he viewed as an attempted coup against his birthright. "This seat in parliament has been in our family for twenty-four years," he told me. "If people here didn't like us, how would it have been stable? Why are they scared of us?"

A lighthearted sheikh from the Sinai leaned over with a bit of wordplay. "We are *ful,*" he said, meaning jasmine blossoms, "not *felool.*"

Hisham el-Sheini took the podium, gloating as he beheld the thousands of men who had accepted the free airfare. "Just by sitting here, you have scared everyone," he said. "Just by showing your respect, everyone ran into their holes."

The whole event appeared staged for the cameras. Men in the audience shouted or chanted only when cued. Off camera, the hosts ignored the other speakers, socializing with one another, talking on the phone, smoking, and relishing the smell of roasting meat from next door. At a signal from Hisham el-Sheini, we decamped to the yard of his three-story villa, where glistening sides of lamb lay on the tables. The flesh was moist and delicious, perfectly cooked. In tribal style, the most senior man at each table ripped off the choicest morsels of meat with his right hand and distributed them to his juniors. Only then did he eat himself. We rushed to eat and board the minivan, to catch a late-night flight back to Cairo.

At the airport, the same group reassembled, now flush with meat, exhaustion, and a sense of righteousness stoked by the rally. But the revolution had another surprise for the *felool*. Domestic flights had been cancelled by an air traffic controllers' strike: another manifestation of the spreading labor unrest. Other passengers in the lounge waited stoically, but not the Horreya members.

"Look what the revolution brought us!" AbdelShafik Sanousi sneered, lighting a cigarette and pacing by the gate. "The revolution of workers and laborers."

A skinny man in a suit stood up and in an even voice confronted this boor from Horreya. "This revolution brought us a lot more than that," he said. "It brought us dignity."

The Marsa Matrouh tribesman was shocked to find a plebeian speaking to him. He had treated the airport lounge, like the bus and the tent, as just another extension of his private domain, where his guests could speak but strangers and servants would remain silent.

"You should think about what you say," the young man continued. "You can afford to eat, but some people cannot. This revolution was about their dignity. People like you caused this revolution."

AbdelShafik Sanousi was the type of bully who couldn't deal with victims that fought back. "Fuck you," he muttered in response, but he already was walking toward the café and the designated smoking area.

It was too much for Iman. First to be insulted by her fellow *felool* and now by an upstart revolutionary. "How dare you!" she screamed, striding over to the man in the suit. "You don't own the revolution." She continued in an almost crazed vein, shouting unintelligibly at the man, who seemed torn between his desire to respond to her ridiculous arguments and his humane instinct to help her calm down. Eventually another Horreya member led Iman, weeping, away from the gate.

The flight was cancelled until the following night. Twenty-four hours later, the same cast of characters reassembled in the same small lounge at the Luxor airport. This time the civilians knew what to expect and eyed the Horreya members warily. Thirty-six hours after they'd left their homes, the regime heavies looked worse for wear, their formal attire wrinkled. At the lounge, I befriended the man with the suit, Aly Malek. He was an accountant and a Revolutionary Youth Coalition member. He told me that in Nag Hammadi, things hadn't changed as much as they had in Cairo. "When we march, the police shut us down," he said. "They try to intimidate us." Hisham el-Sheini, Moataz Mahmoud, and other local enforcers had tried to incite sectarian fear between Muslims and Christians, he said, and now were manipulating their tribesmen in order to protect narrow and corrupt family enterprises.

"What brought down Hosni Mubarak could bring down these guys as well," he said. "But it's harder for us here, because we're nonviolent and we're facing not the army or the police but the armed followers of these guys."

A doctor sitting beside us looked up from his laptop.

"Last night I thought these guys were drunk. But look, there they are, at it again, smoking and disrespecting everybody," he said.

A janitor from the snack bar approached AbdelShafik and pointed to the smoking area, glassed off from the rest of the gate.

"Pimps!" AbdelShafik shouted. Next to me, another traveler, a young professional with a crew cut working on a tablet computer, snapped.

"Who are you?" he screamed, jumping up and running toward AbdelShafik. "Who are you to call us pimps? This country does not need people like you!"

The janitor wasn't cowed either and piped up. "I am responsible for this place, and you cannot smoke here."

The Sanousis, the Sinai sheikhs, and even the Cairene *felool* couldn't have looked more shocked if zombies had lurched into the airport and attacked them. Their own private nightmare was coming to life. At their rally, with the rest of Egypt weeded out, they had felt like big bosses, indomitable, the once and future masters of a meek country. But in the light of day, in a public space inhabited by actual Egyptian citizens, they were exposed as venal has-beens, with dwindling power in their hands but no legitimacy.

AbdelShafik, for a second time, retreated with his cigarette. "Fuck the coffee shop," he said. "They're all fuckers and pimps. Long live Mubarak."

The janitor, victorious, smiled. "Fuck Mubarak," he said.

7.

THE OWNER OF THIS WORLD IS A DEVIL

The Christians were marching again to Maspero, the state media head-quarters. Their predicament had worsened considerably during the year after Mubarak. They had always felt vulnerable because of their small numbers and the constant attacks from Islamist extremists on their legitimacy as Egyptians. Before Nasser, Christians had figured disproportionately in the moneyed elite, but by now, second-class citizenship had long been a reality for them. They could amass financial but not political power. There were no Christians in the top echelons of the army and police. They sometimes held token positions in the government, but never was a Christian preeminent in the ruling party. Christians needed special permission to renovate churches, and that permission often wasn't granted. When they fixed falling-down structures, they frequently were accused of building them taller or bigger than before, which was against the law. Steeple height was perhaps the only construction code in Egypt that was zealously enforced. Mini-pogroms often erupted in response to rural church construction and repairs; another common trigger was rumors, usually unfounded, that priests or nuns had kidnapped a Christian woman from her Muslim husband. Meanwhile, jihadi fundamentalists killed Christians and burned churches with startling regularity. These crimes occurred several times a year, usually in some faraway village in Upper Egypt.

All this abuse and persecution had accelerated since January 25, 2011.

Shortly after the original uprising in Tahrir Square, a group of Christian hunger strikers camped in front of Maspero, demanding equal protection under the law. They were savagely beaten by soldiers and thugs. That first post-Tahrir insult galvanized the Christians; the church had stayed away from politics, trying to cultivate protection from the dictatorship, but its minority flock was frightened into action. They organized a sectarian activist front. Choosing Maspero as the symbolic Christian counterpoint to Tahrir, they called it the Maspero Youth Union, and they began to advocate for religious freedom and Christian rights with an intensity almost never found among Coptic church officials. Soon after, three churches were torched in Cairo's Imbaba neighborhood. Fifteen people died, and two hundred were injured in the riots that followed. On September 30 a Salafi mob burned down a church in the obscure village of Marinab, near Aswan in Upper Egypt. Once again, despite its promises, the government made no investigation.

Whenever the Christians marched, the most principled of the revolutionaries joined them. It was an article of faith among certain Egyptians that they must protect their country's nonsectarian identity carefully. The majority of Egyptians were Muslim, but that didn't mean Islam defined Egypt. Even though the Coptic Church was sectarian in its own way, a core group of revolutionary youth felt a vital moral obligation to stand with it, including Muslims, Christians, and unbelievers. Otherwise, they feared, naked sectarianism would swamp Egypt's transcendent national identity.

The Coptic marches always elicited an almost reflexive spasm of official violence, and no one expected the march on October 9 to be any different. The Copts had so long been taken for granted by the regime that they barely rose to the level of an afterthought. Whatever the state did, it knew the Christians were compromised and afraid: compromised because they had given their support to an oppressive, arbitrary government, and afraid because they knew that, without its peremptory protection, their community might perish. As capricious and insubstantial as it was, the state's protection provided a final barrier against the murderous intolerance that made Coptic life nearly untenable in places that functioned mostly outside the state's ambit, such as Marinab.

As usual, the march began in Abbasiya at the Coptic Church's mammoth cathedral, not far from the Ministry of Defense. Thousands gathered, including the Maspero Youth Union, a delegation from the church, and the most dedicated members of the Revolutionary Youth Coalition. Sally was there; she never missed a march. Among the leaders was Mina Daniel, the charismatic Che look-alike whom Moaz had stitched up during the original uprising in Tahrir. Bothaina Kamal, a former television announcer who was the sole woman running for president (and no relation to Basem), was there. So were dozens of other familiar personalities. Attending protests was part of their job description as activists, and one never knew when a routine demo would suddenly become a turning point. However, the crowd heading to Maspero on that Sunday night thought it knew what to expect, conditioned from nearly a year of controlled violence.

It took almost two hours to reach Maspero as they passed through a succession of working-class and commercial areas, some of them hostile and some friendly. As the protesters approached downtown, thousands more joined them for the finish. Just as night fell, thugs struck. Men with swords and sticks charged the marchers. Others hidden in the dusk threw rocks. Sadly, nothing about that first attack in Bulaq Dakrour felt out of the ordinary. The marchers pushed through, as they had done so many times before. They linked arms, chanted, and sang, punctuating every call with a refrain of unity: "Muslim, Christian, one hand!" They expected a few wounded, maybe a few more clashes, and then they would sweep into the safe area in front of Maspero. Dozens of armored personnel carriers were stationed on the Corniche outside of Maspero, along with several companies of military police. The regime considered the state media headquarters a precious strategic asset and guarded it as smotheringly as the Ministry of Defense itself. The activists knew that they'd be safe once they reached Maspero. The military didn't care about Christian rights but had always protected Christians themselves.

The crowd surged down the six-lane Corniche, bounded on one side by the Nile and on the other by a dense popular quarter that also housed the Foreign Ministry and Maspero. Families with children stood at the head of the crowd in front of Maspero, chanting for equality. Then, as unexpected as a gale, the military struck. Soldiers screamed insults at the demonstrators, and odd disembodied clicking sounds filled the air. People screamed and ran; the noise was gunfire. The assailants were the military police, supposedly there to protect the people they were now shooting. The last upright bastion of national unity, the army—the army!—was killing people, outright and in plain sight.

Gas, fog, and smoke from burning cars distorted the columns of light thrown by the streetlamps. Plainclothesmen appeared at the escape routes. An armored personnel carrier, like a crazed charging rhinoceros, was driven at wild speeds with cold intent toward groups of protesters, running them down by the dozen. Those who couldn't jump out of the way fast enough were crushed beneath the vehicle. Mina Daniel fell, shot once in the head and once in the shoulder. This time Moaz's first aid couldn't be of any help. His friends dragged him away. "If I die, I want my funeral in Tahrir Square," Mina said.

The SCAF's true and vile intent in starting the mayhem at Maspero soon became clear on television. Egyptians saw the terror and confusion of civilians running, soldiers shooting, and unknown knots of men loitering in the darkness on the edge, without knowing what had caused it. Meanwhile, the military junta gave the people its own dastardly explanation of the events on the Corniche. The story was simple: crazy Christians had taken up arms and were attacking the military, in a deranged plot to tumble Egypt into anarchy. They had to be stopped, and the threat these rampaging Christians posed was apparently so great that the army couldn't do it alone. With a speed suggesting they had planned in advance, soldiers raided independent television stations broadcasting live footage of the massacre and cut off their transmissions. Only pro-SCAF television would be allowed on this night.

"Go help the army," one announcer exhorted his viewers. "Our soldiers are being attacked by Christians."

The crawl on state television repeated the fabricated news about murdered soldiers and Christian activists on the prowl. It was textbook incitement, and it targeted an audience already groomed to believe sectarian slander. General Hamdy Badeen, a member of the SCAF and head of the military police, who had been beating, detaining, and torturing with impunity since the revolution, phoned in to a raft of sympathetic stations with entirely spurious reports that Christian demonstrators had attacked the soldiers guarding Maspero.

"The army is with Egypt above all," he told a sycophantic announcer at state-run al-Masriya Television. "We read the *fatiha* for our dead and prayed in the Maspero building. National unity will prevail. Those who created this strife will be held responsible."

The cynicism was breathtaking. General Badeen at that moment must have known probably none of his men had been killed, although evidence later surfaced that one soldier might have died that night. The army was the only party shooting. General Badeen was the one summoning civilians to fight on the streets. If anyone was responsible for trying to start a sectarian civil war that night, it was Hamdy Badeen. He clearly didn't expect to be held to account. General Badeen called on honorable Egyptians to help. It was a direct lie that the unarmed marchers had attacked the army. In fact, the driver of one of the APCs that had driven through and over the crowd was seized and beaten, but then protected by a priest who turned him over to the army. "Honorable Egyptians" materialized throughout downtown, interrogating passersby. "Where are the Christians?" they chanted. "The Muslims are here!" They beat any Copts they found. Regular, "good" citizens had responded to the state's sectarian call.

But despite its best efforts, the military couldn't block footage of the massacre. There were too many journalists around and too many activists with cameras. Grisly loops of video showed the APC hunting like a prehistoric beast among tiny prey, soldiers tossing a body in the river, mobs with homemade guns and spears chasing those who tried to escape. This wasn't the controlled violence that had punctuated the months since the Battle of the Camel. People were dead, and lynch mobs were hunting for Christians. Bullets were crackling: not blanks, not warning shots or tracers, not tear-gas canisters, but spinning, flesh-tearing, bone-crushing bullets, doing their work on the bodies of the demonstrators. This violence spilled onto many levels, much more deadly and widespread than the usual combat between uniformed security forces with tear gas and unarmed protesters with stones.

Mobs of bloodthirsty thousands ambushed the demonstrators from the bridge and the side streets. They had swords and boards and nails and guns and fists, street-fighting weapons and murder weapons. Some were inflamed by what they'd heard and ready to believe the worst about infidel Christians. Many showed the thick, stupid, scarred faces of the veteran *baltagaya* brigades: the Interior Ministry's thugs who came out to beat people on Election Day, at demonstrations, and, sometimes for good measure, out of the blue on a big shopping day downtown. Plain-clothes thugs were seen saluting the uniformed officers. A police officer cursed at a woman from the Maspero Youth Union. "Do you think you'll take the country from us?" he sneered.

The massacre at Maspero felt different from the violence in January and February. It felt out of control. It didn't feel like the calibrated violence of a brutal state. It felt like the furious attack of a wounded system fighting for its life. One of the last remaining zones of safety had evaporated. The army was willing to kill people so casually, so publicly, so prolifically. Even more terrifying, it was willing to unleash the specter of sectarian hate, which would ripple throughout Egypt and dangerously destabilize the country. Even Mubarak's cynical regime had played the sectarian card sparingly. The massacre unfolding in front of Maspero required the active complicity of soldiers, the SCAF, the state media, and whichever intelligence or police service was able to so quickly orchestrate so many well-armed flash mobs all over Cairo. This was evil, pure and simple, and it was the kind of ploy that was easier to set in motion than it was to control. Once ignited, religious hatred could damage Egyptian society irreparably.

Bothaina Kamal, the presidential candidate, had been at the front of the march when the shooting started. She ran past five corpses as she sought shelter down a side street. She hid in an entryway with some others, including a priest. They turned off their cell phones, terrified of being found and beaten or killed. She was covered with blood, and more blood coated the stairs. Policemen and soldiers tried to break down the door, shouting, "God is great!" Bothaina had been expecting attacks from Salafis or riled-up Islamists, but not from the army and the police. "For God's sake!" she called through the door. Finally, she and her companions talked their way past the police. Farther along was a siege line. To cross it, you had to utter the *shahada*, the Muslim profession of faith: "There is no god but God, and Muhammad is his prophet."

Moaz panted as he led a group of activist friends away from the brawl, toward Tahrir Square. Others were trying to get Mina Daniel to the Coptic Hospital, but Moaz knew from the injuries that Mina probably wouldn't survive. He persuaded Mostafa Shawqi, an owl-eyed engineer from Daniel's group, the Youth Movement for Justice and Freedom, and a half dozen others to pack into his car and go somewhere they could be of more use, like the hospitals, where they could document the dead, tend the wounded, and collect evidence. Even as he fled the shooting in front of Maspero, Moaz was aware that the killing was part of a plan. "This is big," he told me, out of breath. "The military wants to stop the elections. They want to say the country is too unstable, and they will use it as an excuse to stay in power." He followed his friend Mina to the Coptic Hospital on Ramses Street. It was nearly midnight. Military police stood by as thugs in civilian dress attacked the hospital.

All Cairo felt like a war zone, more than at any point during the original uprising. Even during the Battle of the Camel, the violence had been limited to the immediate vicinity of Tahrir Square. Now burning cars and mob clashes flared all over the city. I hailed a cab to the Coptic Hospital, which was located a few miles east of Tahrir Square on the road to the Coptic Cathedral and the Ministry of Defense. From the bridge over the Nile, we could see a crowd still surging in front of the state television center. "The Christians were burning the Koran down there in front of Maspero!" the driver told me angrily.

"How do you know?" I asked, curious as to the source of this scurrilous rumor. "Did they say so on the radio?"

"No, some Muslim passengers told me," he said.

We drove on, but the exit from the elevated carriageway for the hospital was blocked. A line of cars had parked to watch the fighting down below on Ramses Street. A man beside me rolled a joint the size of a cucumber and leaned comfortably against the railing, as if for a football match. Battalions of thugs were trying to stop Christians from reaching the hospital. People had to fight their way through with their wounded. I counted five cars burning and one bus.

The state routinely allowed small sectarian flare-ups, allowing vigilantes to burn a church or assault a few Christians. It reminded the Christian minority of its weakness and its dependence on the regime for protection. And it gave the Security Service some leverage over the Islamist fanatics who wanted to purge Egypt of Christians. The extremists might have been a small number, but there was a sizable contingent of Egyptian Muslims who displayed contempt for the rights and rituals of the country's six to ten million Christians. Likewise, many militant Christian Egyptians dismissed Muslims with a rancor that bled into racism, although, to be fair, they had neither the power nor the inclination to harass or harm the Muslim majority.

State Security was accustomed to control. The hooligans it deployed to beat demonstrators, voters, and women were small-time criminals and hoods who owed a debt to the police. They could be beaten or locked up anytime as a reminder. The angry masses of Maspero, however, were harder to control. Some of the men who brought their clubs and swords to Maspero and the Coptic Hospital acted out of patriotism as they understood it, out of a warped but sincere sense of honor; they were under no one's control, including their own. That combustibility made Maspero terrifying. State Security's vile act of self-preservation could easily detonate sectarian war. As I knew from Iraq and Lebanon and Gaza, each home could suffer a world's worth of loss. The thought of the same thing happening here, in a place so recently a font of possibility, provoked in me a bottomless sense of loss, like the death of a beloved friend in his prime. It was terrifying. What would happen if Tahrir failed, supplanted by something as nihilistic as the carnage around Maspero? What would happen not just to Egypt but also to our ability to hope for profound and improbable change? I wasn't sure that my faith could withstand such a blow.

Even in death, the murdered protesters weren't free from persecution. The military exerted influence everywhere in order to delete evidence of its crimes. Under pressure, the coroner issued absurd death certificates that made no reference to bullet wounds or tire marks. The cause of death for a boy who had been shot was determined to be heart failure. An energetic priest named Father Filopatir, who had marched the night before with protesters, was now showing his more reactionary side. He supported Christian protesters within limits, but his main loyalty was the conservative church hierarchy, which definitely didn't want to anger the SCAF. The priest was now taking the lead as the church's fixer, trying to bully families into quick funerals without autopsies. Christians already grieving their personal losses had to contend with a church that seemed more interested in protecting killers than in sheltering its flock. For families reeling with grief, it was a degrading choice: accept a fraudulent death certificate to get the burial over with, or embark on a fight with the bureaucracy in the slim hope of future justice for the murder of a child or fiancé or sibling. There were twenty-four dead, most of them piled in the morgue at the Coptic Hospital. Their photographs already plastered Facebook and Twitter, often in montages that contrasted their mangled, bruised faces with snapshots from earlier times.

Sally roamed the hospital's small interior courtyard, cornering relatives of the dead. Many of them were from rural areas and believed that the dead must be buried within a day. Softly, Sally tried to explain the importance of another small delay. A crime like the Maspero massacre might take years, or an eternity, to be justly reckoned, but it would never happen without a deliberate record, including proof of how the victims had been killed by the army. "We need the autopsy reports if there is ever going to be justice for our martyrs," she explained. Even within her own community, Sally was trying to negotiate between the religious and the secular. After confronting another family, she slumped down on a bench. A diamond cross glittered on her neck where the cross-and-crescent unity pendant normally hung. Her face was swollen from sleeplessness and sadness. "So much superstition," Sally said in frustration. "I can't believe this!"

It was quieter in the courtyard than by the morgue, and the sun was less intense. Moaz, Sally, and Mostafa Shawqi, Mina Daniel's friend, repaired to a long bench to wait.

"We told the families that we should find out how these people died now," Moaz said. "If autopsies prove the military ran these people over, then the protests will be huge."

Moaz had posted photos of the dead on his Facebook page and was looking at them again now. He was mourning the revolution, but also his friend Mina. After the Battle of the Camel in Tahrir, when Moaz had stitched up Mina's temples, the two men had become friends. Mina had a sweet and disarming way of persuading Coptic activists to branch out into broader revolutionary ventures while also alerting mainstream, mostly Muslim activists to the particular injustices visited on Christians. People liked him and listened to him. Mina had represented one of the revolution's best impulses: a move away from parochial self-interest toward a quest for universal rights. He began as a Christian activist and ended his life widely admired for representing everybody.

All along Ramses Street, the crowd exuded dread and anxiety. Thousands outside the hospital waited to escort the bodies to the Coptic Cathedral, expecting attacks on the funeral cortege. Some kept themselves energized with chants: "Mohammed was an adulterer! Muslims are infidels! Down with military rule!" A stench of rot enveloped the courtyard outside the morgue. Twenty-four hours after the massacre, hundreds of relatives and friends were still waiting inside the building for corrected death certificates, accompanied by almost all the revolution's core activists. Moaz, Asmaa Mahfouz, and other Muslim activists tried to calm sectarian fears, but everyone had noticed that none of Egypt's organized Islamic forces had bothered to condemn the massacre or send condolences. No representatives came from the Muslim Brotherhood or the Salafis to offer even pro forma sympathy.

Asmaa Mahfouz wandered around with a legal pad, talking gently, asking questions, and taking notes. "Look to the SCAF," she repeated to everyone. "We were together, Muslims and Copts, marching to Maspero. Suddenly we felt the attack. Why? To divide us, to make us forget about the SCAF and instead have Muslims and Christians fight each other."

A boy leaned against a wall in a small interior courtyard of the hospital, silent, his eyes red. Two friends were with him, one Muslim and one Christian. His brother Sobhi Gamal Nazim, twenty-seven, had been killed by a bullet to the pelvis.

"God will retaliate for what is happening now," said Bushra Basilios, a Christian who quoted scripture nearly every time he spoke.

"Not every Muslim is a fundamentalist," said Ahmed Shaker, a Muslim. "And not all Christians are forgiving. Some of them are bigots."

"The owner of this world is a devil," muttered Basilios.

"We've all lost a lot," Ahmed said. "We ask God: No more, please. Really, it's enough."

Ahmed showed pictures on his cell phone of Sobhi alive and then of Sobhi dead, his life swiped out of this world with a quick flick of the scroll button. The dead man's brother, Wagdy, held his gaze on an indeterminate point in space somewhere above our heads.

"No one will give us our rights," he said. He convulsed in sobs. "God is great," he said over and over, inflecting it like a question.

A man wounded the night before was wheeled into the courtyard. Bandages covered his arms and head. He caught sight of my friend Joe, a Christian who wore a long beard only vaguely reminiscent of the kind that Salafis grew. The wounded man reared up in his wheelchair and grabbed Joe. "Fuck your religion!" he screamed. "Goddamn your religion!"

Wagdy, sobbing for his own dead brother, stepped forward to protect Joe, who was absorbing the blows, and then wrapped his arms around his attacker in a bear hug. Despite the deepening divisions in society, the mourners were trying their best to remain unified.

The consensus among families of the wounded was that Field Marshal Tantawi and his SCAF had engineered the massacre either to put Christians on notice and keep them in line behind the old regime, or to initiate an ethnic cleansing project.

Father Filopatir strode back and forth through the courtyard. Already he had convinced four families to forgo autopsies. Their bodies were about to go to the cathedral for a blessing by Pope Shenouda. A lesser cleric would preside for the remaining families that insisted on accountability. Mina Daniel's family glared at Filopatir.

A scuffle broke out between Wagdy, who had decided to give up on an autopsy for his brother, and his Muslim friend Ahmed, who was trying to change his mind. Their voices climbed until they shoved each other.

"He won't get his rights without an autopsy," Ahmed said.

"I just want to bury my brother," Wagdy replied.

"He's as precious to me as he is to you!"

"Enough!" Wagdy said, weeping. "Enough."

Moaz watched without interfering. "I feel sad," Moaz said. "This is not the new Egypt. This is not freedom."

Moaz had been in the hospital since the early morning and hadn't gone to bed the night before. Neither of us had eaten all day, and with the afternoon sun baking the hospital courtyard, we decided to take a walk. There was little to do other than wait: for the autopsies, for the funerals, for the inevitable nationwide reaction. He led me by the arm out of the hospital. We retreated with a bagful of sodas and wafers to his car, where we sat sweating while he charged his phone. Absentmindedly, he scrolled through Facebook pictures of the dead on his tablet computer.

"Have you seen this one?" For the second time that afternoon, he showed me a close-up of the teenage boy whose head had been run over by the armored personnel carrier. Somehow his face and head had remained intact but were grotesquely misshapen. The photo was widely circulated because of how clearly it suggested a crime.

I blanched. "I don't need to see it again," I said. I'd already seen the actual dead; I didn't need to look anymore. It was hard enough to contemplate the grief and fear of the survivors.

Moaz thought there could be more massacres in the days to come, and that afterward the elections would be ruined. Either sectarian violence would delay the vote indefinitely, or else it would go ahead as planned but without any meaningful participation by revolutionary youth. "This incident will leave marks for years," Moaz predicted. "We are starting something new in our history."

Thanks to the persistent efforts of the activists, seventeen out of the twenty-four families of the dead withstood Filopatir's pressure and insisted on a new coroner's report. At nightfall, they still were waiting for a forensic team. Empty coffins lined the loading ramp outside the morgue, awaiting the bodies once the autopsies were complete. Heaps of gardenia blossoms were everywhere, their scent strangling the courtyard. Posters of the new martyrs covered each coffin.

In the courtyard, Mina Daniel's mother slumped over his coffin. "We were supposed to be going to your wedding," she sobbed, slapping her face and thighs in grief. "The government engineered all this to divide us."

She gripped the hands of her daughters and of a parade of activists who had loved her son. Despite her torment and wailing, she was lucid, looking at everyone with recognition. She turned toward the brick wall and banged her face against it. Mina's sister tried to stop her.

"Enough. Stop," the girl said to her mother, pulling her helplessly away from the wall by the shoulder. *"Bas. Bas."*

We went around the corner to the interior courtyard, now deserted. I leaned against a wall and began to sob. The grief of Mina's mother over-whelmed me. The loss of a child seemed impossible to bear. I thought of my own children at home: my baby girl and my little boy. Even as our children grow up, they are always our babies, and our imperative is to protect them. Mina's mother had done her best, and it had not been enough. I wept for every death and every survivor I had ever encountered until that moment, every individual soul that had been devoured by his-tory in Iraq, in Lebanon, everywhere, a senseless parade of killing. Over the years, I had raged against it, until at some point I had resigned myself numbly. Now the rage flooded back, but along with it came a sense of renewed fellowship. Through wars and uprisings, I had sat in sympathy with mothers and fathers, chronicling their fears, their anguish at the murders of their children, but always I had stepped back emotionally, so that I wouldn't intertwine my own feelings too much with theirs. Today I felt no such distance. I abandoned the idea of removing myself. I could not hold back from identifying with these revolutionaries, and I did not want to. I believed in their hopes and ideals and felt the fear, anxiety, and despair in Mina's mother, in Moaz, in Basem, in all their friends, as if the emotions were my own. It was unbearable, and yet, it had to be borne and transcended, for the sake of the revolution and its ideals. Resistance in the face of death is the most potent weapon of the weak.

Finally, the new death certificates were ready. The activists had won this small battle. "They can't say he died of a heart attack now," Mina Daniel's aunt said, clutching the paperwork.

One by one, the bodies were loaded into the coffins and placed in a line. By now it was nearly midnight, and tens of thousands of mourners had assembled to march to the funeral. Perhaps sensing the desperation of this crowd, the thugs stayed away. Without incident, the mourners marched the length of Ramses Street and through the cathedral's enormous gates, chanting, "Either we get our rights or die like they did!" After the service, a few hours before dawn, Mina's friends honored his last wish, escorting his body to Tahrir, ignoring the stones thrown their way as they approached the square to circle the place that Mina had so loved and for whose ideal he lost his life.

The Maspero massacre unleashed Egyptians' most primal sectarian fears. For Christians, it changed the question from "What can this revolution bring us, as an oppressed minority?" to "Can we survive in this country?" In the immediate aftermath, everyone was sure to rage at the passive church leadership, the SCAF, the soldiers, and state television. But when the shock lifted, they would begin to ask why so many Egyptians had been willing to believe the SCAF and the TV and had rushed into the streets to beat their Christian countrymen. For Christian Egyptians and for the countless Muslims who were neither sectarian nor for military dictatorship, the national reaction would prove as troubling as the massacre itself. So many had come to the aid of the attackers rather than the victims. The Islamic leaders had kept ominously silent, clerics as well as politicians. There were no Muslim Brothers at the funerals or Salafis sympathizing in person or on TV. There was no inevitable nationwide reaction, as Moaz and all the other revolutionaries had expected. There wasn't a chorus of outrage against the authorities or a national reflex against sectarianism. There were almost no spontaneous gestures of solidarity except from the country's dwindling revolutionary community. It soon became clear that hardly anyone in Egypt empathized with those slaughtered in front of Maspero. In the first thirty-six hours, there had been almost no sign that the Egyptian people regretted what had been done in their name. The wider public's silence was the most ominous sign of all.

In the weeks that followed the massacre, Egypt went about business as usual. The organized political class rallied the cadres. Maspero hardly affected the calculations of the SCAF, the Wafd Party, the Brothers, or the Salafis. The people of Tahrir took stock as well. Egypt stood at a fork: it could tilt toward the full-fledged revolution that the January 25 uprising had heralded but never quite wrought; or, in keeping with the normal laws of political physics, it could resume its normal course with some alterations, more continuous with its past than with the dreams of the square. One path required renewed protest on a massive scale not yet seen, drawing workers as well as Islamists. The other path led through elections, which would bring some outsiders, notably the Islamists and a contingent of secular bourgeois nationalists, into the tent where the state's goodies were dispensed. Incremental, contested reform could certainly improve life for Egypt, but that hadn't been the goal of the uprising. Its citizen-leaders had sought to write a new Arab compact, with dignity in daily life as well as before the law, where everyone took responsibility and where the government picked up the garbage and listened to the citizenry. Tahrir's highest hopes depended on citizens, and in the days after Maspero, many activists called for "the Second Revolution" and insisted that if a sectarian massacre couldn't inspire the sofa party to take action, then nothing could. The committed revolutionaries held candlelight vigils, respectfully hoisting signs that called for unity. They marched in small groups. Each foray was met with indifference or contempt. After the Maspero atrocity, the vast majority of Egyptians saw and believed the SCAF's narrative that the noble military guardians of the nation had been attacked by narrow-minded, selfish sectarian rabble-rousers, contemptible Christians demanding far more than they deserved, just like the disrespectful bohemian youth who choked Tahrir week by week.

The military had been tightening the screws of censorship already, and after Maspero, it continued to peddle a brew of lies, delusion, paranoia, and justification. General Adel Emara said it simply wasn't military doctrine to run over people, even though Egyptian police had been known to do so as a crowd-control technique. At a briefing intended to exculpate the army, Emara and another general showed the video of the predator-APC chasing down and crushing people to death. General Emara claimed that the driver was trying to escape the frightening crowd, not to kill. Of course, the general added, it was possible that a Christian fanatic had hijacked the APC and then killed his fellow marchers in order to incite anger against the SCAF. Among such claims, the military also

sprinkled dark accusations of a "hidden hand" at work, a favored rhetorical trope of Mubarak's time.

"We are not circulating conspiracy theories, but there is no doubt that
there are enemies of the revolution," General Mahmoud Hegazy said. Incredibly, the SCAF persuaded much of the public that the army and the
revolution were one and the same, and that the events at Maspero somehow represented an attack by dirty hidden interests against the noble
aspirations of a revolution safely prospering in the military's care. A false
narrative instantaneously subsumed the truth: a parallel history written
and accepted in real time while almost everybody ignored the obvious.

The massacre had unleashed something dark in public opinion. It
also had unhinged many of the revolutionaries. Some members of the
Revolutionary Youth Coalition blamed the CIA for the massacre. Others
wondered whether it was time to plan an armed insurrection against the
junta. Mina Daniel's own Youth Movement for Justice and Freedom was
wracked by baying calls for violence from some members. They were so
persistent that some of the revolutionary leaders thought they were plants
from State Security, trying to divide the group. "The military is leading
us toward fascism by manipulating minorities," one of the few women
leaders among the revolutionaries, Ola Shabha, told her fellow activists.
"We can't take our eyes off the bigger issue."

Barely anyone showed up for the vigils. Nothing came of the cry for
a Second Revolution. The Revolutionary Youth Coalition had carefully
assembled documentary evidence to rebut the SCAF's false narrative and
expose its appalling crimes at Maspero. But only a tiny number of Egyptians exhibited any interest at that crucial point in either truth or justice.
The revolution was right, but there seemed no practical way to carry its
ideas forward. Maybe there never had been. Maybe the only thing that
Tahrir had going for it was a naïve ideal, a cosmic long shot that had
worked once, in January, kind of. Reason offered no evidence that it
could work again; that belief required a leap of faith.

8.

UPSTAIRS FROM THE DEAD COW

The revolutionary zeitgeist swung on a wild pendulum between elation and despair, but Basem Kamel was a study in steadiness. He was older and less radical than most of his fellow activists, more mainstream and well-to-do. He had risked a lot for the revolt, but his concerns were broader than the revolution alone. He cared as much about preserving Egypt as a secular state and blocking the rise of the Islamists as he did about the dream of social justice for all. He thought it shamefully naïve to ignore the political threats to freedom. Islamists and the SCAF could just as readily kill the revolution's dreams as the bullets and blades of thugs. Basem was a self-made businessman, and he brought a can-do pragmatism to his newfound career in politics. He had chosen elections as his preferred path to democracy, and he didn't intend to let anything, even the horrific massacre at Maspero, distract him from the mission.

One Friday afternoon in September, Basem gathered his family for lunch in their Helwan apartment. They saw him now only in passing, usually on Friday mornings or the rare evening he wasn't at a demonstration, a meeting, or a party event. "I'm thinking that I will run for parliament," he said. "What is your opinion?"

His wife grimaced. "Is it necessary?"

His son, Mohammed, who was nine, whooped with joy. "I'll take your posters to school," he said.

"Don't do it," said Sarah, the twelve-year-old. "I don't want you to be a public figure. I don't want to hear all the lies they'll say about you." She stormed off to her room.

"I asked you your opinion," Basem said, following behind her, "but I insist on reasonable reasons."

Ultimately, he did what he wanted, and his firstborn daughter grudgingly forgave him. Basem held his first campaign team meeting just a few days after the Maspero massacre, while most of his fellows from the Revolutionary Youth Coalition were still paralyzed by depression. The Egyptian Social Democratic Party decided to run Basem in the downtown district, where it was confident about winning, although the party would move him elsewhere if it made him more likely to get into parliament. Basem didn't mind the uncertainty. He was willing to start there and shift his operation wherever he was assigned. "Our office is on Parliament Street, just upstairs from the dead cow," he told me. Some Social Democratic Party member had donated an office above a butcher's shop.

While the revolutionary youth were still trying to figure out the basic anatomy of a campaign, Basem was able to draw on the liberal elite's reservoir of funds, connections, and white-collar professionals willing to donate their time to electoral politics. Basem's brother, an engineer, would serve as his chief of staff. A successful marketing executive, Maha Abdel Nasser was already crunching the district's demographic data on her laptop. Mohamed Khalil, a businessman, was raising money, making a budget, and designing possible advertising strategies. It was almost a shock to walk into such a high-caliber campaign strategy session after all the despair among the other revolutionary youth. Basem and Maha and Mohamed Khalil considered themselves revolutionary youth, but they were twice as old as most activists, far more wealthy, and, for the most part, employed in decently paying jobs. They belonged to an entirely different stratum from Moaz, Sally, and the other leaders of the street demonstrations.

Maspero had upset them all. "Sunday was the worst day since the revolution," Basem said as he opened his first staff meeting. "I don't know what to say. It was so dangerous to ask the Muslims to go to the streets."

He wasn't going to let Maspero derail his campaign, however. "We're in a crunch time," he said. "What's my plan for the next forty-five days?"

Over the next hour, they mapped it out, to the day: where Basem would pray on Fridays, which heads of families he had to visit, what

phone calls needed to be made, which neighborhoods were worth evening door-to-door campaigning. They ate peanuts from paper bags,
sipped coffee, and parsed the merits of advertising Basem's campaign on
car air fresheners, napkins, or candy wrappers.

"If I fail, I'm going to hang you all!" Basem joked.

The mood was jovial, confident. I felt like I was witnessing a real
operation. It was hard to imagine how he could lose. There were enough
secular Egyptians in Cairo to guarantee some seats to all the major non-
Islamist groupings, and Basem, as one of the only candidates with Tahrir
credentials, was likely to win one of them. His campaign was just as
much a rehearsal for serving in parliament, which would be an uphill
battle to fend off the Brotherhood and the Salafis while trying to force
the junta back to its barracks.

Maha was already worried about the difficulties of getting anything
useful done with a seat in parliament. "Basem's a good politician," she
said. "He's stable. He's got charisma. The problem is not the race; the
problem is the winning."

Basem's campaign meeting was the most hopeful thing I had seen in
months. In a functioning democracy, it might have seemed unremark-
able, but this was Egypt in 2011. In this small room in an unfinished
concrete building, upstairs from four cow carcasses hanging from hooks
over the sidewalk, Basem and these volunteers were flexing the idea that
they would share in the power that had forever been reserved for the imperious seigneur but which was rightfully theirs. Their talk and schemes
didn't have the tenor of Moaz's and Sally's morally pure revolution, or the
angry second coming so desired by Mina Daniel's survivors in the Youth
Movement for Justice and Freedom. They were in control, they were having a bit of fun, and they expected to win more power and responsibility
at every stage to come. On this day, it seemed to me, Basem had stepped
onto a different track from that of his Tahrir comrades: still stoking the
same flame, perhaps, but entirely at ease with the machinery of politics.
Unless every single gain of the year were erased, a part of the revolution
would find its way to the center of Egypt's labyrinth of power. No one
could say who spoke most truthfully for Tahrir, but Basem's voice was
likely to carry farthest from the square.

Basem still showed up at Tahrir when the Revolutionary Youth Coalition backed this or that Friday protest, but he preferred to work on his political party's business, especially the pressing parliamentary campaign. By now, he said, he spent 90 percent of his time on party politics and 10 percent on the Revolutionary Youth Coalition. "The coalition is a brand," he said matter-of-factly. The casualness of the remark surprised me. He was right, of course; Tahrir was a brand too. Basem wasn't sentimental. He had his convictions and felt no need to dress them up in mystical mumbo jumbo. Yet it felt almost sacrilegious to use the language of marketing to describe Egypt's historical pivot.

As the Islamists were coalescing, the liberals were fracturing into a bickering field of competitors. Even within the Social Democratic Party, disagreements flared over how much selling out was permissible in the pursuit of power. Zyad el-Elaimy sympathized with the moral activists who wanted to boycott the elections or refuse contributions from rich, unsavory donors. But he argued that without tangible power, every single one of the revolution's ambitions would be stillborn. "It's all about politics," he said. "Revolution is politics. It is silly to try to separate them." Winning elections in Egypt would require enough campaign money for expensive radio and television ads, and that money was to be found in the hands of the old elite. The billionaire Christian mogul Naguib Sawiris had founded his own Free Egyptians Party, which appealed to Christians and to classical liberals: people who supported free markets but weren't progressive. The party had plenty of *felool*, corrupt businessmen, and old ruling party members in its ranks. Basem and Zyad pushed for an alliance with Sawiris. They knew he needed the support of revolutionaries so that his party wouldn't be pigeonholed as reactionary and sectarian; Sawiris knew the revolutionaries needed his cash. Ultimately, Basem and Zyad prevailed in the internal vote, and the Social Democratic Party formed an electoral alliance with the Free Egyptians. Without it, Basem and his fellow socialists wouldn't have been able to afford any of the expensive radio and television ads considered indispensable for reaching a largely illiterate electorate. Many revolutionaries quit the party in disgust, while others, such as Sally, grudgingly remained but refused to help with the campaign. It was an uncomfortable compromise that created a rift between those who emphasized their liberal identity and those who valued the revolution above all.

The union, called the Egyptian Bloc, came with lots of funding. Secular liberals had hoped to assemble a grand coalition to challenge the Islamists, but it fell apart over the question of *felool*. Moaz and the Revolutionary Youth Coalition wanted a total ban that would exclude several million National Democratic Party members from politics. Basem and Zyad were willing to settle for a coalition that excluded only former members of parliament and National Democratic Party members under criminal investigation. Personal vanity and sincere ideological differences between left, center, and right also came into play. Most of the secular or liberal party activists wanted to be king and had no instinct for sharing a podium, much less political power. As a result, most of the liberal parties fell apart, leaving only the Social Democrats and the Free Egyptians. Even they could not agree on a unified slate of candidates, finally deciding to split up the country, with each party running alone in half the districts. By the time they had figured out how to coordinate, the campaign was halfway finished. Basem had to move to a new district, yielding his Parliament Street district to a Sawiris candidate.

The Egyptian Bloc formally debuted two weeks before voting began in the first round of parliamentary elections, which were to take place in three stages from November to January. Under a bland corporate logo of two hands and a stylized Egyptian flag, the bloc's motto urged somewhat generically, "Together we will get our rights."

Sawiris's fortune made him the single most important bankroller of secular liberal politics. He made an unfortunate symbol. He was a hard partyer known for boozy nights at Cairo hot spots and lavish cruises around the Mediterranean. He already had enraged Islamists by tweeting a cartoon that mocked the face-covering *niqab*, or full veil, worn by some Muslim women. Sawiris had alienated revolutionaries with his brazenly plutocratic lifestyle and lack of concern for the poor. He was articulate but off-color and clearly out of step with the pious lifestyles of most Egyptians, Muslim or Christian. He had made his billions during the old regime, which made him suspect even though he hadn't been a favored Mubarak crony. This was the best hope of the liberals: a partnership between a tone-deaf mogul and a group of earnest, secular, well-to-do socialist professionals. The Free Egyptians traded on fear, recruiting Christians by harping on the threat of Islamist domination. Their money felt dirty and their politics divisive. That could be what it would take to win.

Sawiris launched the Egyptian Bloc ostentatiously from the Shepheard Hotel's tenth-floor ballroom overlooking the Nile. Slabs of marble cake towered on crystal platters. A few hundred men and women in formal business attire celebrated on Naguib Sawiris's dime. Zyad was in full swing, seeking to frighten and then inspire his listeners. "On Kandahar Friday," he told the fancy crowd in the ballroom, "I went to Tahrir Square because I felt it was our square, and I didn't want to let them take it over from us. But I felt like I was not in my own country. If we don't want our country to turn into Saudi Arabia, the Egyptian Bloc is our only choice. We don't want Kandahar Friday to happen again." Zyad strode off the stage and headed to a television studio for an interview.

Basem skipped the big show at the Shepheard Hotel. He didn't want to waste any energy on activities that didn't translate directly into votes. Every night in November, Basem dedicated the two hours after sunset to neighborhood stumping. His team picked a street in his new district, the jam-packed and heavily Christian enclave of Shoubra, and Basem shook as many hands as he could. He wanted people in his district to see his face and learn his name. If a voter appeared receptive but ambivalent, he would engage in a five-minute debate. For two-thirds of the seats in their district, voters would select a party from a list of more than a hundred. For the remaining seats, voters would choose individual candidates from an equally long list. The first struggle for any candidate, or party, was simply to get voters to remember his name and the symbol by which he would be identified on the ballot for the illiterate.

Basem's opponents, the Muslim Brotherhood, had been campaigning nonstop since Ramadan: four months of constant barnstorming. The Salafis, whose cash-rich clerics preached to ready audiences, were finding remarkable success with their ultraconservative message. They campaigned on a platform of rigid enforcement of sharia. Their female candidates were represented by a sketch of a rose because women ought not to be seen in public. A devout, Koranic Egypt could overcome all its problems, the Salafis said.

Meanwhile, the secular Egyptian Bloc, the rump end of a fragmentary and elitist liberal coalition, was hitting the streets at the last minute with a vague message. Most of their candidates looked visibly uncomfortable on a sidewalk, and even more so in the company of a *shaabi*, or lower-class Egyptian. Basem, however, loved it. It brought him back to his days at construction sites. His new district stretched north and east from downtown. He was now operating out of a first-floor apartment at 138 Shoubra Street, across a wide boulevard from the police station. He'd been interviewed by all the major television hosts. On the street, many people recognized him, even if they weren't always sure why. "We have no idea how well we are doing," Basem said as he set out for his nightly meet and greet. "We have no money for polls." Two young boys from the neighborhood fanned out ahead, distributing orange pamphlets with a photo of Basem, the Social Democratic Party platform, and the slogan "Egyptians deserve a real choice. Together we will get our rights."

Two of Basem's brothers, Ahmed and Sameh, walked with him that night. The Kamel family operated as a unit. All four brothers still lived in the same building as their parents, and their sister, Ines, lived nearby. Basem's kids routinely spent the night with their aunt or uncles. Three of the brothers worked at ABC Architecture and Design, the family business. Basem's campaign was a family operation as well. The brothers went to the office during the day and helped Basem run for office in the evening. "How to feed the kids?" Basem said. "We don't have the luxury not to work."

Tonight a film crew was following him with a bright light. "People pay more attention," Basem said. "They think you must be important." He was wearing a beige suit and a blue plaid shirt, with no tie. Everyone else in the entourage shivered in sweaters.

"I don't like members of parliament!" a minimart proprietor shouted. "We've seen nothing since the revolution!"

"What's important is that you vote, even if not for us," Basem replied.

"When are the elections, anyway?" a customer in the shop asked.

Citizens who in the past had passively ignored or accepted political theater now felt free to express their gripes. Many responded to Basem with suspicion as he approached. One man crumpled Basem's flier and threw it on the ground. "It doesn't even list your profession!" he sneered. Another said he would vote for no one. Another accused Basem of being a grifter.

"*Izzayak?* What's up?" Basem approached a group of men smoking *shisha*, or waterpipes. "Will you vote?"

"We don't know who these people on the lists are," one of them said. "I don't know you. I don't know who you are, what you are after."

Unfazed, Basem plowed forward, in his zone. As aides handed out fliers with the party's platform, Basem hit the highlights. "We're Social Democrats," he said. "We believe in rights for everyone. We believe in social justice. The state must make sure the poor have housing and food and jobs. And it is the responsibility of the state to help our economy grow."

He bear-hugged a man with an enormous beard. "Don't vote for the Salafis!" he said.

"Long live the revolution!" the Salafi replied. "I don't support you, but I like your arguments."

Unlike Basem with his slick campaign, the Revolutionary Youth Coalition was in disarray. Some of its smartest members were immobilized. Alaa Abdel Fattah had been arrested on ridiculous charges of conspiring to shoot the army at Maspero. Even Mina Daniel had been charged posthumously with perpetrating the massacre that killed him. Others seemed terminally distracted. A few weeks before Egypt's first serious opportunity to wrest control of the country away from the old regime and the authoritarian Islamists, the parliamentary elections, Ahmed Maher, founder of the April 6 Movement, and Asmaa Mahfouz, the inspiring orator, were both in New York City marching with the 99 percent in the Occupy Wall Street movement.

On principle, the Revolutionary Youth Coalition had refused to join the well-funded Egyptian Bloc. Now it was left with a pure, idealistic, and penniless parliamentary campaign. The coalition branded its slate of candidates "the Revolution Continues." Moaz took a table beneath the vaulted ceiling at café Groppi, a now decrepit icon of Cairo's glory days, and solicited ideas from everyone he knew about how to organize a national parliamentary campaign. "Failure is close," he said. His glasses were bent; he had sat on them. Moaz noted people's suggestions but found himself stymied. "That's a great idea," he kept saying, "but how can we do it if we have no money?" The Revolution Continues didn't even have a few hundred dollars to rent a megaphone to mount on top of a car. Its candidates were untainted, but also unknown.

Moaz was running in his neighborhood. Although the Brotherhood had formally cut ties with him, Moaz still relied on his old Brotherhood *usra* and his friends to organize campaign events. They were going to stencil the campaign signs in Moaz's family's garage and hang them around town. Meanwhile, Khaled el-Sayyed, a chant leader from Mina Daniel's movement, was running against his old friend Zyad in the same district. They had worked together closely to plan Tahrir, but now they avoided even speaking to each other. When they buttonholed passersby on the street, the Revolution Continues candidates had more of a plea than a program. "We won't bribe you," Khaled el-Sayyed told prospective voters in his district. "We look like you. We live like you. Vote for us." He sounded like an angry teenager demanding respect.

Elections required an entirely different set of muscles from protests. Whatever knack young revolutionaries had for electrifying an audience at a march or a clash clearly didn't transfer to electoral politics. Now Egyptians wanted to hear a long-term plan and evidence that candidates could deliver. The revolutionaries were willing to work hard, but their genius was tactical, not strategic. The Revolutionary Youth Coalition was as ill suited to plot a grand election campaign after Tahrir as combat infantrymen would be to govern and rebuild a country they had just destroyed in an invasion. On Saturday, November 19, violence broke out on a spur street off Tahrir Square. Riot police beat a demonstrator to death, and soon an all-out battle raged between cops and demonstrators. A police sniper was shooting people in the eyes. Tear gas wafted over the entire city center.

It was almost with relief that the revolutionary youth activists suspended their political work to rush to Mohamed Mahmoud Street and buttress the random demonstrators who had begun to fight the police over a meaningless stretch of street. The fighting was intense but bizarre because it was contained to a single city block. The army held tight control over the city, but was allowing a lethal war between police and revolutionaries on one circumscribed proving ground. The military could have cleared and sealed the area within minutes using only tear gas, stopping the battle and saving lives. In fact, it did so all around Mohamed Mahmoud whenever the fighting spilled out. But the soldiers let it rage on in one small area, cleverly calculating that it would prove a final, fatal distraction to the revolutionaries. They were right. The Revolution Continues judged it indecent to seek office while friends were dying, so Moaz and company suspended their parliamentary campaign and joined the battle. Even Basem stopped by, if only for a few hours.

The Revolutionary Youth Coalition leaders visited Mohamed Mahmoud and stood in solidarity with the motorcyclists working as volunteer ambulance drivers. "Stand your ground! Stand your ground!" Basem shouted in encouragement. Moaz treated the wounded while Sally and Zyad flushed with pride at the resilience of the young fighters. Sally's nose twitched at the tear gas. "This smell," she said. "It reminds me of beautiful days." But this was someone else's fight, not theirs. It was an almost nihilistic spasm of frustration and rage. The people fighting at Mohamed Mahmoud did so only because the police were there and fighting back. If the police had left, the revolutionaries would have too. This was a natural sequel to the Maspero massacre. Violence had been normalized. First they came for the Christians, and no one cared. Now they were shooting college students, teenage soccer fans, and revolutionaries in the face, and still no one cared. It would only be a matter of time before the regime would turn its guns on other, more organized competitors. Entities like the Muslim Brotherhood and the old ruling party ignored the military's murderous tendencies at their peril.

The government, it was now clear, had only been decapitated, not overthrown. Knowing what it was up against, it embarked on a long game to outmaneuver its opponents and sometimes seemed more sure of its goal than the revolutionaries. Once Mubarak was gone, the disparate groups that had come together to oust him couldn't agree on what to do next, or how: Electoral politics or street protest? Constitution first, or elections? And what kind of society should the new Egypt be, anyway? As activists without experience, funding, or institutional power struggled to organize politically, state media filled the void, calling the revolutionaries disruptive and destructive and spoiled. The sofa party, conservative and cautious, was easily swayed, and the revolution was losing the masses. By the time of the Battle of Mohamed Mahmoud, the young activists were in a state of suspense. Would they be able to finish the revolution they had started, or would the new Egypt prove worse than the old? As exhilarating as it was, their reunion in the square also had a darker edge, one that heralded the fraying of the revolution.

Unlike partisans of the Revolution Continues, Basem didn't view this latest outbreak of violence as a pivotal litmus test. It was unfortunate, that was all. He had a major rally that night in his district, and he found it preposterous that Moaz and other comrades thought he should suspend his campaign. No one else was taking a break. Why cede the contest to the Muslim Brotherhood, the Salafis, and the old regime? Some of the voters in Shoubra, Basem's working-class district, groused about the latest events in Tahrir as they waited in a café for the candidates to speak. One flung his dominoes to the table in disgust when his friends spoke of the fighting in the city center. "Fuck Tahrir, the cunt of the mother of the revolution," he said. "Fuck the revolution."

Basem spoke with fluid confidence, a much more natural-sounding orator than he'd been just a few months earlier. He sought the support of women, whose rights would suffer under Islamist rule, and of people who were tired of the state's abuses. "Nothing justifies the police killing people and putting hundreds in the hospital," Basem said. "The police are our servants, not our masters. Their time will come." He warned his listeners about the new burdens of citizenship. "If you don't vote today," Basem said, "you can't complain tomorrow."

Egypt was splintering. The Muslim Brotherhood was enjoying a new alliance with old enemies in the military as the two joined in condemning the anarchists fighting on Mohamed Mahmoud Street. Basem and Zyad advanced toward the prize of parliament and the possibility to shape new laws. Meanwhile, around Tahrir, the revolutionaries somehow kept fighting for days over the same block. They were completely disconnected from the rest of the country, which was applauding the SCAF's authoritarian tone and pondering whether to vote for Islamists or establishment secular candidates. Almost no one was contemplating voting for the Tahrir candidates of the Revolution Continues.

Moaz found the simple life-and-death chase in the square easier to digest than the complex realities outside. "We will have revolution after revolution, like a cascade," he said with glee. He let himself believe that government atrocities would inevitably draw people to the streets like on January 25. But his party, al-Tayyar al-Masry, had recruited only a few dozen former Muslim Brothers, while the establishment parties were mobilizing millions of voters.

Mohamed Mahmoud itself had devolved into a weird, contained, and violent ritual. Tahrir Square was quiet, and so were all the surrounding streets. The army kept things under control everywhere except for that single block, where it left the police in charge. And so, on that one spot, wave after wave of young Egyptians expended themselves. The army could have stopped it at any time by taking over the checkpoint from the police. The protesters could have simply stood back and stopped dying. But like wasps drawn to a honey trap, they came and fell. Kids who were afraid to tell their parents they were heading to Tahrir fearlessly attacked the police. They wrote their names and birthdays on tape affixed to their chests and sleeves, so they could be identified easily if killed.

Power relies in part on the willingness to kill. In the early days of Tahrir, revolutionaries had shocked the regime with their willingness to die. They had dared the regime to kill them all, and the regime had flinched. Nearly a year later, however, the regime seemed to have shed its reluctance. The revolutionaries had changed too. Before, they had been willing to fight; now they seemed eager.

On the third day of the clashes, there was a march from Shoubra to the square. Basem joined because he opposed the force being used by the government, although he didn't endorse the street protest itself. As he walked for three hours with people from his district, a woman confronted him.

"We stood up to the old regime. They were all dogs!" she sputtered. "Now all the political parties are the same."

"So you have no hope?" Basem asked. "All these people in the square cannot take power. They have to elect someone."

"Everyone is fighting for chairs," the woman said contemptuously. "This is the worst moment in the history of Egypt."

That was the nihilism of this incarnation of Tahrir. The SCAF was the worst group to ever rule Egypt, and yet many of the young people in Tahrir now believed that anyone willing to engage in politics against the SCAF was just as bad as the dictators. In their view, the only people who were noble were the ones rushing headlong toward violent confrontations with the police. This disregard for complexity, for political thought, for the nuances of citizenship, was just another recipe for apathy and indifference. Even if this fight won a concession from the SCAF once again, it had succumbed to a form of vanity; many of the activists in Tahrir no longer had faith in practical agents of change, only in their ability to oppose authority. To some, violence perversely brought solace.

The fights over politics seemed abstract and procedural, the odds long against radical change. To seize power in politics, one had to draft laws, raise money, and woo defectors from the military and the former ruling party. To seize a street required a more straightforward asset: great numbers of people willing to die. By the end of the five-day Battle of Mohamed Mahmoud, nearly fifty people were dead and more than three thousand wounded. It wasn't entirely in vain. The Supreme Council of the Armed Forces finally set a hard deadline to surrender power to an elected president: June 30, 2012.

The day before the fall parliamentary elections, a few thousand revolutionaries huddled in Tahrir as if awaiting a miracle. Some of the most dogged campaign workers had now decided to boycott. They gave up and sat in the square. A young activist who had spent almost every week on the road for two years, first for Mohamed ElBaradei and then for the

Social Democratic Party, had impulsively decided not to vote. "I am with Tahrir," he said. Candidates from the Revolution Continues list didn't even intend to leave the square to vote for themselves. They imagined that their boycott would somehow erase the power and legitimacy of those who would win. The revolutionaries didn't realize that they had yet to woo most Egyptians, who were still unconvinced that the January 25 moment could or should translate into anything enduring. Whatever else it meant, boycotting the election represented yet another abdication from the public sphere. The revolution felt like it was all out of ideas.

Tear gas–infused dust choked the city. Irritation lingered in the tear ducts and lungs, a hangover of violence. The late-winter sun made everything a sickly gray. Then, all at once, the sky broke open, and warm rain poured over the square, washing away the toxins. A murmur swelled from all corners, first sounding like a hum and then like a roar. Everyone was praying: "May this rain bring us blessings and not harm." Even the secular and atheist revolutionaries were turning to one of the last forces that hadn't disappointed them: God. They needed help anywhere they could find it.

On Election Day, November 28, the Muslim Brotherhood erected tents at every polling station, in direct violation of the law. Liberals complained, and some were dismantled. Basem awoke early to vote in Helwan and then head to his district. He phoned me to ask how people were voting in Moqattam, the hilltop district where Zyad lived.

"Everybody I talked to in the line told me they're voting Brotherhood."

"That's not good," Basem said.

"Maybe the liberals come out in the afternoon?" I offered.

"We can hope."

Basem lived in Zyad's district and was voting for him. Both of them were voting for their own party rather than for the Revolution Continues list, which theoretically represented their origins. For Basem, the Revolution Continues candidates seemed out of touch with reality. "Khaled el-Sayyed is too crazy, too young," he said. "I don't trust him to represent me."

We met a few hours later at Basem's Shoubra office. Three Social Democratic Party lawyers were collecting reports of fraud from around the district and preparing official complaints. Most were for minor violations, such as the Brotherhood tents and banners. Basem rushed in. He had just inspected polling stations at the Shoubra Engineering College, where judges were using ballots that had not been stamped properly. "We shook a lot of hands before today," he said. "Now our only role is to monitor."

His Bluetooth earpiece lit up. "Move, move, move!" he cried. "Some women were caught trying to smuggle ballots into a polling station."

"It's an incredible year, 2011," Basem said as he rushed down the street with his aides a few minutes later. "For me, for all of Egypt."

He pushed past the military police into the polling station at the Shoubra campus of the University of Banha Faculty of Engineering. He made a big show of standing by the judges in each classroom, but he knew he had little power here.

"They told me there were problems here, but I did not find anything," he said after a quarter hour. "What can we do? Earlier I saw an old woman ask for help, and a volunteer pointed to his party and said, 'Sign here.' If I tell a judge, what will he say?"

Back at his office, Basem sat at a desk surrounded by friends. A pile of posters of his face, printed on high-end plastic, lay crumpled on the floor. They never had been used. "At first we didn't have any posters," Basem said with flat amusement. "Then we didn't have any rope to hang them up with. Then we got rope, but we didn't have enough guys to hang them."

He turned to his team. "Tonight we will meet, see our mistakes and good points, and make a plan for tomorrow," he said. "After the elections, I will turn off my phone and sleep until Friday."

"Congratulations on your campaign," I said.

"It's bad luck," Basem scowled. "It is still early."

With nothing left to do, the candidate fidgeted. He didn't like to wait passively. He turned to his friends.

"If I win," he joked, "I will get in parliament, and I will forget all about the revolution. I will tell the people in Tahrir to go home."

"Seriously," I asked, "how will you avoid changing?"

"You cannot!" Basem retorted, his expression a little more serious. "It happens to everybody."

The country would vote in three waves. This was just round one. The first results surprised almost everyone. The Muslim Brotherhood was winning about 40 percent, a little more than expected. The Salafis were winning 25 percent, a lot more than expected. The Wafd, the old, corrupted, and officially sanctioned opposition, was polling about 10 percent. The remaining quarter of the votes were split among the other secular movements. The *felool* parties that wanted to resuscitate the old regime won barely 5 percent. The results wouldn't be official until just before the seating of parliament at the end of January, but Basem and Zyad appeared to have won comfortably.

In the second round of voting on December 15, the Islamists cruised forward. This was also Moaz's round, but his campaign had never recovered after November. He paraded through his neighborhood with about fifty volunteers, chanting, "Revolution in the square! Revolution in parliament!" but didn't shake people's hands. It wasn't even clear that he was a candidate. When polls opened, Moaz couldn't find his ID card. He was too disorganized even to vote for himself.

The army had erected a stone wall across Mohamed Mahmoud Street to shut down the fight there. Immediately after the second round of voting, soldiers violently cleared a small group of revolutionaries from a sit-in beside the parliament building. Impervious to the rolling news cameras, security men threw furniture from the parliament roof onto the unarmed revolutionaries five floors below. One soldier unzipped his fly and urinated languorously on them, his piss stream tracing a line across the slogan affixed to the side of the building: "Democracy proves that authority rests with the people." Indifferent that Zyad was a member of parliament–elect, soldiers punched and clubbed him. "To hell with your parliament!" they said.

Their disregard was a hint of the future relations between the military and Egypt's elected politicians. A young woman was thrown to the ground, and soldiers tore off her *abaya*, revealing a neon-blue bra. In what became an iconic image, a soldier leapt energetically in the air and landed a foot in her rib cage. An older woman who tried to intervene was clubbed over the head until she collapsed. The entire assault was video-taped and viewed widely.

The generals were sending a blunt message that, elections notwith-standing, the military was the final arbiter. Every time the military mur-dered or humiliated civilian demonstrators, the state media and the ruling generals lambasted the victims, and each time they were met with more public approval. They were weakening the revolutionaries and dis-crediting them in the eyes of much of the public.

Whatever its motives, the SCAF had created a Pavlovian cycle. The generals changed course only in response to huge crowds or violent clashes at Tahrir. They taught the revolutionaries that protest was the only tool that worked, and therefore the revolutionaries returned to Tah-rir in response to every crisis. At the heart of the revolutionary move-ment was a tiny number of extraordinarily motivated individuals, a few thousand at most, who organized the rest. Each time the state opened the spigot of force, it sent some tens to the cemetery, some hundreds to the hospital, and some hundreds more to detention. Each casualty required inordinate attention from the activists: the prosecutions must be resisted, the torture documented, the wounded healed, the dead mourned. Four days of clashes might exhaust the following month's energy. All that time spent cleaning up the aftermath was time *not* spent appealing to every-day Egyptians. Whether that was the SCAF's plan or merely a collateral benefit, it was in any case to the SCAF's advantage.

There was some talk about whether the revolution had been lost. Basem believed it would take a generation to change national attitudes, and that the best way was through sustained, grinding work in parlia-ment, state institutions, and political parties. Success would take years. Moaz dreamed of a more radical transformation for the country but had no idea how to bring it about. Like so many revolutionaries, he suffered from a kind of political attention deficit disorder, always juggling too many ideas to concentrate fully on one.

"We've got to leave the square and make many Tahrir Squares all around Egypt," Sally Moore told anyone who would listen. "We've been talking about this idea for a long time, getting to the neighborhoods and breaking the isolation of Tahrir Square. We need to do it." She'd had a breakthrough after the assault on the woman in the *abaya*. Now that she was choosing to work away from the party and outside the square, she felt rejuvenated.

Sally wasn't alone in the sentiment. Revolutionaries had ghettoized themselves geographically and culturally, encouraging one another in isolation from the mainstream. Now they had an idea: Why not campaign against the SCAF's lies block by block, village by village? They borrowed the name for their new citizen's movement from a newspaper headline about the blue bra beating: Askar Kazeboon! ("the Military Lies!"). Activists and filmmakers assembled many short videos that juxtaposed lying SCAF members with footage of the military crimes they were denying. It was powerful and simple, with an important, easy-to-understand message: at last, a distillation of a revolutionary idea that could reach a wide audience.

Sally and her friends held Kazeboon! screenings all over Cairo, even projecting films onto the wall of Maspero above the heads of the soldiers guarding it. The idea was designed to go viral. Activists anywhere in Egypt could download the clips or make their own and get out into the neighborhoods to declare: The military lies! Emotionally, the campaign marked an almost Oedipal breakthrough. For a year, revolutionaries had chanted, "The army and the people are one hand!" even when the army was standing by indifferently while police officers murdered civilian demonstrators. The revolutionaries had avoided blaming the military directly for its abuses because of the hallowed place the military held in Egyptian life, even long after it was clear that the military was all too willing to kill or suppress the people it pretended to protect. Finally, the young revolutionaries were abandoning their false pose of national unity and calling out the army and its leaders on the SCAF for their tyranny.

The new parliament would be seated on January 23, 2012. The week that followed was scheduled as a national holiday to commemorate the previous year's uprising. No matter how incomplete the revolution seemed, the election was a tangible accomplishment. Egyptians had voted, and despite widespread instances of small-scale fraud, all the parties involved had endorsed the results. Egypt would have a parliament with a diversity of voices that roughly approximated the people's actual choices. The old system remained intact, but it had not been able to shut down entirely the mechanisms of protest and dissent. Egyptians still were able to exercise the rights of free speech and assembly that they had won a year before. Though they might be killed for demonstrating, now their deaths would be reported in Egyptian media, in some cases even accurately. All this fell short of a revolution, but it was more movement toward freedom and dignity than Egypt had ever seen.

Two days before parliament was to take the oath of office, the government finally published the election results. The most heartening number was the tally of ballots: twenty-seven million, the most votes ever cast in an Egyptian election. The high turnout was a sign of faith in the democratic process. Most depressing was the number of revolutionary youth who made it into parliament: three. Zyad, Basem, and Mostafa el-Naggar, a former Muslim Brotherhood and ElBaradei activist who'd founded his own Justice Party and won an independent seat in Cairo. (There were dozens of parties with indistinguishable names blending the words "justice," "freedom," "revolution," and "democracy.") After a year and a thousand or more deaths, after a tyrant had been tried and an entire system of governance cast into doubt, the revolutionaries had managed to capture only three seats in a parliament of 508. Just half of 1 percent. Moaz wasn't elected, and neither were any of the other young activists; the only victories for the Revolution Continues came from a batch of seasoned older socialist politicians who ran as coalition partners.

Even before the official results were posted, Moaz figured that his compatriots had been shut out. He already had moved on. He was organizing *salasel*, or human chains, in which supporters of the revolution silently lined streets, holding signs with slogans. Anyone who wanted to engage them in conversation could, but there was no chanting or disrupting traffic. This was an attempt to reach the Egypt left behind by the revolution.

One Sunday night along Abou el-Ezz Street, a commercial boulevard in Mohandiseen, about fifty people showed up for one of Moaz's *salasel* gatherings, most of them women. Everyone dressed in his or her best. They held up signs that said things like "I am not a thug" and "Our battle is with corruption, poverty, ignorance, and injustice." The links in the human chain stood about arm's length apart alongside the slow-moving traffic.

"Who's in charge?" asked a woman clutching a bag of posters. Moaz was nowhere to be found; he was running late for his own event. He made it after a half hour.

"Dude, you said five minutes!" said his childhood friend and erstwhile campaign manager.

He blamed the traffic. "It's Egypt," Moaz said haplessly. "What can I do?"

Moaz also was running security for a January 25 anniversary march. He met some of his team in Tahrir at the Belady Café, an upscale establishment replete with faux vintage photos of January 25 that marketed itself as the new revolutionary hangout. On state TV, we could hear an announcer heaping scorn on the upcoming anniversary marches. "These rabble-rousers want to burn down the country," he said. Moaz had tried to persuade the revolutionary groups and the Brotherhood to have a single, unified stage in Tahrir. He had failed. He was recruiting as many strong, athletic people as he could to provide security on January 25. He was afraid of thugs. "The revolution started with a few tiny protests, and in the end, there will be nothing left of it but a few tiny protests," he said.

Across town at the Golden Tulip Flamenco Hotel in Zamalek, the twenty-two elected members of the Social Democratic Party were plotting their legislative agenda. They spent the entire day in a conference room upholstered in burgundy velour. Late on Saturday evening, they unveiled it to the world. Only a half dozen reporters were interested enough to show. Basem and his colleagues waited an hour, but there were no more comers. Their performance was a harbinger of the embarrassment to come inside parliament. Each elected member of parliament gave a short, vacuous speech with no specifics. None of them listened when the others spoke. The gossiping delegates were so loud that the reporters had to move closer to the front to hear the vapid presentations. "We want to help the poor," they all said.

A few reporters asked pointed questions. Each time the candidate deferred: "Basem will take that question. He is our revolutionary." When Basem's turn came, he walked through the audience, handing out papers with every official's personal cell phone number and email. The others didn't look so happy about it. That day, Basem changed his profession on Facebook from "architect" to "politician."

During the campaign, Basem had shaken fifty thousand hands. He rarely saw his children anymore, and his wife was usually asleep by the time he got home and fell into bed. He had spent the last two months canvassing his working-class district, and he felt acutely the difference between the clear, revolutionary agenda of his old Tahrir comrades and the spectrum of overlapping, sometimes contradictory interests of his constituents. The most pressing problems remained simple to describe and nearly impossible to solve: unemployment, rising food and fuel prices, inadequate housing. Questions of politics and rights felt secondary to the Egyptian majority struggling every day with individual poverty and a broken national economy. When Basem asked about politics in Shoubra, some people simply wanted a new president elected, with no more protests in the meantime. Others wanted the military to stand down immediately. Many Christians were more concerned about the Islamist surge than about the junta's powers. Few evinced sympathy for the revolutionary youth. The previous week a Kazeboon! team had set up a screening on a Shoubra street, and irritated neighbors cut off its electricity; they didn't want to hear any complaints about the army. Basem invited the Kazeboon! team to plug into his district office on the main avenue and project its videos against the wall.

A year in, Basem said, the revolutionaries had achieved symbolic victories by putting Mubarak on trial and holding elections. People had stopped being afraid, but the system that controlled them remained obstinately in place. Parliament and his own election notwithstanding, Basem said, street demonstrations remained the only tool by which people could affect the government, but even the effectiveness of protest was in question now. On January 25, 2012, Egypt would celebrate the one-year anniversary of its uprising, but it wasn't just the Revolutionary Youth Coalition planning a commemoration in Tahrir. So were the Muslim Brotherhood and the SCAF. With everyone claiming the revolution, it was hard to agree on what, if anything, it meant.

"It's not clear to me what people want," I said.

"It's not clear to me either," Basem said. "That is the problem."

At ten o'clock, early in the morning for these late-rising revolutionaries, Egypt's first meaningful parliament since World War II was sworn in. It was a Monday, just two days before the anniversary of January 25. The inaugural session was a balm to some and a source of rage to others. For the Islamists, who had won a commanding majority, it was a victory and vindication. The new parliament wouldn't end their struggle, but it marked a sea change in their political status. For the hard-left revolutionaries such as Sally, the new parliament meant nothing; they had boycotted the vote. Today they would protest an assembly they considered powerless, packed with fools, chauvinists, and religious obscurantists. In the middle fell those like Basem, who believed that politics and revolution were not mutually exclusive. They were conflicted, for they knew that a hall full of Salafis and Muslim Brothers would be unlikely to organize sustained resistance against the military junta or to showcase clever consensual lawmaking. Nonetheless, they believed in the democratic process. To them, the seating of parliament marked a decisive, if tainted, step toward rule of law.

Zyad made a symbolic walk through Tahrir Square to the swearing-in. Over his untucked shirt, he wore a sash that read, "No to military trials." All the Social Democrats would wear them, an affirmation of their revolutionary pedigree. "I'm from here," he said, pointing at the square. Then he pointed at the gates of parliament. "Not from there. The street for me is the most important thing." A street vendor shouted at him, "Don't forget the poor!" We walked through a maze of barbed wire and concrete barriers, a new martial geography designed to make downtown protests impossible. He walked along the same route he had taken nine months earlier to vote in the constitutional referendum, when the possibilities for Egypt and the revolution had seemed so much happier. He morosely passed a crowd of Muslim Brothers who were singing and waving carnations; today marked an outright victory for them. "The people want God's law!" the Islamists chanted.

It took all day for the speaker to swear in the 508 members. All over the country, Egyptians watched on television. When it was Basem's turn, he spoke the oath: "I swear to uphold the law and the constitution." Before the speaker could cut him off, he added his own extra twist: "And I swear to continue the revolution."

Immediately, the Muslim Brotherhood stepped from the ranks of underground opposition into a state of intoxicated power. No sooner had the members of parliament taken their oaths than the Brothers sidelined everyone who opposed them. There wouldn't be any legislating by consensus or even minority consultation. The Brothers and the Salafis installed supermajorities on every committee. The chamber they envisioned would have no meaningful minority power.

It rained overnight before the revolution's anniversary on January 25, leaving puddles everywhere. Some of the streets leading to Tahrir were flooded ankle-deep with water from sidewalk to sidewalk: makeshift reflecting pools. Cold humidity sapped the city.

This was the Brotherhood's celebration. Whereas the original January 25 marches emerged more or less spontaneously, the first anniversary was an exercise in organized power. After dawn prayers, tens of thousands of well-instructed Muslim Brothers took to Tahrir. They were polite and impeccably dressed, and all elaborated on the same talking points.

For the Muslim Brotherhood, all was not won, but Egypt was heading in its direction. For the revolutionary youth, all was not lost, but little had been achieved. A secretive and repressive junta had succeeded Mubarak, and now two mammoths sat astride Egypt: the military and the Muslim Brotherhood. Moaz and his peers felt an urgent need to rejuvenate a stalled revolution. Should the January 25 anniversary be a celebration or a protest? On this semantic hook hung the future of the relationship between the Muslim Brotherhood and the revolutionaries.

All the original revolutionaries were marching on Tahrir to re-create the feeling of the year before. Zyad and Moaz marched from the same mosque where they had gathered on January 28, 2011. Ayyash marched from Café Riche in Talaat Harb Square, five minutes away. Basem and Sally joined a march that began outside Basem's parliamentary office in Shoubra. In a gesture of tribute and unity, the Coptic Maspero Youth Union had built a thirty-foot-tall obelisk out of lacquered canvas stretched on a wooden frame, on which its members had carefully painted the name of every martyr of every persuasion since January 25, 2011. As he walked, Basem chatted with constituents about the Brotherhood's alarming behavior in parliament. Moaz and the other ex–Muslim Brotherhood Youth patrolled the march perimeter, making sure no one harassed the women. This was a march for all the revolutionary youth, no matter their affiliation or sect, the last place where dissident Brothers and secular liberals still worked in tandem.

The different branches of the march united and crawled up Talaat Harb Street, but when the revolutionaries reached Tahrir, the square was already full to capacity with Muslim Brothers and Salafis. Rainwater blocked the way forward where the street met the square. The memorial obelisk was stalled. The march stopped. The crowd was so densely packed, it was hard to move in any direction.

"I have an announcement!" Basem said in a mock-serious announcer's voice. "We did all this to fill the square. The square is full! So I will go to the party headquarters, make some phone calls, and take a nap before my flight." He was traveling to Ethiopia that night to try to negotiate a fair system to share the Nile's water with the countries upstream from Egypt.

Another hour passed before the rest of the somber revolutionaries picked their way into the square, where they were swallowed by throngs of jubilant Islamists. By sunset, they finally managed to erect their memorial to the martyrs on a barren patch of dirt in the roundabout at the center of Tahrir. It faced an enormous banner on the Muslim Brotherhood's stage: "The Victory of the January 25 Revolution."

The Brothers partied in Tahrir for the rest of the week. By Friday, the revolutionary youth could not mask their disgust. The Brotherhood's dutiful millions had boxed them out of their own uprising. Paramilitary Brothers sprouted all over downtown like muscle-bound mushrooms after a rain. Their tight T-shirts showcased their bouncer's chests, and they had the uninflected facial expressions of the riot policeman or thug, only slightly less mean and dumb, or perhaps merely less practiced. Outside parliament, they formed a cordon to distance protesters from the new Brotherhood members of parliament. In Tahrir, they created a buffer around the Brotherhood stage. By Friday, they proved necessary. The Brotherhood's celebratory crowds had dwindled, and the revolutionaries were commemorating their Friday of Rage from a year earlier. The Brotherhood's festivities made an irresistible target.

Moaz and hundreds of the original revolutionary youth marched across the Qasr el-Nil bridge toward Tahrir. They had prayed at noon at the Mostafa Mahmoud Mosque in Mohandiseen and had retraced their pivotal January 28 march route. They stopped by the stone lions on the bridge, where a year earlier the police had drenched them with fire hoses while they prayed. Here they had conclusively overrun the brutish cops. Now they met no resistance, but ahead lay what many considered their new enemy: the Brotherhood. Today they were technically allies, but these youth felt a special resentment for the Islamists in the square. The regime was the enemy they'd expected to fight. The Brotherhood, they thought, should have been on their side, on the people's side.

"Fuck the mothers of the Brothers," one said. Moaz, whose mother was one of those being insulted, wore a manic frozen grin. "This is a revolution, not a party!" the revolutionaries chanted. They were like somnambulists retracing a path that once had led them to glory.

When they reached the square, they swarmed in front of the Brotherhood's stage like angry drunks. "Leave, traitors, the square is ours, not yours!" they sang. Hundreds of burly Brothers linked arms. People waved their shoes at the leader behind the microphone. Then someone actually tossed one onto the stage. More projectiles followed: water bottles, corncobs, garbage. The man on the stage droned on. Someone shimmied up the lamppost and began worrying the electric wire until he pulled it free. He had cut power to the sound system. Now the Brother onstage was barely audible. The crowd grew rowdier. Some kids now held rocks. Another brandished a broken bottle. "This is crazy," someone next to me said.

"Liars!" the crowd shouted. "Sellouts! Leave!"

"You can't make us leave," the Brother onstage said smugly. "We are the real revolution."

"Fuck your mother!" came the reply, chanted in unison from the crowd.

"We love you, youth," the man said. The Brothers played the national anthem and, as a concession, covered the word "Victory" on the stage banner.

On the anniversary of its best moment, Tahrir had buried its most beguiling promise: the dream of pluralism. In the first days of the revolt, the words "revolution," "dignity," and "freedom" had as many meanings as there were mouths brave enough to utter them. Pluralism had been part of the explicit accord of the men and women who had marched a year before. There was to be a multiplicity of voices. No one should have a monopoly on power; no one could have a monopoly on truth. Truth and power were to be contested, negotiated. A year after that dream had burst into the open, a hail of shoes had banished it. Tahrir in its infancy embraced everyone's right to speak, even those who were wrong. Today no one cared what anyone else had to say or whether they were speaking in good faith. The white noise of shouting had drowned all voices.

9.

I DON'T FEAR MY PEOPLE

Another massacre propelled the country into its second revolutionary year. This one had nothing to do with politics, at least not overtly. It happened when the country's powerhouse soccer team Al Ahly traveled from Cairo to play its rival El Masry in Port Said.

Revolution might have motivated a few Egyptians in the past year, but soccer inspired everyone. The games commanded universal attention. Obsessive youthful fan clubs called ultras fueled the rivalries. They fought with abandon after every major match. Mubarak had kept a tight grip on the ultras, instinctively grasping that their hooliganism could drift easily into political rebellion.

On February 1, as Egypt turned away from its observance of January 25, Al Ahly and El Masry clashed on the field alongside the usual scuffles in the stands. The underdog home team, El Masry, won 3–1. Then thugs stormed the Ahly visitors' stands armed with clubs and machetes. While viewers watched on live television, they hunted Ahly fans with the intent to kill. The police knew from long experience how to contain soccer violence, but on this night, inexplicably, they did something they'd never done before: they turned out the lights and locked the gates so that no one could escape. Some lucky Ahly fans took shelter in their team's locker room, but within minutes, seventy-four people had been slaughtered. One died in the star striker's arms. At a minimum, police negligence had turned a riot into a massacre. But because nothing like this had ever happened before between soccer fans, many suspected some sort of police complicity with the armed thugs.

Immediately, all the ultras suspended their feuds in solidarity. The league cancelled the rest of the season. A few angry Ahly partisans focused their ire on the Port Said fans, but a quick consensus formed among the ultras: the state was to blame. Such killing could not have taken place without either an unimaginable level of negligence or government complicity. The SCAF blamed anarchic forces and declared that the country needed tougher law and order.

Revolutionaries were shocked that the state was displaying such callousness toward salt-of-the-earth Egyptians, regular folk who tuned their TVs to the Premier League rather than to Tahrir. They expected violence against political demonstrators, not sports spectators. The SCAF was simply displaying the casual accounting practices of the ruling class. When passenger ferries sank and trains crashed and landslides buried apartments, killing hundreds, government officials would literally shrug. The country was poor and crowded, and the rulers had found they suffered no adverse consequences if a few dozen died here or a few hundred there, even if government neglect or malfeasance was the cause.

The Port Said killings shook Zyad. Over the past year, thirteen of his friends had died, but every single one of them had joined the revolution by choice and knew the risks. The people murdered in Port Said had made no such decision. They were just cheering their soccer team. Zyad believed the state had killed them, or encouraged them to be killed, in order to distract Egyptians from the revolution. He felt partly responsible; he and his friends had pushed this revolution, and now innocents were being punished for it. In parliament, the Muslim Brothers in charge had condemned the deaths but didn't want to anger the military junta by holding anyone important accountable. Zyad's rage grew. For him, the blame rested with the SCAF's leader, Mohammed Hussein Tantawi. The field marshal was the head of state, the supreme commander, the one who gave the orders that filtered down to the rank-and-file cops.

Angry voices around Egypt were calling for a blockade of Port Said to punish all the city's denizens for the deaths in the soccer stadium. But those people were not at fault. In a show of solidarity with them, Zyad organized three buses filled with revolutionaries to travel from Cairo to Port Said. They toured the site of the massacre and held a rally. Thousands of shell-shocked Port Said residents, grateful for the moral support, cheered the visitors from Cairo.

The soldiers who had beaten Zyad in December had reminded him that being a member of parliament provided him with no special protection. He was as vulnerable as anyone else. But as he addressed the shaken denizens of Port Said, he grew livid. He wanted them, and all the Egyptians watching him on television, to feel as angry as he did and to focus that rage on Tantawi, Egypt's latest dictator.

"Why do we beat the saddle and forget the donkey?" he said, quoting an old proverb. It meant: Don't let the ill-fitting saddle distract us from the real cause of our problems, the uncooperative donkey.

"Who is the donkey?" someone in the audience shouted. Zyad repeated the adage. He was asked again.

The third time, he finally answered with a wry smile: "Field Marshal Tantawi."

As soon as Zyad descended from the stage, he realized that Tantawi would not allow such an insult to pass. He confided his surging anxiety to a television host who had traveled with the convoy to Port Said. She squeezed Zyad's arm. "The SCAF will ask you to apologize," she said.

"Only when they apologize for killing people," Zyad said.

She was right. Within days, Zyad's case was a national priority. The prosecutor charged him with insulting the head of state, a crime that could easily lead to three years in prison. The other parliamentarians could talk of nothing but the effrontery of the young member who had dared compare the field marshal to a donkey. The Muslim Brotherhood lambasted Zyad in public and ordered him in private to seek forgiveness from Tantawi.

"You should not insult an old person," a senior Muslim Brother told Zyad.

"He killed my friends, and in return I can kill his friends also," Zyad retorted, citing another time-honored Egyptian tradition. "If he wants to insult me, I will not feel humiliated."

During the final decade of Mubarak's rule, Zyad had collaborated with Muslim Brotherhood dissidents, defending them when they were persecuted by the state. As soon as they made progress in their pursuit of power, however, the Muslim Brothers abandoned Zyad in order to curry favor with the military. The speaker of parliament ordered Zyad to apologize, in public.

"The only reason we don't expel you from parliament is because the revolutionary groups might set the building on fire if we do," the speaker told Zyad privately, after the regular session had concluded.

"That is your problem," Zyad said, "not mine."

A year after the revolt that felled Mubarak, it was still more risky in Egypt to call a dictator a donkey than it was to shoot unarmed civilians in the face. Even Zyad's family pushed him to apologize. They were afraid. In late February, one of his uncles met with some generals and brought an offer home to Zyad: if he apologized to Tantawi in person, the charges would be dropped.

"They want to humiliate me," Zyad told his uncle. "They want to break me, and break the revolution. I won't do it."

———

Parliament had quickly devolved into a circus show. Members fell asleep during the proceedings and spoke on their cell phones in the chamber. A Salafi Noor Party member tried to drown out the speaker with the call to prayer. "Do you think you are more Muslim than the rest of us?" asked the speaker, a senior Brotherhood official pious enough to have a *zebibah*, a bump from grinding his forehead into the ground during his five daily prayers. Muslim Brothers ignored major issues, from the continuing state of emergency to the military trials of civilians, pushing only on matters that would increase their share of power, such as election rules. The once-persecuted Islamists now controlled impregnable majorities in the parliament and in the constituent assembly that was to draft the new constitution. It irked them to see young revolutionaries outside parliament protesting the Brotherhood the way they had all once protested Mubarak's National Democratic Party. The Brothers enlisted the army and the police to push critics far away from the assembly hall. The Brothers' original promise to govern by consensus vanished when they realized they could control the government as long as the Salafis were on board. Their authoritarianism quickly killed any revolutionary excitement about the people's assembly.

Fruitlessly, the Social Democrats tried to interest their colleagues in substantial legislation to address the gaping problems in Egypt. Zyad wrote one bill establishing a minimum wage and another abolishing the military code of justice. The Muslim Brotherhood killed both in committee. Basem proposed laws to reduce income inequality and alleviate the housing shortage, which suffered a similar summary death.

Never one to be deterred, Basem convened a forum outside parliament on rent control and the Egyptian housing shortage. Millions of Egyptians lived in substandard housing while hundreds of thousands of apartments sat empty because of mid-century rent control laws that kept rents at five or ten dollars a month. Basem brought together housing advocates, landlords, and economists, convinced that there was a way to free up this decaying housing stock to the benefit of the poor, the middle class, and the wealthier owners. He had a ten-year plan.

This was the kind of wonky social justice issue that really inspired Basem. He didn't want to tell a cop to fuck off. He wanted to midwife an urban planning renaissance that would help the poor and make money for Egypt. Basem wasn't trying to connect to the street, he was trying to invent policy. Eventually, Basem reasoned, the government would need to solve the real problems facing the nation, and then it would turn to anyone who had taken the time to design a workable solution with input from powerful constituencies. From the beginning, Basem mistrusted the parliament, but he thought it would be a useful place for the vulnerable liberals to sharpen their ideas and buttress their organizations. After the swearing in, Basem avoided speaking in the chamber. Instead, whenever it was his turn, he gave his time to Social Democrats from the provinces who felt detached from the party's Cairo power brokers. The move cost him little but earned him enormous trust and loyalty from the rest of his party's caucus.

A sustained bureaucratic assault was called for to preserve the Social Democrats' position in parliament, and Basem was perfect for the task. He took charge of organizing the party's provincial branches. He planned for the next election campaign, which could come at any time on the SCAF's liquid transition calendar. He set up a policy division for the party and a research bureau to serve its members of parliament. When he wasn't in parliament, Basem was on the road: every evening, every weekend. Few others in the liberal bloc wanted to do this thankless work. Some liked making speeches and appearing on talk shows but dropped key tasks that Basem then picked up. Others were simply discouraged.

It was easy to see why. All sides agreed that the most important task of the transition was the new constitution, and it wasn't being created by the parliament. The Constituent Assembly, a special body controlled by sixty Islamists from the Brotherhood and the Salafi Noor Party, was in charge. There were forty seats on the Constituent Assembly for a pastiche of other groups whom the Islamists clearly disregarded as minority special interest factions: the Coptic Church, establishment Islamic clerics from Al-Azhar University, labor unions, secular liberals, and six women. The Islamists could force through anything they wanted, and it became clear that they would, starting with making Islamic sharia the primary source of law in the land. "It's a farce," Basem said of the drafting process. Every single suggestion the liberals made was roundly ignored. Eventually they walked out. Soon even the more conservative delegates followed. Egypt had limped along for decades under a halfway decent but heavily abused constitution. Now elected Islamists were in the process of writing a constitution that would uphold the military's existing special privileges while also creating new mechanisms of religious authoritarianism. Egypt was losing its chance to draft a set of rules that would set a revolutionary precedent for the Arab world.

Meanwhile, Egypt's military custodians steadily constricted the free space that remained for revolutionary activity. Some activists were conveniently conscripted, disappearing for years to distant army bases. Civilians continued to vanish into military custody, where they were often tried and sentenced before secret military courts. Most of them were apolitical poor people arrested at checkpoints for vaguely defined crimes such as thuggery and violating curfew. The "No to Military Trials" campaign had documented more than ten thousand such cases. Higher-profile cases against activists were designed to intimidate the community of dissidents and critical thinkers. The blogger and revolutionary strategist Alaa Abdel

Fattah had missed the birth of his son during two months in jail after the Maspero massacre. A Christian blogger who had written critically about the military was imprisoned for nearly a year. Those who were jailed on trumped-up or spurious charges were usually released by special pardon, to emphasize that justice was a gift from the ruler, not a transparent process equally available to all. Almost every activist had some charge pending; Moaz was one of dozens under investigation for thuggery.

"We all have cases against us," he said. "They save them so they have a reason to lock us up when they want to."

The most extreme case was the SCAF's crackdown on civil society groups. Ever since the summer of 2011, wags like a retired general I interviewed had been peddling a bizarre brew of conspiracy theories about human rights groups and other nongovernmental organizations secretly serving the agendas of the CIA and of global Zionism. By December, that paranoia had permeated official policy. The SCAF arrested forty-three civil society activists and charged them with a variety of crimes bordering on treason. Those targeted weren't the revolutionaries of Tahrir; they were lawyers, researchers, and trainers laboring in bread-and-butter civil society efforts: human rights and election monitoring, organizing, political party and democracy training. These weren't the most visible activists, but they were among the most important. Since the time of Mubarak, they had tallied the accusations of torture, election fraud, harassment, and slander. The SCAF was sending a clear and chilling message to Egyptians: they could be imprisoned easily as foreign agents if they scrutinized the government.

Of those arrested or charged, nineteen were Americans, including Sam LaHood, the son of US Secretary of Transportation Ray LaHood. He had been helping to train new political parties. The SCAF didn't expect this move to jeopardize the next $1.55 million that Washington was due to send it, but an Egyptian military delegation to Washington in February got an earful. Pursuing the son of an American cabinet official triggered a level of irritation that the massacres had not. The Egyptian judges in charge of the case relented immediately, allowing the Americans to be released if each posted $300,000 bail. The supposedly independent judicial system had exposed the depths to which it had sunk.

That spring of 2012, the presidential campaign swept over Egypt in a dazzling display. All the country's political forces emerged into the open. The old regime's organization and supporters had largely stayed out of sight during the fall parliamentary campaign, but they were done hiding. The presidency was too important, and none of the new liberal parties was strong enough to absorb the old elite. Until now politics had played out mostly between the SCAF, the Muslim Brotherhood, and the revolutionary protesters. But there were others to be reckoned with, and the most important was the old regime, which fielded two candidates: Ahmed Shafik, Mubarak's prime minister, and Omar Suleiman, the elderly spymaster who ran Mubarak's intelligence services. Suleiman in particular cut a terrifying figure to many Egyptians: he was a quintessential man of the shadows, and he had been in charge of all the most important business of Mubarak's regime, from squelching terrorism and domestic dissent to handling relations with Israel and Palestine. When it came time to file official candidacy papers, Suleiman's henchmen delivered hundreds of thousands of signatures, far more than required, and leaked that the state intelligence services had gathered them.

The Muslim Brotherhood had insisted it would not put forth presidential candidates, but broke that promise and announced two: Khairat el-Shater, the organization's de facto strongman, and Mohamed Morsi, the loyal enforcer, as backup. Morsi was quickly labeled "the spare tire." Another phenomenon was the Salafi Sheikh Hazem Salah and his fanatical followers, the Hazemoon. They had managed to glue posters of the sheikh everywhere, unnerving secular Egyptians and mainstream Islamists too.

Suddenly Egypt's political landscape appeared in a different light. The dominant candidates represented the old regime's intelligence service, the extremist Salafis, and the hard-line wing of the Muslim Brotherhood. There was a wide array of candidates in between with more nuanced and moderate views, but until the first round of voting in May, no one could gauge their popularity. There were no credible opinion polls. Unlike the parliamentary elections, which featured broad coalitions, the presidential race would serve as a precise measure of voter preference. There was a secular Arab nationalist who had worked for the old regime (Amr Mousa), and another who had not (Hamdeen Sabbahi). There was a lawyer with impeccable revolutionary credentials but no direct involvement in rabble-rousing protest (Khaled Ali). There were the Muslim Brothers and the Salafis, and then there was a lifelong Muslim Brother who had been thrown out because of his independence and his willingness to work with secular people (Abdel Moneim Aboul Fotouh).

Unless a single candidate captured more than 50 percent of the vote in May, there would be a runoff a month later between the top two finishers. Egypt faced the clearest test yet of the population's political tastes. The field of candidates was huge. The extremes frightened many people, who didn't want to be governed by a Salafi or an intelligence man. The Muslim Brothers and former regime candidates had the most polished campaigns because of their organizations' long histories, but on occasion, they veered into rhetoric as mad as Sheikh Hazem's. The moderate majority was fragmented among conservative Arab nationalists, secular liberals, Christians, old regime sympathizers, secular revolutionaries, and religious revolutionaries. It was obvious to all the campaigns that if the moderates could agree on a single candidate, they were almost guaranteed to win. They would need someone who was untainted by the old regime and could make at least a nod to revolutionary sentiment, and who was committed to a secular, liberal state, as well as someone who could rally the support of Christians, big businesses, and people who wanted stability but didn't seek a full restoration of Mubarak. It was also obvious to every candidate that he himself should be that unifying representative. No one could agree, and the field remained split.

In the first round, Basem was drawn immediately to the campaign of Hamdeen Sabbahi, a handsome Nasserist politician who delivered rousing, revolutionary-sounding speeches in a sultry rasp. His actual views were quite reactionary. Sabbahi liked a robust military, and he wasn't much concerned with due process and minority rights. His vision was of a resurgent Egypt that would dominate the Arab world. Sabbahi spouted xenophobic nonsense and conspiracy theories just like the old regime. His slogan was "One of us." Basem happily campaigned for him. He liked that Sabbahi wouldn't kowtow to the United States, and he found it reassuring that for all the blather about Nasser and the patriotic army, Sabbahi argued that the military should stay in the barracks, away from the presidential palace, Ittihadiya, in the Cairo suburb of Heliopolis. Other secular revolutionaries stayed away from Sabbahi, gravitating instead to the little-known but more thoroughly liberal lawyer Khaled Ali, who never managed to gain even tiny name recognition among voters. (He ultimately won just 1 percent of the vote.)

Revolutionaries with religious backgrounds joined the campaign of Abdel Moneim Aboul Fotouh, who for a few weeks seemed poised to bridge the divide between secular and Islamist Egyptians. Aboul Fotouh convinced an impressive group of notable secular academics and doctors to join his campaign, and at the same time he won the backing of Salafis. Young activists, including Moaz and Ayyash, gushed; they were convinced this campaign was inventing a new form of Islamic liberalism. However, Aboul Fotouh never committed overtly to basic liberal principles: he acted like an open-minded pluralist, but he never said whether he wanted Egypt to be a secular state, and he never said he would guarantee freedoms for minorities, political parties, and the nonreligious. He grew popular, but because of his silence on central questions, Aboul Fotouh never could gain the trust of Christians or resolutely secular Egyptians.

As a reminder that the old regime's arbitrary enforcement of the law still prevailed, the supposedly independent commission overseeing the presidential ballot disqualified the three most alarming candidates: the Brotherhood's el-Shater; the old spy, Omar Suleiman; and the Salafi Sheikh Hazem. The outraged Hazemoon besieged the Ministry of Defense, camping in tents outside the gates and stockpiling weapons. They seemed crazed, a genuine threat to the state. The Revolutionary Youth Coalition begged them to disperse, but they refused. Some secular revolutionaries even joined the sit-in, a move that the coalition leaders knew would only discredit their cause. Moaz thought he could end the standoff: he planned a march called the "the Final Friday" at the end of the month of May, and assembled a big tent of youth groups, secular and religious. They would walk from downtown to the Ministry of Defense, gather up the Salafis, and take them away, providing a face-saving way for the Hazemoon to back down. The idea did not seem likely to work. Once Moaz's march reached the ministry, most of its participants joined the Salafis in throwing rocks at the army.

"Selmiya! Selmiya!" Moaz shouted in vain. "Peaceful! Peaceful!"

But a different chant from the crowd drowned him out: "Death, not humiliation!"

The army moved quickly, sending phalanxes of soldiers into the crowd. Some fled, others stood and fought. Men from the neighborhood armed with buckshot rifles, clubs, and Molotov cocktails came up from the side streets; they had grown sick a long time ago of revolutionary interlopers. As the fighting intensified, Moaz ran through the tear gas pleading.

"This is not what we should be doing!" he shouted, his voice giving out from overuse. "It is not to our benefit to fight here!"

"I've been waiting a year for this," a leftist answered. "I want to send the SCAF messages carved in dead bodies."

Against such bloodthirst, politics offered little. Moaz knew that with this clash the revolution would lose yet another sizable chunk of public opinion. Presidential elections were just a few weeks away. The SCAF had promised to cede power by June 30. Couldn't these impatient young people wait even a little?

Basem was in the provinces meeting with Social Democrats when he heard about the fighting outside the Defense Ministry. "All we're going to reap at the end of the battle is more martyrs and martial law," he remarked in disgust. The revolutionaries had impulses but no grand plan. A few days later, Moaz, Sally, and a few hundred activists marched on parliament, demanding an investigation of the violence outside the ministry. They phoned Basem, who was inside. He refused to come out and join them.

A week after those Final Friday clashes outside the Defense Ministry, most of Egypt watched the two perceived front-runners interrogate each other on live television in the nation's first-ever debate: Abdel Moneim Aboul Fotouh, the doctor and former Muslim Brother, versus Amr Moussa, Mubarak's former foreign minister and recent head of the Arab League, the diplomatic forum for the Arab states. In classic Egyptian style, Aboul Fotouh was a half hour late to the studio because of traffic, and the debate itself stretched nearly four hours, long after midnight. In a polity where pointed questions had been extinct in political life, the debate was a revelation. The former diplomat and the former Muslim Brotherhood strategist went after each other high and low. Aboul Fotouh embarrassed his opponent by asking how he had acquired his expensive home and large fortune after a lifetime as a public servant. Moussa cornered Aboul Fotouh over his historical ties to radical Islamist positions that he still had never repudiated. In the cafés, people followed attentively. Audiences seemed to love that the candidates were exposed, but they hated the candidates themselves. The polls that established the two men as front-runners were suspect in the first place, but after the debate, both of them lost support. Once people saw their prospective leaders chafe at critical questions, they seemed to reject them. These consequences were so distressing to the other candidates that they all cancelled the debates they had scheduled for the following week.

After the vote, the first-round results surprised everybody except for the Brothers and the *feWool*. Morsi, the Muslim Brotherhood's uninspiring backup candidate, finished first, and almost even with him was Ahmed Shafik, the bumbling man who had all but spat on Tahrir at its beginning and who, as prime minister, had declared among his achievements that he had killed and been killed. Morsi and Shafik each drew on well-organized constituencies, enough to put them atop a crowded field. People who yearned for stability—including Christians who saw a grim future for themselves under Islamist rule—had gravitated to Shafik's hard secular law-and-order rhetoric.

It was a dispiriting result. The most regressive candidates had come out ahead. No matter how one sliced the numbers, the revolution had screwed up. Aboul Fotouh and Sabbahi, the two overtly revolutionary candidates, had failed to merge their campaigns. Together they could have dominated the race. Apart, they finished third and fourth, a million votes behind Morsi and Shafik. People had voted in droves, and a decisive majority had voted for candidates who explicitly supported a secular state, and against the old order in the person of the *feloot* candidates. And yet, divided among themselves, the reformist, revolutionary public hadn't managed to back one single candidate for the presidency. Therefore, they were left with no one.

The Muslim Brotherhood and the National Democratic Party would go to a runoff. It was a choice between two evils, both soundly rejected by the majority. The Muslim Brotherhood had been Mubarak's insurance policy. He had erased all other opposition so that he could tell his critics: It's either me or the Islamists. Now Egypt faced a choice of Mubarak's devising: his handpicked successor or his handpicked opponent.

Moaz was distraught. A vote for Shafik was impossible: the man embodied everything that January 25, 2011, had opposed. Reluctantly, Moaz would vote for Morsi in the June runoff, but he knew the Muslim Brotherhood cared nothing for the revolution, only for its own power. "In one year, I have lost everything," he said. "I lost the Muslim Brotherhood. I lost the revolution. I lost our country." All he had left was his family, with whom he spent less and less time.

For other revolutionaries, especially the secular ones, a vote for Morsi was impossible as well. "We don't want to trade the old fascists for new fascists who claim God is on their side," Basem said. "Shafik will bring out the old weapons. We can deal with them." The Islamists, he feared, had more potent tricks in store.

"If the Muslim Brotherhood takes over, they will put Islamists everywhere," Basem said. "They will take to the streets and call us infidels." Even if the old regime retained power, he believed, it would be vulnerable because it had no legitimacy. The Islamists were different, because they could reimpose authoritarianism while claiming democratic legitimacy; they could tyrannize secular Egypt and say they were doing it in the name of the people.

In parliament's last session before the election, Basem made his first speech. He addressed the Muslim Brothers as hypocritical authoritarians.

"You used to say you wanted consensus," Basem said. "But in the back rooms and at the negotiating tables, you always talk about the majority. We will never again follow you and fight your battles." Immediately afterward, he was slammed in the Muslim Brotherhood press.

Shafik was campaigning on people's fear: of instability, of greater poverty, of Islamism. He had all the style and confidence of the old regime, with the added fuel of the real concerns about the Brotherhood. The Islamists purged their own organizations of any internal dissent and pluralism; how, then, would they be able to tolerate pluralism and dissent in the country as a whole, especially if they found themselves suddenly in the control room with all the levers and buttons at their disposal? Shafik promised to at least keep Egypt secular, if not free.

Two days before the presidential runoff, two momentous rulings came from the Supreme Constitutional Court, which, like the US Supreme Court, was the final arbiter on matters of law in Egypt. The first was a decision on whether Shafik's membership in the old ruling party disqualified his candidacy. The second was whether to shut down parliament because of flaws in the way it was elected.

Long ago, Egypt's judges had earned a reputation for independence and legal dynamism. Mubarak had eroded that critical streak steadily, and by the end of his reign, the courts remained powerful but reactionary. Now the Supreme Constitutional Court was unapologetically connected to the military and the old regime. Its vice chair had made herself one of the most prominent public voices arguing that the military should take a stronger hand and should outlaw all Islamist political parties. Even before the new Muslim Brotherhood–dominated parliament was sworn in, she told a friend of mine, "Don't worry, we've written a legal decision disbanding parliament. It's in a drawer waiting until we need it."

Apparently the time had come. With the possibility of a Muslim Brother in the president's office, it wouldn't do to have a Muslim Brotherhood majority in the legislature. There was ample historical precedent for the court to send an entire parliament home. It had happened several times before, under Mubarak. Politicians had figured that the court, despite its tremendous power, would leave the status quo intact, allowing Shafik to run but also leaving parliament in place. Instead, late in the day, the court announced that Shafik was fine, but the parliament had to go. As if to emphasize that true power still remained in that ill-defined constellation of security forces, bureaucracy, and anonymous officials that formed the deep state, the SCAF announced that it would assume legislative powers in the parliament's absence. It was in every sense of the term a judicial coup, and perhaps it was a precursor of worse to come. If Shafik won, the deep state would have an ally in Ittihadiya Palace, and the SCAF now had insurance in case its preferred choice didn't make it. A victorious Morsi would come to an office with castrated powers.

For liberals, the real battle was over the constitution, and the court's decision made it even harder to imagine a new charter that would exile the military from politics forever. Yet some were glad to be rid of the Islamist parliament, even if its demise came by an illiberal judicial mugging. "I'm happy," Basem said as soon as he heard the news. "You cannot imagine how much we suffered under the aggressive Islamist majority." I thought he should have been worried about how his desired result came about.

That night, Moaz joined a delegation of revolutionary youth who met with Morsi.

"Drop out of the race," they told him. "These elections are a sham. Even if you win, the military will not let you govern. They control everything."

Morsi refused. As the Brotherhood entered this round against the regime, its members felt so sure of victory that they didn't even bother to court the young revolutionaries. They had made it to the brink of power despite never once joining wholeheartedly with the revolution. The Brothers hadn't consulted or communicated with the revolutionaries at any of the vital junctures, and they didn't plan to now.

Moaz felt stymied, facing two enemies at once: the Muslim Brothers and the old police state. "How can we make strategy," he asked, "when our only weapons are strikes and protests, but they have guns?"

That weekend, Egyptians made their choice between Shafik and Morsi. A devil's choice, but twenty-five million voted. The 52 percent turnout was the highest in any presidential election in the country's history. Egyptians were assuming their new role as citizens with agency. In the delta province that both Morsi and Shafik were from, the party organizations ran strong. I talked to people whose votes were bought for fifty pounds—about nine dollars—and to people who gave their votes freely. Some had high hopes for their candidate; others voted for the lesser of two evils.

Abdelrahman Ayyash was boycotting. The court decisions had killed his last shards of faith in the transition. He took me along to interview rural voters. Ayyash came from this region of the delta, but among the *galabiya*s and *abaya*s, the baggy pleated pants and the polyester dress shirts and trucker caps, he already looked, in his striped polo shirt, like an envoy from the elite in the capital. In this area, all the Christians had voted for Shafik; all the Islamists for Morsi. Most people explained their votes in thoughtful ways, but there was an alarming undercurrent of unsustainably high expectations; supporters of both candidates expected an economic boom within months of the election. They were sure to be disappointed. At the end of the day, we paid a visit to Ayyash's uncle, who ran a language school in the provincial city of Zagazig.

"We are lost!" his uncle cried theatrically, wiggling his eyebrows. "This is the worst choice. We thought when we removed Mubarak, we had removed the biggest stone."

"It's all a game," Ayyash agreed. "The president won't have power over the SCAF."

The results were not even in, but already the Tahrir chapter was drawing to a close.

As Egypt voted, Zyad had gone on vacation to the beach. He returned to Cairo late on the second day of voting, just in time to despoil his vote in protest. Across his ballot, he wrote: "Shafik is a criminal and Morsi betrayed us. My vote is for the martyrs." He posted a picture of his vote online.

What made Zyad a useful revolutionary made him a flailing reformer. He mistrusted all leaders, including himself. However, he said he would probably run for parliament again in the next election, unless he was in prison. He wanted in, but he also wanted to be considered an outsider. He would remain on his party's ticket, but as an adamant party skeptic. Whoever was in charge, he'd prefer to be in the opposition. Zyad's reflexive dissidence could go only so far in the effort to design a new order. As he put it himself, "We learned how to destroy the tyranny. Now we have to learn how to construct an alternative."

Basem had long settled on his preferred method for building that alternative. On the first day of the presidential runoff, he boycotted, not even bothering to go to the polls to cast a null vote. He didn't mind if Shafik won, and he thought that even an Islamist victory, while more complicated to contend with, would have the benefit of precipitating the Brotherhood's downfall. He was confident that Egypt eventually would embrace his brand of Third Way secular socialism.

In the coming months and years, Basem believed, Egyptians already disgusted with the old regime would grow equally disenchanted with Islamists when they saw how they behaved in power. The long race would go not to the swift or the popular but to the diligent and organized. Eventually voters would look for politicians with realistic ideas, and Basem was sure that a plurality would finally support the liberals, including his party. He was ready to go to prison under any regime, he said, and he wasn't worried about the decay of revolutionary ideas and the absence of dialogue between secularists and Islamists. When there was a need, Basem thought, Egyptians could come together as they had in Tahrir. Right now what was needed was something else, something boring but crucial: new identities, new ideas, and institutions to nourish them. "Once the Islamists make a big mistake, it will be easy to gather people in Tahrir Square and make a revolution again," he said. I wasn't so sure.

Basem was much more interested in the internal elections of his party than in the presidential contest. He was convinced Egypt had taken a turn for the better into an era of open politics and free speech. The country needed the patience of a gardener to cultivate institutions more than it needed the flair of a revolutionary infantryman ready to die. Basem was wasting no time; he had a party to tend. At nine o'clock in the evening, he was meeting with his Shoubra team to lay the groundwork for his next parliamentary election campaign, whenever it would be. The first parliament still had not been disbanded, the next president had not been chosen, the SCAF still was completely in control, and already he was running for reelection.

Basem, Ayyash, and Zyad had acclimated to the new order by seeking accommodation within it, settling into roles that they expected would make them players in the country's political future. Moaz and Sally, how-

ever, remained on the outside shouting in. Sally had receded from public view but was working with the same intensity. The Kazeboon! team
was producing an ambitious series of films to propagate ideas about citizenship and community through compelling stories: a cultural populist
revolution to follow the political one. Meanwhile, Moaz had gone back
to his day job. It had been fifteen months since he'd drawn a salary. He
had been politicking so long it was a surprise to remember that he had a
parallel career as a pharmacist.

The Revolutionary Youth Coalition had nothing left to do. These
once inseparable partners had become atomized, each operating in a
realm of their own. Tahrir had altered the state forever, and more change
was coming. A president would take office, and he would be beholden to
the people who elected him. He would have the authority to confront the
putrid judiciary, the malignant security services, and the arrogant army.
And he would govern knowing that in four years' time he would face another competitive race for president. Egypt, the revolutionaries believed,
would never again tolerate the kind of stage-managed charade that had
reelected Mubarak to his final term in 2005. Police misdeeds would continue, as would political shenanigans and the reflex to shout down or silence opponents. Yet this was an undeniably freer Egypt, and it was in the
throes of transformation. The hardships suffered in revolutionary Egypt
were symptoms of a society in transition rather than slumbering in an in-
duced coma. Egypt was going somewhere—somewhere that was unlikely
to be worse and would probably be better—and it was thanks to Tahrir.
The revolutionary youth of Tahrir could very well become the next generation's political elite. Today, though, they were rolling about like spilled
ball bearings, incapable of steering the process they had unleashed.

The Muslim Brotherhood's inimitable vote-tracking operation showed
that Morsi had won. Not by a huge margin, but a comfortable 3.5 percent, nearly a million votes. A tense week followed; the official results
from the Presidential Election Commission were delayed. The generals issued a new fiat that would supposedly give them control over the
next president's budget and office. The Islamists sent a million protest-

ers to the streets in a staggering show of force against the military; their numbers also served as a rude reminder of how tiny the revolutionary demonstrations were in comparison. By its second day, the protesters at the Brotherhood sit-in had built new bathrooms in Tahrir out of brick. A year and a half after the revolution, the square was full again, but it looked nothing like a revolutionary youth affair.

Authorities finally announced the results a week after the vote. A great suspense gripped the millions outside in Tahrir and in front of their televisions all over the country. If victory were declared for Shafik despite the overwhelming evidence that Morsi had won, it would be outright war. If the presidency went to the man who had won it, a grinding struggle would follow between the Islamists and everybody else. It would be unpleasant but not, it was generally felt, cataclysmic. The fatuous judge in charge droned on for an hour. Finally he read the results: Morsi: 13,230,131 votes. Shafik: 12,347,380.

Only the Brothers celebrated without reservation. A Morsi aide preposterously invoked Nelson Mandela, saying, "We will surprise you with our generosity." In the square, Moaz stood near one of the officials who had supervised his expulsion from the Brotherhood. The man kissed Moaz's forehead as if they were comrades again, but Moaz knew Morsi's win was not his own. "Yesterday we were working together against Shafik. Tomorrow I will work against the Brotherhood," he said. "It's not the end of the revolution, it's the start of our work." In a few minutes he would report for his fourth overnight shift at the Rushdi pharmacy. He hadn't slept in three days. "The revolution will continue, but I cannot," he joked hoarsely.

As I walked out of Tahrir that night, crowds lined the overpass. Thousands poured in every second, mostly men, with the same slightly menacing air of indiscriminate celebration that had swept Cairo the night Mubarak resigned: jubilant but lacking joy, ready to quaff Tahrir's mob energy. The square was suffocating and airless, too crowded to move, the kind of scene punctuated invariably with sexual assaults and groping. The elections had ended a tortuous period in the country's history. The junta had been unable to stop Egyptians from choosing their own leader, for the first time in history. But the coming inauguration would be a far

cry from a revolution. It was a step, with some undeniable progress away
from state terror and toward free speech, but only a tiny one. The day-to-
day hardships of life in Egypt persisted. For most people, the revolution
had yet to begin, but at least they would have some say over the mess.

The most encouraging thing I saw that week took place not in Tahrir
Square but in Ayyash's living room. One of the revolution's most powerful weapons had been its ability to persuade elders to abandon fearful habits of thought. As the Brotherhood prepared to take the throne,
Ayyash and his brother shared an after-work lunch with their father. The
two sons had left the Brotherhood, but their father was still a trusting
member, still ready to blame every single nasty act by its leadership on
"outside pressure" or a conspiracy rather than any bad judgment or mal-
ice on the part of the Brotherhood.

For decades, and at great risk, the entire family had lived by the Brotherhood's daily rhythms and exacting commitments. Now there was real
vitriol in their arguments. Ayyash's father thought the Brotherhood wise
and expected it to lead Egypt a step closer to the promised land. Ayyash
and his brother thought the Brotherhood feckless and self-serving, and
expected it to lead Egypt a step closer to a remodeled era of religious
dictatorship. Yet, unlike so many other revolutionaries who had severed
ties with their families as they had with mainstream Egyptians, Ayyash
still shared his ideas at home with a reciprocated love and respect. In this
house, between this reactionary father and revolutionary son, the connection was as strong as ever.

"I believe in my sons," Ayyash's father said. "They will not leave the
righteous path." He was confident that his boys would be doing right
even when they were rejecting their father's way. He was more pleased by
their dedication, by their seriousness of purpose, than he was wounded
by their break with the Brotherhood. Ayyash and his father would keep
talking. And the revolution would continue.

Morsi held his symbolic inauguration in Tahrir Square a day after
he had sworn his oath before the Supreme Constitutional Court. The
new president's words sounded right for the occasion. "We used to look
around us and say: When will Egypt and its people become the owners
of their destiny? Today you have become the source of authority," Morsi

said, to a tumult of cheers. "As for myself, I have no rights, but I have duties."

His future failures would not stem from callous indifference or from the abusive prerogative of a despot who considers an entire nation his personal property. They would be the mistakes of politics and ideology. The Muslim Brotherhood had committed political errors already, and President Morsi would add his own to the stew. On this day, he made a convincing case that, whatever his faults, he would not be guilty of tyranny and careless ownership. When Morsi first took the stage, dressed casually in a blazer that hung loose around his belly, he pushed aside the officious presidential guards who stood between him and the crowd. Then came a hair-raising moment that framed this middle-aged professor from Muslim Brotherhood as a president distinct from the regal despots who preceded him. Morsi stepped forward and pulled open his jacket. No tailored suit, no tie, and, most importantly, no bulletproof vest. "I don't fear my people," Morsi exulted. "I don't fear anyone but God." It was an electrifying gesture that momentarily transcended the triumphalism of Morsi's Islamist supporters and the fears of his secular opponents.

A year and a half earlier, at the close of those first eighteen days in Tahrir, anything had seemed possible. All of us had imagined an entirely new society: Basem and Moaz, Sally and Zyad, Ayyash and his friends. A true revolution hovered within reach. I too had believed they might achieve it. My own experiences had taught me to be cynical and to expect little. Tahrir had smashed through that cold realism, creating possibilities from the impossible. A year and a half later, Tahrir's ultimate legacy still lay in the future. The revolution had transformed many people, even if it hadn't changed the entire world in an instant. In a generation or two, Egypt might be led by wise women and men whose identities and values were forged in those eighteen days at Tahrir. Like everyone else, I would have to be patient.

For most of the revolutionaries, any fleeting sense of triumph had dissipated already. One catastrophe had been averted, as Shafik and the old regime had failed to seize the presidency and turn back history. All was not lost, but little was won. The Tahrir revolutionaries hadn't worked so hard in order to elevate the Muslim Brotherhood to the presidency. They would march on, in opposition to military rule and Brotherhood authoritarianism, scratching and hoeing and shuffling and planting in the little beds of citizenship they were cultivating. In the meantime, I would have to keep my faith in Tahrir and wait for the harvest.

10.

THE ENEMY WITHIN

President Mohamed Morsi unveiled a plan for his first hundred days with the flourish of John F. Kennedy presenting his New Frontier a half century before. Everything was going to change, from the state of law to the state of garbage collection. Only the most ardent of Brothers took this program literally. Never during his campaign had Morsi wholly embraced the revolutionary agenda, even though he hired some reputable outsiders as advisers (including Mohamed Fathy Rifaah al-Tahtawi, the former diplomat who had joined the revolutionaries in Tahrir). He had pledged to listen to young revolutionaries if elected, but he had never actually promised to adopt any revolutionary or reformist policies. Once in office, he kept close counsel, consulting only his colleagues from the Brotherhood.

At any rate, Morsi's power was fundamentally circumscribed. There was no parliament, and the old SCAF leaders remained in charge of the security establishment. Field Marshal Tantawi was still defense minister, and General Sami Enan still ran the military. In June the Supreme Constitutional Court had dissolved parliament and assigned all its legislative powers to the SCAF. These unaccountable and capricious judges, carryovers from the Mubarak era, had reminded everyone that the military wasn't the only old regime institution still thriving in the shadows; the judiciary system wielded tremendous powers, which it was willing to use to defend its own prerogatives.

The Brotherhood had betrayed the rest of the civilian political forces repeatedly over the previous year and a half, most notably by making deals with the SCAF about the elections and endorsing military crack-downs on protests. As a result, even before Morsi had made a single decision as president, he lacked any reservoir of goodwill to draw on. Mainstream liberal parties, including Basem's Social Democrats, the Free Egyptians, and Mohamed ElBaradei's Constitution Party, joined forces with older non-Islamist movements such as the Nasserists to warn Morsi: they would accept no religious fundamentalism from the presidential palace, and they refused to stomach Brotherhood unilateralism. Already they were worried. They had seen the Islamist electoral machine, and they had watched the SCAF and a compliant judiciary pursue the con-struction of a new authoritarian regime. They could easily imagine being crushed between two fascist poles. At the Social Democratic Party head-quarters, Basem tried to set an invigorating example, keeping people fo-cused on small, achievable goals so they would not think too much about the dispiriting big picture. A party aide named Hala Mostafa slumped in a chair outside the conference room where Basem chirped away with his colleagues. "We were tricked," she said. "Betrayed on all sides."

Some revolutionaries were more willing to entertain the notion of partial collaboration. "The Muslim Brotherhood will be in power for four years. You can't make clashes for four years," Moaz said. "So we will work with them for three years, and in the fourth year we will make clashes against them." The revolutionaries knew that the Brotherhood was rigid, hierarchical, and insular, but they thought its members shared a desire for some important things, such as police reform; after all, the Brother-hood had suffered more than any other group from torture and indefinite detentions. The Brotherhood might also cooperate to put boundaries on the military's unchecked power. Over the years, unscrupulous military judges had imprisoned many Brotherhood leaders in court-martials in-stead of trying them in civilian courts; this continuing travesty of justice united much of civil society, secular as well as Islamist.

In the turbulent year and half since Tahrir, Egyptians had deposed a dictator, approved a constitution, and, for the first time in history, freely elected a parliament and a president. Street protests and vibrant, open dialogue had become established ingredients in public life. There was a widespread feeling that, after all that swift change, whatever was to come next was probably going to be gradual and incremental, the product of politics and negotiation rather than uprising and revolution. Over the next year, Egyptians planned to draft a new constitution that would conclusively replace the Mubarak order. They would elect a new parliament. And then they could set forth on the long, arduous process of enshrining the rule of law and repairing Egypt's broken structures of daily life. There was never enough housing, enough gas, enough jobs, enough foreign currency reserves in the central bank, enough water, enough crops, enough schools, and so on. After a year and a half of revolution, Egypt was bracing itself for a steady, arduous climb toward reform.

––––––––––––

Inside the Revolutionary Youth Coalition, the divisions had hardened into dogma. Basem missed months of meetings and finally resigned. Zyad said he believed that the revolution had permanently unseated the old order, and that now it was time to turn to the ideological fights between socialists and neo-liberals, secularists and Islamists. I thought he was delusional. He began to talk about the Revolutionary Youth Coalition in the past tense.

Against this pressure, Moaz still toiled for the revolution, increasingly alone. He was sure that the old regime was strong as ever. He was among the few who recognized that the protesters in Tahrir Square on January 25, 2011, had succeeded not because of their youth and vigor, or because the deep state was dying, but because of their unity: Islamist and secular together; right and left. Bumbling Moaz was right, where his more polished and urbane colleagues were mistaken. He had traveled a great distance from the years before the uprising, when he defended the Muslim Brotherhood's doctrinaire leadership. From his Brotherhood education, he had learned that any effective political message had better make sense to regular folks. "If the Revolutionary Youth Coalition cannot trust Islamists, then there's no hope for the rest of Egypt," he said.

One by one, Zyad confronted the other coalition leaders and told them it was time to vote to dissolve, and he insisted that the decision be unanimous. Moaz refused, and spoke in public about the internal fight. Zyad phoned him.

"We are going to end the coalition, and you had better not say anything in public against this decision," Zyad said. "Do you fucking understand?"

Moaz hardly ever raised his voice, and he never cursed. "I understand you're nervous," he answered. "I respect you because I have broken bread with you in your home. But this decision is wrong, and I will say whatever I choose."

"What the fuck—" Zyad began, but Moaz cut him off. Now they were both shouting.

"This is not a personal disagreement, it's political!" Moaz said. "I will hang up now, and I don't want to hear your voice again unless you can be polite."

Quietly, the Tuesday before the presidential runoff, the Revolutionary Youth Coalition voted to dissolve. Its union was already so moribund that most of the members didn't bother to show up for the last meeting. Zyad phoned in his vote. Basem didn't need to, since he'd already quit the coalition. Moaz had tried to dissuade his colleagues and couldn't bear to attend the last vote. "It's a mistake," Moaz said, but he was one of the only ones who wanted to hold it together. Sally presided over the Revolutionary Youth Coalition's last formal action: the composition of a letter to the public that enumerated the coalition's hopes and failings. The members catalogued their mistakes and missteps, and pledged to lead by example one final time. Their experiment wasn't working; their organization was no longer accomplishing its revolutionary aims. Rather than cling to power, they would disband and hope to reconstitute in a more felicitous shape.

In this diagnosis, they were once more naïve. They believed new forums would emerge where Islamists, liberals, socialists, and anarchists would band together to talk ideology and tactics, to dream up a better Egypt. But, in fact, the centrifugal forces that had spun the young revolutionaries apart were pushing on all Egypt. With the Revolutionary Youth Coalition, a handful of young people had nurtured a shared space in the lee of violence and authoritarianism, but it hadn't just sprung up organically. They had forced it into being, and then, through vanity or neglect or simply irreconcilable differences, had let it erode to nothing. By letting even its shell go, they reduced the chance that it could ever be rebuilt.

The failure was signal and momentous, even if it felt anticlimactic. The Revolutionary Youth Coalition was the one entity in Egypt that respected cooperation without forsaking ideology. Its members didn't pretend they had no principles or beliefs, or that they all agreed among themselves; this wasn't the fake, imposed harmony of the National Democratic Party or the Brotherhood. They acknowledged their profound disagreements and still found a way to work together for the aims they shared: the end of tyranny, the advent of law, and a barrier of dignity for average people against the twin injustices of poverty and political oppression. This revolution belonged to them as a group, but they had gradually given it up. They no longer could communicate effectively enough to forge a common project. And if they couldn't do it anymore, what chance was there for the old and stultified peacocks who'd never once shown the slightest interest in empathizing with their fellows and merging their political arcs?

"No entity should speak for the revolution," Zyad said to me. "The coalition didn't have an identity." I disagreed. The coalition's identity was so simple that its own founders overlooked it. It was the one place where Egyptians were required to behave like citizens, to exercise their rights and take responsibility. It was the one place where people believed that they owned their government. It was the first and only place where people were required to have opinions, to foreswear passivity, and where they were allowed to disagree without seeking to destroy one another. It was the place where politics was born in Egypt, and the only place where it was nurtured with passion and integrity. Politics is the art of talk, of negotiation and compromise, and Egypt had had no politics whatsoever until these young activists began to work together across ideological lines. Some Arab exiles had enjoyed meaningful searches for consensus, but Mubarak had allowed just enough political space inside Egypt to thwart a motivated opposition movement abroad. The coalition had initiated something vital and human that had previously been absent. From the left, the center, and the right, from both secular and Islamist spaces, they had established common ground. They had achieved unimaginable goals in their early months agitating against the regime. These youth had been the lone adults who dared to subvert the dominant notion that moral people of principle never talk with their ideological enemies, much less work with them.

Now they too had split along the old lines dividing Islamist and secular, left and center. They too boycotted and walked out of meetings rather than talking to the end. They had meant to set an example for Egypt, and so they had. Their example no longer gave anyone much cause to hope.

A week after Morsi's June 30 inauguration, the Revolutionary Youth Coalition made public its decision to dissolve. Its leaders had postponed their final press conference until the presidential succession was settled. With the political horizon safe and clear, they could now announce that the coalition was no more. Egyptians possessed avenues to seek their rights; the revolutionary period was over. Moaz refused to attend the final press conference at the el-Sawy Culture Wheel, a modernist complex of theaters and meeting spaces perched on the edge of the Nile beneath a bridge. He thought that Zyad and the rest were crazy to believe that Egypt was ripe for normal electoral politics.

"People have not changed from the way of thinking that kept Mubarak in power for twenty-nine years," Moaz told me, explaining his absence from the Revolutionary Youth Coalition's final event. "Right now the people's problems aren't whether to be Islamist or secular. Their problems are how to find a job, get married, get a good education."

He made a final plea to save the coalition and expand it, inviting all the new youth groups that had emerged over the last year and a half. "We should not give up what we have," he warned his friends. No one was interested. Even in its demise, the Revolutionary Youth Coalition caused a stir with its final public self-criticism, reading aloud from the lengthy "political audit" its leaders had drafted. The group wanted to set an example of accountability, even in its moment of terminal failure. "Even though it is not standard operating procedure in Egypt, we believe it is necessary for every group to submit a clear and transparent account of what it has done, good and bad," Sally explained.

They confessed that they had screwed up by not keeping open channels with the institutions of power: the military, the intelligence agencies, and the elected government. They acknowledged that it had been a mistake not to expand their membership. They said that at times they had been too eager to speak on television even when they weren't sure what or whom they were representing. The members took turns at the podium, seeming to almost relish their last moments in the spotlight as spokespeople for something much bigger than themselves and their fragmented movement. Afterward, the political audit was dutifully posted online, and, in a final funerary gesture, the Revolutionary Youth Coalition closed its Facebook page.

The coalition's honesty would have been rare and refreshing in politics anywhere, but was especially so in Egypt, where such a performance had never been seen. Yet the leaders of the Revolutionary Youth Coalition still avoided the questions that had undone them and that were poised to undo the entire promise of the original uprising a year and a half earlier. The revolution concerned many things, but at its core, it was about an attempt to seize power. The young people in Tahrir wanted to take power away from Mubarak's system and give it to someone else. They had ideals, but in the end they needed to wield some sort of force in order to achieve them. The people of Tahrir, far more so than revolutionaries in other times and places, were uncomfortable with that necessity. They sanctified vague Platonic ideals such as revolution, "the people," and youth while scorning dirty and earthly practices like politics, compromise, and "chairs," the symbol of power.

Some saw this as evidence of the coalition's strong principles and some simply thought them excessively innocent, but by the time the members disbanded, it was clear to me that they were guilty of an obstinate intellectual failure. After so much time, blood, and work, these activists insisted on ignoring the central questions for which they were responsible, even though they were smart and well-read enough to address them. What were the rights and responsibilities of citizens and those who governed them? Who should have power in Egypt? What universal rights did human beings possess? Avoiding these questions was neither naïve nor principled; it was simply an evasion. They had no excuse.

Very few of the activists had been truly committed to revolutionary goals. Few and far between were the firebrands who wanted to topple the state and usurp power. Many of the leaders of the Revolutionary Youth Coalition were miscast; they were reformists, not revolutionaries. Even at the apex of Tahrir fervor, the youth activists never had the power or institutional support to force their will, and while they could be blamed for not having issued bolder demands, it was also fair to acknowledge that they'd never made very deep or broad inroads outside their narrow ranks. There was also little that unified the revolutionary movement beyond a rejection of Mubarak's worst excesses.

It was mind-bogglingly difficult to imagine a way forward from Egypt's endemic poverty and misrule—so difficult that many of Egypt's most talented revolutionaries refused to grapple with the most pressing questions. What compromise was acceptable? What could an Islamist and a secularist agree on? What did it really mean to stand in favor of the people, the nation, freedom? Basem and Moaz, at least, were trying to answer these questions, in thought and in deed. For their trouble, they were both derided as sellouts by some of their revolutionary peers, even as they parted ways with each other over the acceptable boundaries between religion and government.

With the revolution and the regime at a temporary impasse, for the first time in his adult life, Basem took a rest. He sensed the respite wouldn't last long. At its peak, the family business had employed three Kamel brothers and a half dozen others, but a free-falling economy had eliminated almost all ABC Architecture's clients. Basem's brothers found other jobs. Ramadan began in July, and Basem slept late. In the evenings, he ate with his wife and children. He took his children to the movies, the ice-skating rink, the fun park. At Family Land in the suburb of Maadi, he sipped mango juice with his wife, Rasha, while the kids rode bumper cars.

"I can't remember the last time we spent a day like this," Basem said.

"A long time," Rasha said. "At first I thought life would go back to normal after the revolution. When you started building the party, I realized it never would."

They sat comfortably in silence. "Every day I worry you'll get arrested," Rasha confessed.

Basem raised his eyebrows.

"It's a new world," his wife said with equanimity and a hint of a smile. "We don't know anything about what all this will bring."

Despite all the ominous signs, Moaz felt that grand possibilities still beckoned. At last, he believed, Egypt's revolution was on track. There was a civilian president in Ittihadiya Palace, and for all the problems Moaz had with the Muslim Brotherhood, he was sure it would do a better job than Mubarak or the SCAF. New parliamentary elections were supposed to come in the fall, and Egyptians would have the chance to resolve their differences through flawed but fundamentally free politics. Flush with a sense of achievement, Moaz traveled to Syria for Ramadan to help the rebels fighting the dictator Bashar al-Assad. The Arab world was interconnected and suffered from a plague of dictators who displayed a similar contempt for the lives of their subjects. Moaz was sure that his experience as an Egyptian revolutionary could be of use to his Syrian brothers. In 2011 he had traveled on a medical convoy to Libya in the early stages of the uprising against al-Qaddhafi, and he felt a historical confluence. The Arab world was moving in concert into a new age of self-determination, with popular uprisings inevitably redrawing the blueprints of power. It seemed only natural to work in solidarity across borders with other civil society activists, providing help when possible and exchanging ideas about this bright new future.

"The revolution isn't only for making protests but also for advising other countries how to secure freedom and build better lives," Moaz said. The Free Syrian Army had seized a sliver of territory in the north, and Moaz joined a mission organized by an international confederation of doctors, the Arab Medical Union, to help Syrian civilians, rather than militiamen, take control of the liberated areas. He joined activists in the town of Azaz, which the government bombarded daily. They were struggling to staff clinics, pick up garbage, and distribute food.

"The people with guns shouldn't be running bakeries, warehouses, cooking gas distribution," Moaz counseled the Syrian activists.

It was his first time in a combat zone, but it didn't feel that different to him from the many battles with police. He sheltered in the basement with the few remaining doctors when the hospital in Azaz was shelled. Afterward, they zigzagged through deserted streets to pray the Eid al-

Adha prayer in the town mosque, ignoring the occasional sniper bullet.

"You won't hear the bullet that kills you," a Syrian advised Moaz. "So relax, don't be afraid."

The activists decided to abandon the clinic at Azaz and smuggled Moaz over the border. It was time to go home; his visa was up. The war in Syria was more sprawling and lethal than anything Moaz had encountered during the Egyptian Revolution, and he realized that his type of civilian activism would make little difference. The best he could hope to accomplish for Syria, he thought, was to raise awareness and money to help refugees. Syria's political problems seemed even more irresolvable than Egypt's. "You can choose to start a war, but you cannot choose the end," he reflected.

He returned home to Egypt depressed and deflated, but more than ever committed to nonviolence. A psychologist friend suggested that change might shake Moaz out of his funk. He shaved his beard and resigned from the Egyptian Current Party, which had failed to sign up even three thousand members after a year of effort. Without members, money, or a clear idea, he saw no point in political parties.

For all its machinations since January 25, 2011, the military had held to only two constants: it had grabbed any authority it could, and it had exercised that authority poorly. The Egyptian public adored the military, but it was a mediocre military at best: bad at the basics, such as training conscripts and organizing battalions, and worse at everything else. While the military happily expanded its powers, it also avoided responsibility for governance and for matters like Egypt's international loans. When charged with providing basic security during the revolutionary transition, the military, uneasy and unfamiliar with filling the role of domestic police, had arrested tens of thousands of innocent people, while street crime spiraled to never-before-seen levels. The military was authoritarian and guilty of greedy overreach; it was also incompetent.

As President Morsi took over, the SCAF went about its business, confident it could simply ignore him. As Ramadan drew to a close in mid-August 2012, however, jihadists in the Sinai attacked a military base.

They killed sixteen poorly trained conscripts, stole their armored vehicles, and stormed the Israeli border. The Israelis quickly repelled the attackers, but the ineptitude of Egypt's military had been exposed publicly.

At that moment, as the SCAF was apologizing for its embarrassing failure, Morsi made his move. He fired Defense Minister Tantawi, military chief Sami Enan, and all the other top generals. The SCAF was vulnerable, and Morsi saw the opportunity to remove Mubarak's old henchmen and replace them with new officers whom he thought would be loyal to the elected president. It looked like a bold and sweeping transformation: the president righteously enforcing civilian primacy, firing the corrupt and senescent generals who had stifled Egypt as the backbone of Mubarak's regime and later as his successors.

In truth, though, the move was far less radical and significant than it appeared. The initiative to replace Tantawi and Enan came as much from the junior generals on the SCAF as it did from the new president. Morsi wanted Tantawi's inner circle gone, but so did most of the younger SCAF generals, who had chafed as their superiors lingered on for generations after retirement age. There had been no renewal in the upper ranks for two decades. Morsi's interests coincided with those of the SCAF, and he found a willing replacement for Tantawi: General Abdel Fattah el-Sisi, a religious man with a veiled wife and a solid record in military intelligence. El-Sisi was wily enough to prevent internal dissent in the armed forces and pious enough that Morsi considered him an ally. The SCAF generals had fumbled a lot of important decisions during their tenure as Egypt's rulers, but they had maintained a fabulous discipline in their public appearances. There were rumors that influential officers disagreed about whether the military should run the country more directly or maintain a dignified distance as the power behind the throne, but this internal struggle never filtered out to the public. The generals always presented a united front to outsiders. They did so now as well. Tantawi and Enan accepted their forced retirement with public grace, and they had cause for satisfaction: they were granted immunity from crimes committed in office. El-Sisi and the other generals on the SCAF presented the changes as an amicable shuffle, chosen by the general staff and approved by the civilian president.

At the same time, Morsi also claimed the powers of the dissolved parliament for himself. The president wanted to reassert civilian primacy, and, again, his interests on this front converged with those of the military, which wanted to take a step back from day-to-day politics. In another country, it might have been hard to imagine that any single person could temporarily hold the authority of the entire legislative branch. Under a less arbitrary system, new elections would have immediately followed the dissolution of parliament. But Egypt's rulers liked to improvise. Faceless judges had dissolved the parliament, the SCAF had claimed authority, and two months later, this awkward Brother-turned-president had reached out and taken the power of law from the SCAF. It didn't look anything like a democratic transition, but at the moment it did look like an improvement; better that unfettered, unregulated power rest with an elected civilian than with a secretive clan of violent, intolerant generals.

From that first shift in August, however, some liberals and secularists warned that Morsi was amassing his own dictatorial powers. It was already considered a poor omen that he hadn't tried to form a national unity government or a cabinet of neutral technocrats, instead preferring an ideological alliance with the Salafis to the Brotherhood's right. The new president had not yet done anything that could be construed as authoritarian, but his detractors predicted it was only a question of time. Here was one man, an alumnus of an underground authoritarian religious order, who now possessed the entire power of the executive and legislative branches of government, along with total control over the body that would write Egypt's next constitution. It was bound to go wrong, the liberals believed. Basem's colleagues in the Social Democratic Party opposed military rule, but many of them, from the moment of Mubarak's fall, had seen the SCAF as the only force that could check the Islamists. If the military retired from politics and returned to the barracks, the Social Democrats said, the Muslim Brotherhood would control everything.

In short order, their fears proved justified. Morsi began packing the government with sycophantic cronies. A trusted hack was put in charge of state television and newspapers. During the campaign, the Muslim Brotherhood had promised to avoid "culture wars" and focus on rescuing Egypt's broken economy. However, now that they were in power and goaded by their extremist Salafi allies, the Brothers proposed banning alcohol, censoring internet pornography, and closing down the all-night cafés that had been a mainstay of Egyptian social life for centuries. The Brotherhood abandoned one of the most pressing issues of its campaign, reforming the police and Interior Ministry, for a bigger priority: using the tools of the old regime for its own ends. The Brotherhood didn't care if the police abused citizens, so long as it could insert its own loyalists into police ranks. As new cases of police brutality and torture piled up, the Brotherhood remained silent. The presidential advisers who really mattered were all Brotherhood loyalists: the prime minister, the justice minister, and the informal kitchen cabinet that helped Morsi set foreign policy. The Brotherhood's influence was so widespread that its supreme guide felt obliged to hold a press conference denying that he controlled President Morsi, only intensifying the belief that he did.

These were broken promises that very quickly merged into far greater breaches of trust. The Brotherhood wrote a parliamentary election law that gave it unfair advantage. The Supreme Court, which had final authority over election laws, requested changes. The Brotherhood made the revisions, but then refused to send them back to the court for a final review. Even more alarming to the liberals and the secularists was Morsi's stewardship of the Constituent Assembly: the hundred Egyptians tasked with writing a new charter for the country. The assembly had been formed by the now-disbanded parliament, which had been controlled by a veto-proof supermajority of Brothers and Salafis. Most of the reputable non-Islamists had already quit the Constituent Assembly in protest before Morsi was elected, including Basem's Social Democratic Party and the liberal groups that identified as revolutionary. By October, almost all the remaining non-Islamists resigned in protest from the Constituent Assembly, including conservatives representing the Coptic Church and the Mubarak-era political class. Now Morsi was acting unimpeded, in concert with the fundamentalists in the assembly.

Liberals believed the situation had become irreversibly grave. After all the struggles of the previous two years, a single, relatively extremist faction controlled the presidency, the government's legislative powers, and the Constituent Assembly. Carried away with their power, the Brotherhood and its allies had discarded their conciliatory rhetoric about the Islamic requirement for *shura*, or consultation, and the need to pave a durable way forward by including all Egyptians in the constitution. Instead, they were now forcing their way through with a winner-takes-all swagger. Morsi and his Islamist allies began to justify all their actions with a perverse misreading of democracy. The Brotherhood had won fair elections, they said, and now could write whatever laws it pleased, minorities be damned. They claimed the Brotherhood had the blessing of a democratic majority to do anything it wished, whether in government or in the drafting of Egypt's permanent constitution. It had no need to consult or include anyone else; the Brotherhood state had the blessing of both God and the ballot box.

In the Constituent Assembly, the Brotherhood and the even more extreme Salafis appeared completely indifferent to the rights and privileges of others: women, Christians, secular Muslims, liberals. Instead, they were moving forward with a document that would preserve centralized misrule (but now in the service of the Brotherhood), while advancing a particularly fundamentalist brand of Islam. In practice, no one was interested in negotiating the compromises necessary for a legitimate constitution. The liberals had aspired to write a document that would simply ignore the aims of Egypt's conservative, Islamic citizens, who probably made up the single largest bloc of the population. Now the Islamists held the levers, and they were going to write the constitution their way. This wasn't Philadelphia in 1787; this was the Wild West. There were manifold areas of contention, but three threatened to overwhelm the entire constitution.

First was the process itself. This constitution was supposed to be the product of negotiation among all Egypt's factions, a departure from the norm of dictatorial rule. Instead, it was being written in secret by one group alone. For many, the lack of inclusivity and transparency was as big a problem as the Brotherhood's actual policies.

The second was the military's special privileges. For decades already, its budget had been secret, and it operated without de facto civilian oversight. In exchange for allowing civilian politics to proceed, the military wanted these protections enshrined officially and permanently in the constitution. The military would get to select its own chief and its own defense minister, who would dictate national security policy independently of the elected president. Almost everyone except the fringe revolutionaries was willing to accept this toxic demand as a necessary evil, but the liberals and the Islamists each had very different ideas about what kind of deal they wanted to make with the military in exchange for its immunity and autonomy.

This disagreement pointed to the third and final point of contention: religion. Secularists had tried once already in 2011 to circumvent the democratic process by negotiating a bill of rights in a secret deal with the military. Known as the Selmi document, this bill would have guaranteed a secular state (along with the military's special status), but the Islamists rightfully shot it down because of the unacceptable backroom manner in which it was conceived: liberal goals by illiberal means. Once they were in charge, however, the Islamists were just as undemocratic and self-serving. They ignored the few token secularists, liberals, Christians, and women in the Constituent Assembly. The Islamists made their own backroom deal with the military: the same special privileges the SCAF was always pursuing, in exchange for a new provision to define Egypt as an Islamic state that gave clerics the power to review laws, and that left little to no room for religious minorities, secular Muslims, and laws based on universal rights rather than the Koran. The reflex of both the secularists and the Islamists, when in power, was to dictate to the other side rather than negotiate. Even on so fundamental a question as the constitution and the source of all laws, the Islamists and their secular counterparts behaved like little dictators, pursuing a winner-takes-all strategy, Egypt be damned.

The crisis came to a head at the end of November. Another war had flared up in Gaza. In the past, Egypt had acted as a willing enforcer for Israel and the United States. Mubarak, Israel, and America shared a common distaste for Islamists. The Brotherhood, however, stood firmly on the other side of the conflict. The Islamist militant faction Hamas, after all, had begun in the 1980s as the Palestinian branch of the Muslim Brotherhood. There was a rare moment of geopolitical suspense. Would President Morsi break with the Egyptian military on a key matter of national security policy and side with Hamas, spreading the instability from the Gaza war into Egypt? To the surprise and pleasure of the Egyptian military, the Israeli government, and the White House, Morsi took a pragmatic tack. He used his leverage over Hamas to broker a cease-fire, acting less interested in the Hamas cause than in preserving Egypt's longtime role as the regional leader and neutralizing any outside distractions to his domestic rule. President Obama rewarded Morsi with a long, friendly phone call and copious positive press. A few months earlier, Obama had snubbed Morsi's efforts to visit the White House; now he was praising Morsi as a statesman.

On November 22, basking in the glow of tacit approval from an American government that suddenly realized how much it needed him, Morsi went further than anyone had imagined he would. He issued a decree that gave him unlimited dictatorial powers, just two days after the Gaza cease-fire and just one day after Secretary of State Hillary Clinton visited Cairo. Egyptians were stunned, but the US government barely uttered an objection. To all appearances, the United States had given Morsi its blessing. The president's decree concentrated all the nation's power in his hands. It took away the judiciary's power to dissolve the Constituent Assembly or the Shoura Council, the relatively impotent upper house of the legislature, which remained in place. Judicial review was gone. Morsi had assumed legislative authority already, and now he took the authority of the judiciary as well. This was more formal power than any of Egypt's dictators had ever held.

The fallout was immediate. Everyone except the Muslim Brotherhood and its Salafi allies viewed Morsi's new powers as a coup against the state. His moderate advisers resigned in protest. Secularists, liberals, and nationalists who had been bickering among themselves now found common ground in opposing Morsi's new tyranny. Morsi tried to rally support. "The *felool*, remnants of the old regime, are hiding under the cover of the judiciary!" he shouted in a raspy speech. "I will uncover them!" Tragically for the prospects of consensus and democracy, he was right in his diagnosis if not in his cure. The judiciary was acting unconscionably as the long arm of the deposed regime, overturning elected institutions capriciously and thwarting reform and transition. Unfortunately, the only solution that Morsi and the Brotherhood could concoct was to banish the entire opposition and erect their own dictatorship.

The power grab climaxed on December 1. President Morsi announced that the hallowed constitution, which was supposed to be the studied product of deliberation and consensus, would be completed that very night. Incredibly, it would be put to referendum just two weeks later. The Constituent Assembly, with only its Islamist members present, rushed through in a single all-night session more than two hundred articles meant to govern every aspect of life in Egypt. Clerics and jurists shouted down one another, inserted sloppy last-minute language, and fell asleep in an appalling spectacle that was broadcast on live television. In the past, the Islamists had argued plausibly that regardless of their faults, they were smart, competent, and had an overarching vision. This constitutional fiasco proved otherwise. The hastily drafted legal language was sloppy and prone to multiple interpretations. Clerics got their authority over lawmaking. The military got its total immunity and independence. Countless other provisions weakened the civil state. This was anything but a revolutionary constitution.

This contest for Egypt's future deranged all sides. Morsi gave screaming speeches about his legitimacy and the conspiracies of the *felool*. The secular forces, frightened into cooperating, couldn't decide whether to campaign against the constitution, seek Morsi's impeachment, or boycott all politics. Most of the anti-Morsi secular political groups united under a new banner, the National Salvation Front, but it was as illiberal as the Muslim Brotherhood. The Salvation Front rambled endlessly about the evils of Islamism, but its leaders never discussed liberties, individual rights, due process, or the primacy of elected civilians over the military. They talked only about how the Islamists were the new dictators and had to be turned back.

A week after Morsi's decree, protesters surrounded the Ittihadiya Presidential Palace. They called Morsi a new pharaoh and demanded his immediate resignation. They called his followers sheep, *khirfan*, which in Arabic rhymes with *Ikhwan*, Brothers. They were filled with righteous indignation and hunger for vengeance. Some tried to drive a bulldozer toward the palace. Others attacked and killed Muslim Brothers who were counterprotesting in support of the president. Police stood by and let the two sides fight it out.

Morsi could have responded to the protesters' demands by reconvening the Constituent Assembly, or he could have ignored the demonstrations outside his palace. Instead, he called on the Brotherhood's supporters to gather at the palace and defend his legitimacy. It was a recipe for war. Thousands of partisans swarmed Ittihadiya. Muslim Brothers detained and beat people they suspected of *felool* or revolutionary sympathies. In tents outside the palace, Brothers tortured and interrogated activists in sessions that were videotaped and leaked. Brotherhood lawyers and presidential advisers then cleared some detainees for release; others they transferred to the police for detention. Egyptians were already veterans of all the depredations of a police state. Now they were experiencing a new abuse: makeshift torture chambers on the grounds of the president's house, staffed by members of the president's religious organization.

Moaz and Basem had both joined the first protest at Ittihadiya. Once the Brotherhood called out its thugs, Moaz left. As more and more of his friends were captured and beaten, Moaz worked the phones. He called his old contacts in the Brotherhood hierarchy, pleading for them to release the activists they had tortured. He helped secure the release of Ola Shabha, an eloquent young leftist, who appeared on television that week with her face bruised and swollen and a black eye, a living testament to the thuggishness of Morsi's presidency. "It was a big mistake," Moaz said of the Ittihadiya clashes. "There were mistakes on both sides." In the final count, more than ten people were killed and thousands injured.

Confident he would win the constitutional referendum, Morsi rescinded elements of his presidential decree and restored some powers to the courts. But the palace fight galvanized the secular opposition. The secular National Salvation Front briefly stopped its dithering. Mohamed ElBaradei joined forces with former presidential candidates Amr Mousa and Hamdeen Sabbahi. Most of the secular, nationalist, and liberal political parties were aboard too. Three days before the nationwide referendum on Morsi's constitution, the Salvation Front initiated a "no" campaign.

It was too late and outmatched but still managed to convince one-third of the voters to oppose the constitution. Crucially, the "no" vote won in Cairo, signaling that the Muslim Brotherhood had lost the capital.

The National Salvation Front offered a final chance for liberal re-demption. Over the previous year, secular groups had failed to unify in a single coalition for the parliamentary elections, and then even more spec-tacularly had lost a chance to win the presidency by squabbling among themselves and splitting the secular vote. Morsi's missteps opened an op-portunity. The Muslim Brotherhood had exposed itself as power hungry and eager to use violent tools of repression to silence opponents. It was mismanaging the economy, and had restored neither dignity nor law and order. The anti-Morsi forces could now unite, if they chose, and advance a positive agenda that appealed to Egypt's moderate center. There was a vast pool of citizens who identified as Islamic supporters of a secular state and had voted in the presidential race for the mild ex-Brother Abdel Moneim Aboul Fotouh. There were avowed secularists who ran the gamut, from outright liberals and progressives such as Basem and his friends, to right-wing authoritarians who hated Islamists but hardly qualified as demo-cratic. Pumped with anger at Morsi's behavior, the electorate was ripe for a message of civil rights, reconciliation, and competent governance.

But the National Salvation Front was riven by egos and indecision. Its leaders couldn't even agree on a strategy against Morsi's constitution until the last minute. They couldn't settle on a single leader. They didn't embrace any positive agenda, and it became impossible to fairly describe the alliance as "liberal." It was simply anti-Morsi and anti-Islamist.

Even more alarming was the Salvation Front's chauvinist prejudices. Sadly, the National Salvation Front was so obsessed with rooting out Islamist influence that it rejected a partnership with Aboul Fotouh, since the independent politician had roots in the Brotherhood. Aboul Fotouh's Strong Egypt Party criticized authoritarian overreach by both the mili-tary and the Muslim Brotherhood, endowing it with unique political credibility of the sort painfully absent from the Salvation Front. Even Basem dismissed Aboul Fotouh: "Once a Brother, always a Brother," he said. When I asked how he felt about his old friends from the Revolu-tionary Youth Coalition, Moaz and the other activists whom I considered religious liberals, he was equally negative. All of them had been expelled from the Brotherhood, and all of them had toed a delicate line, resisting Brotherhood policies but not succumbing to anti-Islamist intolerance. Apparently, to Basem, this ambiguity made them suspect.

"I like them personally, but there is always some screen between me and them," he explained. "I never fully trust them. They say one thing, but they mean something else."

An active member of the Muslim Brotherhood takes an oath of fealty and must always follow direct orders. That unquestioning obedience distinguished the Brothers and left a lingering mark even on those who left the organization. Moaz, for instance, had challenged his Brotherhood bosses, but he had retained the strict commitment to an idea. Now he was a liberal revolutionary and not a Brother, but he put his principles first. Basem found the Brotherhood's groupthink and discipline disturbing. He had noticed how longtime friends still in the Brotherhood had severed ties completely with Moaz and the other dissident Brotherhood youth.

"The organization means more to them than friendship," Basem explained to me. "I don't think they ever really consider us friends."

This profound mistrust coursed through Egyptian society, often taking a much more virulent form than Basem's skepticism. Brothers were portrayed as drones serving a power-hungry secret society: robots, automatons, fanatics willing to kill on an order from the supreme guide. The caricature wasn't entirely removed from reality, as had been evidenced in the Brotherhood's vile display at the presidential palace. Yet it carried its own ugly whiff of prejudice. The elite looked askance at the type of head scarf worn by Morsi's wife and marveled that a great nation like Egypt had a president so ill versed in matters of etiquette. In September Morsi fumbled with his testicles on live television during a meeting with the Australian prime minister, a move taken as further testament that the new president was a coarse rube. Eventually nearly three million people watched the clip on YouTube. Morsi fed the ridicule with his bumbling English. Although he had a doctorate from the University of Southern California, Morsi spoke awkwardly, calling world history a "spaghetti-like structure," comparing modern politics to the film *Planet of the Apes*, and warning against drunk driving at an international conference in Germany in heavily accented English, admonishing that "gas and alcohol don't mix." That final phrase spawned an entire genre of satire, including a popular song and ultimately an opposition slogan: "Egypt and Morsi Don't Mix." Satirist Bassem Youssef's popular show *El Bernameg*, modeled on Jon Stewart's *Daily Show*, won spectacular ratings mocking Morsi. Even Moaz made it onto the program, subjected to a withering takedown for a talk-show clip in which he argued that it was possible to oppose some of Morsi's policies without opposing everything about the man and the Brotherhood.

Morsi made an easy target. There were weekly outrages, some great and some small. As Egyptians struggled under increasing economic hardships and international setbacks, mocking Morsi's malapropisms helped boost the people's morale. Bassem Youssef got great mileage off a bizarre hat that Morsi wore while receiving an honorary doctorate in Pakistan. When the comedian was summoned to the general prosecutor to be investigated for insulting the sovereign, Bassem Youssef wore an oversized replica of President Morsi's doctoral cap. Furthering his image as a thin-skinned and imperious ruler, Morsi initiated more prosecutions for the crime of offending the head of state than Mubarak, Sadat, Nasser, and King Farouk combined.

Along with a handful of liberals and ex-Brothers, Moaz joined in the National Conscience Front, a rickety effort to counter the reflexive antireligious sentiment of the secular National Salvation Front. The Conscience Front was supposed to showcase Egyptians able to engage in honest criticism of the president without resorting to rote anti-Brotherhood and anti-Islamist propaganda. Many of its members were apologists for Morsi, however, and as the sole young revolutionary in the Conscience Front, Moaz was attacked for carrying Morsi's water.

"You are doing the Muslim Brotherhood's dirty work, cleaning up their mess," one of Moaz's old revolutionary comrades accused him during a televised debate.

Moaz said, "My conscience makes me follow the right path even when it's hard and I don't like it. I don't like the Muslim Brothers; they fight me and make problems for me. But I want to do the right thing."

Although his motives appeared earnest, Moaz was being manipulated. He was serving as a kind of useful idiot, a cover for the Brotherhood's increasingly inept presidency. And he was caught in an increasingly deserted middle ground. With every passing day, fewer and fewer Egyptians were interested in seeing the merits of both sides and willing to cooperate with secular liberals as well as with Islamists. Liberalism's first tenet is freedom. It depends on laws and rights that allow disagreement and protect minorities. Increasingly, no one from the secular or Islamist camps believed that their opponents had the right to so much as express their opinions in public. In this corrosive atmosphere, Moaz's efforts appeared vain or even foolish.

On the second anniversary of the uprising, Moaz felt deflated. He was trying once again to revive the ethos of the Revolutionary Youth Coalition. He had managed to assemble some soccer ultras and some Salafis, along with representatives of the Revolutionary Socialists and the breakaway Brotherhood Youth, to proclaim a renewed revolutionary agenda that focused on ending police brutality and improving the quality of life for workers and the poor. It was a noble but marginal effort. Moaz marched with the now-fractious remains of the revolutionary youth on the same route they had followed two years earlier, but the commemoration lacked passion. Only a few thousand walked the whole route. In Tahrir, Moaz saw Basem.

"You're still in the square?" Basem asked.

"Yes," Moaz said.

"You accept the actions of the Muslim Brotherhood?" Basem asked archly.

"No, that is why I am in the square," Moaz said, his voice tinged with fatigue.

"We should fight together against the Brotherhood," Basem suggested.

"We should not just fight against the Muslim Brotherhood," Moaz replied. "We should fight for ethics and the revolution against everyone who opposes them."

They conversed almost pro forma, knowing they weren't going to work together again, and that each was unlikely to shift the other's view.

Basem excused himself. He was expected in a television studio to discuss the National Salvation Front's latest demands.

Some intangible restraint was cast aside after the 2013 anniversary of the uprising. President Morsi no longer went through the motions of sounding conciliatory. His advisers threatened the opposition on television. Morsi screamed himself hoarse in speeches and went after dissenters in court. Riots broke out in Port Said because the runaway courts sentenced fans to the death penalty for the previous year's soccer stadium slaughter but failed to convict any of the senior police and military officials who were ultimately responsible for the killings. Police fired indiscriminately, killing forty people. Morsi failed to condemn or curtail the police violence. The military occupied the canal cities to quiet things down but refused to enforce the curfew that Morsi had ordered. Videos circulated of soldiers playing football after dark with Port Said residents. The police had reverted completely to their old ways, wantonly beating citizens, with many of the most gruesome incidents recorded in videos that the police shamelessly dismissed as fakes. Meanwhile, the Brotherhood's media began a sectarian drumbeat, portraying opposition forces like the upstart anarchist "Black Bloc" as Christian fronts.

It was the most promising moment yet for the secular forces. The Brotherhood's mistakes opened the way for a change of fortune at the polls. Yet as quickly as it had coalesced, the political opposition collapsed. Already its leaders had deadlocked over whether to invite or exclude members of Mubarak's ruling party. Formed as a non-Islamist alternative to Morsi, the National Salvation Front had devolved into a bickering company of narcissists. Just a whiff of power had driven them mad. Basem was methodically preparing for an election that was expected sometime in late spring. A grand coalition of all the secular and liberal forces was the only effective counter to the domineering Islamists, but Basem wanted to be ready to run with just his own midsized party if that was all that remained. He found himself arguing even with his fellow liberals and Social Democrats. Many wanted to boycott any election organized under Muslim Brotherhood rule because they believed it would be inherently unfair.

"We have to participate, so that we don't leave everything to them," Basem urged his fellow central committee members. "We have to work hard and be ready for elections whenever they come."

But there was a deep-seated culture of boycott in Egypt that far predated the revolution. Under Mubarak, most ballots had been rigged so heavily that the only way to protest was to stay home. Dissenting votes would be thrown away, the thinking went, but a national election with a 5 or 10 percent turnout at least would embarrass the dictator and make it hard for him to claim a popular mandate. This idea had survived into the age of Tahrir, and time and again it had prompted revolutionaries and liberals to squander any serious chance at shaping the electorate. Twice they had hesitated until the last moment to campaign against flawed constitutional referendums because they had been tempted to boycott. Most revolutionaries and many liberal and secular voters had boycotted the parliamentary and presidential elections because they resented the authoritarian conditions under which they were held and the lack of acceptable candidates.

Mohamed ElBaradei, the feckless symbol of secular liberal Egypt, managed to undo the opposition campaign with a single tweet. "Called for parliamentary election boycott in 2010 to expose sham democracy," ElBaradei tweeted in late February. "Today I repeat my call, will not be part of an act of deception." What arguably had made sense in Mubarak's waning years made none in the revolution's third year, when secular and liberal Egyptians were trying to establish themselves as an alternative to the Islamists. Within days, the entire opposition agreed to sit out the forthcoming parliamentary elections.

No one wanted to defy ElBaradei, the wise man who had been so inspiring in the early stages of the uprising. He had been right about a few major points. He had always insisted that, after Mubarak's fall, the first step was to carefully draft an inclusive constitution before moving on to a contest for power. No one had listened. He had also pushed for a revolutionary presidential council as a way out of crises, but he never managed to persuade any powerful constituencies. He never decided whether he wanted to remain aloof, the conscience of the revolution, or to enter the fray and seek to lead the country. When it came to politics, ElBaradei was a total failure. He never resonated with the public. He was a terrible, uncharismatic speaker. He was indecisive and often misread the situation. Almost every tactical call he made was wrong. He had declined to establish a political party for more than a year while his followers forged organizations without him. He had kept channels open with the Brotherhood and with old regime figures without ever managing to hold either side accountable for its abuses of authority. He had courted the military without effectively condemning its control of public life.

At this key moment, the opposition could have outgrown and cast aside this once inspiring but now handicapping figure. Other leaders in the National Salvation Front could have disagreed with "the doctor" and insisted that the only way to win power in a democracy was to run for office. Contesting elections didn't forfeit the right to protest afterward if they were rigged or stolen. It was almost as if ElBaradei were so afraid to lose, so afraid that the secular front would never manage to attract a sizable electorate, that he preferred to sit out every competition or only enter it halfheartedly. Most of the opposition chose to follow ElBaradei's lead. Either they shared his diagnosis or they were too deferential to him. Basem fell in the second camp, as did the majority of the Social Democratic Party: they wanted to run, but they felt for reasons that were never entirely clear that they couldn't break ranks. "We have to respect the decision of the Salvation Front," Basem said.

A few days later, the courts stepped in and postponed the elections because of the imperious process by which Morsi had forced through the law. The public mostly forgot about the whole boycott brouhaha, distracted by the shortage of diesel, electricity, and foreign currency reserves. But the supposed liberals had shown their hand. ElBaradei had led them in a retreat from democratic politics, and he had begun voicing in public the secular side's trump card long bandied about in private: the military. "If law and order is absent, they have a national duty to intervene," ElBaradei said. "They will just come back to stabilize. And then we will start all over again." Of all the senior secular statesmen, ElBaradei had seemed by far the most liberal, but barely a half year into the first elected presidency in Egypt's history, he was tacitly endorsing a military coup.

Law and order were slipping away fast, and the blame couldn't all be laid at Morsi's doorstep. Most of the government bureaucracy was

in outright revolt against the president. The judiciary was doing everything it could to thwart the Brotherhood's agenda. Police were actively
fomenting chaos. Officers joined a mob attacking Christians at the Coptic Cathedral in Abbasiya. They stood by as vigilantes sacked the Muslim
Brotherhood's new headquarters on the Moqattam plateau overlooking
Old Cairo. Public transportation shut down over diesel shortages that
had no obvious explanation. Power cuts were more severe than ever.

Somewhat adrift, Moaz joined the Ghad Party, led by Ayman Nour,
the dissident who had run for president against Mubarak in 2005. He
liked it because it was a party committed to liberalism and pluralism, and
the leadership was willing to accept a former Brother. However, some of
his new comrades accused him of only pretending to have been expelled
from the Brotherhood so that he could operate as some kind of faux
liberal sleeper cell. In a still more bitter sign of the times, Moaz returned
from a short visit to Lebanon in March to learn that he was under investigation as a terrorist, allegedly for plotting with Hezbollah, the militant
Lebanese Shia party. Every activist faced a web of pending investigations,
but the charges seemed increasingly dangerous.

All over the country, people were understandably afraid and angry.
Life was getting harder and more disorderly. The police were clearly at
cross-purposes with the Muslim Brotherhood, and the military's cryptic
statements left the public unsure whether it would protect Morsi's regime
or act against it. The people of Egypt were caught in the middle. Egyptians who supported one side found they that had almost no common
ground with the other. Trust was scarce. Moaz met with one of Morsi's
advisers and pleaded, "You need to be more pluralistic. You're not meeting people's needs, and you never will unless you work with the people
with whom you disagree." The adviser disagreed. He thought Morsi was
doing as good a job as could be expected under trying circumstances, and
that his detractors would hate the president no matter what because they
were Islamophobes.

A new movement capitalized on this disconnect in May. Tammarod,
founded by five young activists, began as a simple cry of frustration at

Morsi. In an echo of the anti-Mubarak Kifaya movement of 2005, their "Rebel" petition proclaimed "We reject you!" and listed Morsi's failures: no security, no wealth, no jobs, no dignity, and no justice. The petition laced fear and xenophobia into its bill of particulars. "We reject you because Egypt still follows in America's footsteps," Tammarod declared. "Morsi is a total failure in every single goal . . . he is not fit to govern a country as great as Egypt." The movement's only affirmative demand was Morsi's exit and new elections. All of the five were veterans of Tahrir, and a few hailed from the April 6 Movement. They spoke well and knew how to organize. At first Tammarod was barely taken seriously, considered a symbolic stunt even by its supporters, but by the end of May, after only a month, Tammarod announced that it had gathered seven and a half million signatures. The number was stunning, although Tammarod declined to submit its petitions to any outsider for verification.

The anti-Morsi campaign revealed just how much of Egypt had lost faith in its president. Tammarod attracted onetime Brotherhood voters, people of all social classes, and fans of secular and religious government. Extreme secular nationalists thought the Brotherhood never should have been allowed into politics; a handful of die-hard democracy proponents wanted a referendum or early elections so that Morsi could be tested at the ballot box. Disenchantment with Morsi was a unifying cause, and important players took note, opportunistically jumping to support Tammarod as its nationwide popularity soared.

Tammarod's success also raised questions about whether the old regime was backing it, with or without the knowledge of its founders. The five volunteer coordinators worked out of a simple borrowed space in downtown Cairo, and yet the campaign seemed to command vast resources in virtually every town in Egypt. *Felool* businessmen and political parties backed the campaign, while the police left it free to work. Local strongmen who had kept out of sight since Mubarak's time felt comfortable openly embracing Tammarod. Whispers spread that the campaign had the blessing of the former ruling party, the military, the police, general intelligence, general security, and most civil servants who weren't Brotherhood supporters. Police let Tammarod gather signatures in public spaces where politics were legally prohibited, such as train stations. Conservative billionaire Naguib Sawiris and his Free Egyptians Party quietly contributed their national network. Established *felool* bosses in the countryside backed the Tammarod volunteers, understanding that this was finally a national movement that had buy-in from the secular security establishment as well as revolutionaries. Tammarod's momentum was unmistakable. By the time of the first anniversary of Morsi's inauguration on June 30, Tammarod hoped to present eleven million signatures, more than the number that had voted for Morsi. Organizers intended a protest so large that it would force him to call early elections, although the petition specified no political path forward, only a total rejection of the president.

A vast groundswell had turned against Morsi and the Muslim Brotherhood. Remnants of the old regime were casting their lot with Tammarod, but genuine public outrage had peaked against the sanctimonious and incompetent Brotherhood. People were sick of the unreliable gas and power lines, and the political grandstanding, while Christians feared that with each passing month they would be more likely to hear of a church burning or a lynch mob killing a Christian family in a distant village. The Coptic pope and even the most senior Sunni Muslim cleric in the country, the sheikh of Al-Azhar Mosque, endorsed the right of the faithful to join the anti-Morsi protests. The military began to issue public warnings. Defense Minister el-Sisi claimed he didn't want to take sides, but if forced would always choose "the people." There was much confusion in the political class about whether the military was signaling support for Tammarod or warning against destabilizing new protests. "The men of the armed forces don't gamble with the present or the future of the nation," el-Sisi said, clarifying nothing.

In private meetings, the defense minister warned politicians from the government and the opposition that the military wouldn't tolerate unrest. Both sides read what they wanted into el-Sisi's messages. Members of Morsi's inner cabinet were convinced that the military had no intention of taking charge. The opposition understood that if the crisis escalated, the military would step in. Because each side was convinced it had the military's support, there was no incentive to negotiate a political compromise. Basem worked feverishly on a June 30 Committee that

brought together most of the opposition youth movements and political parties. Their sole focus was to maximize the protest turnout. They
planned marches in every Cairo neighborhood, every provincial city,
every market town.

"It could end up being nothing," Basem said. "But if it's big, June 30
will be the end of Morsi." Basem predicted that the Brothers would fight
in the streets to defend Morsi, and that if people died, even more Egyptians would turn against the Brotherhood. None of the Tammarod supporters imagined an outcome that left Morsi in office. They weren't out
for conciliation or a shift in government.

Moaz thought that early presidential elections would undermine the
entire revolutionary transition since Mubarak's removal from office. He
knew several of the Tammarod founders. One, Mahmoud Badr, was an
old friend who had worked with the Kifaya movement in 2005, and
another was active in Moaz's most recent political home, the Ghad Party.
He met them at cafés and tried to persuade them to pour their energy
into a revolutionary campaign for parliament and then impeachment by
constitutional means. Moaz worried that throwing out the first elected
president so quickly would doom whoever came after. Badr wasn't convinced, but he agreed to debate Moaz on television.

"Wait until parliamentary elections. If we succeed, we can kick out
the president," Moaz said in the broadcast. "We have a democratic option to solve the problem."

"Mohamed Morsi is a criminal," Badr replied. "He is killing the people."

Inside his party, Moaz had better luck. Some Ghad members wanted
to join the Tammarod protests and the June 30 Committee. Moaz said
that as a liberal party, Ghad should leave its members free to follow their
consciences but should institutionally oppose a movement that was setting the stage for the military to return to power.

"Should we accept that any time a president makes mistakes and the
military disapproves, there can be a military coup?" Moaz said at the internal party debate. "These things will make our country unstable, with
coups for generations." He prevailed. Ghad members voted not to endorse the Tammarod rebellion.

Morsi dismissed everything about Tammarod, despite his mounting and measurable failures in governance. "I am the legitimate, constitutional president," Morsi insisted. He ignored the demand that he govern less like a dictator and more like a civilian elected by a narrow margin. Although he didn't seem to know it, Morsi's mandate was to steer an enormous, poor country out of authoritarian rule and toward democracy, and not to replace Mubarak with the Muslim Brotherhood. Until June 30, Morsi had plenty of options. On the drastic side, he could have scheduled a referendum on his presidency, buying time. He could have called for early presidential elections rather than serving his full four-year term, in the process ridding the Brotherhood of responsibility for a declining Egypt. Less radically, he could have pushed for immediate parliamentary elections, so there would be another branch of government to balance his powers. Or he could have dismissed his cabinet and appointed a new team of non-Brotherhood technocrats, dispelling the charge that he had mismanaged the state and appointed only cronies.

Instead, with the support of the Brotherhood, Morsi took the most extreme tack possible. He acknowledged none of the criticisms of his presidency, and he dropped all pretense of moderation. He appointed as governor of Luxor a member of Gamaa Islamiya, the group that in 1997 had derailed Egyptian tourism with its terrorist attack on a temple in the province. At a rally for Syrian jihadis, he praised Islamist extremists willing to seek martyrdom. He smiled as clerics on the stage condemned the Egyptian opposition as godless infidels. Some of the clerics urged Egyptians to join the jihad in Syria, which was against Egyptian law and crossed one of the military's historic red lines. It was a chilling performance: the president of Egypt sharing a platform with extremist clerics, blessing a religious war against anyone who opposed President Mohamed Morsi.

Questions about Morsi's competence grew, particularly in military circles. Mysteriously, a private meeting was aired on television. Morsi presided as advisers argued about a dam under way on the Upper Nile, in Ethiopia. The Egyptian government considered the dam a threat to the national water supply, and politicians had argued over the most effective way to persuade or force Ethiopia to abandon it. Senior politicians made incendiary proposals to sabotage the dam or arm Ethiopian rebels. To members of Egypt's security establishment, the meeting made Morsi look like a dangerous amateur who might carelessly plunge Egypt into a regional war.

The most charitable explanation for the Muslim Brotherhood's obstinacy was that long decades underground had ill prepared it for public life. After a history of state suppression and anti-Brotherhood propaganda, even a well-intentioned Brother might find it confusing to distinguish real criticism from propaganda. So out of touch was Morsi that he told his counselors he was confident the armed forces would stay out of the fray; he believed in el-Sisi's loyalty. The Brothers also exhibited unmistakable signs of messianic fervor and religious primacy. Morsi declared repeatedly that God had blessed his group, so it couldn't ever be all that wrong. He was also shockingly comfortable with religious violence. The Brotherhood itself had foresworn violence long ago, in the 1950s, and had condemned its alumni who turned to *takfiri* murder of those deemed unbelievers. But now President Morsi had very notably failed to condemn the spate of anti-Christian attacks and the mid-June lynching of four Shia Muslims in a Cairo suburb. The more the Muslim Brotherhood considered itself under political assault, the more it resorted to menacing sectarian rhetoric. Morsi didn't contradict his supporters, who went on television warning that a challenge to Morsi's "legitimacy" could unleash the hellfires of Islamist jihadi extremists. For now, the jihadis were holding their fire only because the Brotherhood's electoral success had given them the notion that maybe, just maybe, Islamists could gain dominion through politics rather than holy war.

The two sides appeared determined to hold a collision course rather than negotiate, dooming Egypt to a destructive showdown. The Tammarod people wanted to erase Morsi and the Muslim Brotherhood from Egyptian politics, going further than Mubarak ever had. Morsi and the Brotherhood, meanwhile, branded their opponents as traitors. In his last opportunity for conciliation a few days before June 30, the president dismissed those protesting his reign: "We will deal with them decisively, and there will never be a place for them among us."

It would be either them or him.

———

On June 30 anti-Morsi demonstrators clogged every major square in Egypt. The military made absurd claims that twenty million or even thirty million had joined the protests, a number that would have been physically impossible. But the Tammarod protest was the largest ever in Egypt, larger even than the Tahrir Square demonstrations that had toppled Mubarak. Almost every demographic was represented, including some Salafis and religious folk who had voted for Morsi before turning against him. There were tried-and-true revolutionary youth who had braved the regime's bullets, and there were veteran reactionaries who had never displayed a trace of sympathy for the uprising. The crowds were jubilant and diverse, and included vast numbers of government employees and first-time demonstrators from the lower, middle, and upper classes. Revolutionary protest mania had finally reached even the pro-stability crowd and the *felool*. Women in bouffant hairdos and pricey jewelry joined their husbands and children to demand the fall of Morsi. Some of them had complained about past protests disrupting traffic and business, but this time they were willing to make an exception. Unlike the ragtag, improvised protests of the past, Tammarod had high production values, thanks to its well-heeled backers. Everywhere were glossy signs that read "Irhal!" in Arabic and "Go Out!" in English. Military helicopters flew overhead, dumping flags on the people. Green laser pointers flickered everywhere. Men kissed policemen and danced in circles around them, welcoming them back into the fold.

Again and again when I asked people what they hoped for, I heard the same refrains: "We have to ask the army to intervene." "The Muslim Brotherhood is brainwashed; it is not part of Egypt." "Morsi is an idiot. Morsi is a criminal." Several told me they hoped the Brotherhood would be outlawed once again. The demands were almost careless. "I don't care who will lead the country. We just want Morsi to leave," said a lady in a fine tailored dress, sipping tea on a terrace near the presidential palace on a break from chanting. Many of the first-time protesters who joined Tammarod sounded remarkably similar to the *felool* supporters of the Horreya Party whose revival I had attended nearly two years earlier. A police officer, his white uniform freshly starched, announced that as soon as the Brotherhood was banished from the palace, the police would finally start doing their jobs again. "We can reestablish security overnight," he said with a grin.

Basem led a march of thousands from his old parliamentary office in Shoubra to the Ittihadiya Palace. To Basem, however, this day of rage felt no different from the first dogged parade from the pastry shop on January 25, 2011. Both were products of careful preparation and spontaneous popular anger. "God willing, we will liberate Egypt from the Muslim Brotherhood's occupation!" he shouted, as if Morsi and his cohorts were foreign invaders. He didn't mind that elements of the old regime, along with the army and the police, were overtly backing the June 30 protests. To Basem, that only highlighted the justice of this latest popular revolt: it had animated the powerful and the armed and the privileged as well as the disenfranchised and dispossessed. Moaz approached the edges of the protest to get a sense of its size and composition. He saw thousands of regular people, but he also saw among them the police and bureaucrats of the old regime. A knot tightened in his stomach.

Egypt under Morsi had reached an impasse. Some of the millions who filled the streets on June 30, 2013, believed they were continuing a popular revolution that had begun two and a half years earlier. Most of them didn't see any legal or constitutional way to thwart Morsi's budding repression and religious dictatorship. And those who could imagine other ways to challenge the despot didn't think it was worth waiting. Basem, for instance, had come to believe that the Muslim Brotherhood was incapable of respecting freedom, the law, and anyone who opposed its project to transform Egypt into a backward caliphate. He thought any delay in stopping the Brothers could be fatal for secular Egyptian democracy. Tammarod dangerously twinned two inaccurate dictums from Egypt's revolutionary period: that vast crowds outweighed the authority of a ruler, and that the people's will would restrain the military from resuming the history of abuse and incompetence that had continuously characterized its role in Egyptian life since 1952.

The next day, July 1, the defense minister issued an ultimatum to President Morsi: Address the demands of the protesters, or else the military would issue a road map for a "transition to democracy." The ultimatum didn't come from the young Tammarod leaders or from the civilian politicians on the June 30 Committee. It came from el-Sisi, who theoretically served at the pleasure of the elected president to whom he was giving forty-eight hours notice. Until now the general had been almost a complete unknown, but now he appeared on television in oversized aviator sunglasses, looking every bit the military strongman. Basem was euphoric. He believed that el-Sisi and the other generals were bowing to the will of the crowds on the street. It never occurred to him that the military might have promoted the Tammarod protests behind the scenes in order to step into the breach and assume direct power once more.

The Brothers had initiated their own counterprotest at Rabaa al-Adawiya Square in Nasr City, a quiet neighborhood of middle-class government employees that wasn't a natural Brotherhood stronghold. The men and women in Rabaa were incredulous. They supported a leader who, for all his shortcomings, was the country's legally elected civilian president, a man who had been in power for only a year, and who had contended the entire time with obstruction or outright rebellion from the most important branches of the government that he supposedly directed. Morsi's supporters reflected the president's cloistered worldview. They saw none of the Brotherhood's guilt, only the hypocrisy of its critics. They didn't recognize or acknowledge that the Brotherhood had trampled on pluralism, ignored the rights of secular Egyptians, and also displayed contempt for justice, accountability, and rule of law. Now, as the confrontation climaxed, they also hinted at violence.

"There will be an Islamic revolution," a man from the Gamaa Islamiya told me. He was a forty-nine-year-old construction worker named Taha Sayed Ali, wearing a hard hat and carrying a wooden pole. "I am not here for Morsi, I am here for legitimacy," he said. "If they threaten our legitimacy, everybody will pay."

Everyone was waiting for Morsi's response. As soon as General el-Sisi had imposed a deadline, Moaz understood that a military coup was under way. He saw only one way out: for Morsi to fire the insubordinate defense minister but at the same time admit his own mistakes and resign, effective once a new parliament was seated. But he knew firsthand the arrogance of the Brothers. He spent the day phoning every Brotherhood official he knew.

"What's your plan?" he asked. "Your time in power is finished. Find a way to avert a coup."

"God is with us," one assured him. "Things will be fine."

After midnight, Morsi finally came on television. He rasped and ranted and shouted about his legitimacy. He didn't relent an inch. It was the speech of a man who planned to go down fighting. It was a speech that comforted the men and women in Rabaa al-Adawiya Square who expected martyrdom. Moaz watched at a Brotherhood hospital with one of Morsi's advisers.

"It's all over," the adviser said. "There might have been a way out, but not after this speech."

"You know how a chicken keeps running around after you cut off its head?" Moaz remarked. "Morsi is like that."

After that, the coup proceeded clinically. The deadline passed, and Morsi had not stepped aside, so the military took charge. Soldiers arrested the president and took him to the presidential guard barracks. One by one, senior Brotherhood leaders were also taken into custody. Brotherhood television stations went off the air. Late in the afternoon of Wednesday, July 3, el-Sisi appeared on television, in uniform, sedately presenting his road map, flanked by leaders who should have had every reason to stand against the military and for the revolution: the Coptic pope, the sheikh of Al-Azhar, and Mohamed ElBaradei. The top judge from the Supreme Constitutional Court would serve as a figurehead interim president. A new constitution would be written, and then a parliament and president elected. It was the original order of operations that ElBaradei had sought after January 25, along with Basem, Moaz, and many other activists. This time it came with a military guarantee that religious forces would be kept in check.

The Tammarod crowd went wild. Fireworks, screaming, dancing, mob euphoria. Hundreds of green laser pointers followed the choppers overhead, draping them in an eerie green glow. At the moment of the coup, only a few Morsi critics still had the presence of mind to realize that a crime had been committed against democracy in the name of revolution, and the vast majority of them were ex-Islamists. Abdel Moneim Aboul Fotouh, the ex-Brother and presidential candidate, had supported

Tammarod but instantly decried military rule, in any form. So did the young ex-Brothers in al-Tayyar al-Masry. And so did Moaz. Perhaps their history made them sympathetic to the Islamist movement they had left, or perhaps their religious convictions reminded them to concentrate on the injustice in play. But their voices were lonely. Around them Egypt celebrated, while the deep state swiftly encircled the Brotherhood and began to dismantle it.

The next day, Basem strolled down Shoubra's central avenue. Everywhere there were victory parties in the street. Ultras beat oversized drums and sang football songs. Men and women stopped Basem to kiss him or shake his hand. His phone rang nonstop with calls from well-wishers. There were no speeches, and it was a few days before the street would be plastered with banners of el-Sisi beside his model: Nasser.

Only one man in the entire crowd wasn't grinning. I'd seen him before; he was one of the activists at Tahrir who had gradually drifted away from the scene. "Don't celebrate too much," he muttered in the direction of the celebrants, although only I could hear him. "This scar on my face: I got it from the SCAF, during the cabinet clashes. I don't forget."

A woman stopped Basem and gripped his elbow. "Thank God the Brotherhood is gone," she said. She told him she looked forward to voting for him again the next time he ran for parliament.

"Thank you," Basem said. He smiled. "Long live Egypt."

Basem didn't think it was right to pursue all members of the Brotherhood and all its media outlets; he thought it would be enough to arrest those who had committed crimes. "We must do everything according to the law," he cautioned his constituents.

"What do you think?" he asked, turning to me. "Was it a revolution, what happened on June 30, or was it a coup?"

"Whether you support or not, it's a coup," I said. "There can't be any debate about that." I was wrong; the semantic debate raged for months, because supporters of el-Sisi and the military's status as final arbiter couldn't countenance the unvarnished truth that military rule was inimical to democracy. So they had to hide it in circumlocutions. Basem didn't mind one silly term that was making the rounds: "popularly legitimate coup."

"It's a revolution, not a coup," Basem replied. "The military didn't remove him. The people asked Morsi to go, and he said no. Only Morsi's people think it's a coup. He lost his legitimacy."

He explained that legitimacy came from the people and could be passed like a baton. The people had withdrawn this coveted legitimacy from Morsi, Basem went on, and had bestowed it upon the June 30 Revolution. "We have returned to square zero of our revolution, to start it again in the right way."

"What about the Islamists?" I asked.

"If we make a new country without including them in the system, it will be a great way to make sure this country collapses," Basem said. He was sure the Muslim Brotherhood would be integrated into the new system, one way or another.

"Aren't you worried about the military's power?" I asked. "You saw what they did the last time."

"They've had this power the whole time," Basem said. "We need a long time to change the mentality of the military and the people."

"How can you trust the military now?" I asked.

"There is no guarantee," Basem answered with his habitual ambiguity. "The guarantee is the people. El-Sisi said he will not enter politics or take charge. People learned very well the lesson from the SCAF the first time. We will be in the streets again if el-Sisi tries to take charge."

He turned out to be right. A few weeks later, when the general decided that he did, in fact, want to run Egypt, people flooded the streets. But they didn't come out to oppose him; they wanted to say thank you.

———

Now there was a sad echo of the days of Tahrir in the people's lockstep unanimity. All Egypt spoke in one voice about restoration, thanking el-Sisi and the great military in ever more hysterical and fawning tones. Private television and newspapers followed the script set by state media. El-Sisi had instantaneously been crowned the savior, and every guest on every show implored the general to do the nation a favor and deign to serve as its next president. Only in one isolated square, behind barricades, did supporters of the Brotherhood maintain a world apart, preparing for martyrdom in the name of legitimacy.

"If Sisi has an army, Morsi has an army too," warned a burly professor of statistics. "We will apply legitimacy even if it is with our own blood. We will not move even if we are killed here."

"They are brainwashed," a man beside the professor added. "They believe everything they hear on state media."

He was right that the anti-Morsi mania sounded like the bleating of brainwashed fools, but so did the menacing rhetoric in Rabaa al-Adawiya Square. Uncritical adulation of the army was just as bad as uncritical adulation of the Brotherhood.

"We'll never believe in democracy again," the man went on, as if the abridgement of democracy rendered democracy itself repugnant. Would he blame God if someone blasphemed? I didn't get the impression that he or many of the other men and women in Rabaa Square had ever really supported democracy that much in the first place. They were glad when the Brotherhood won power, but they displayed only the shallowest commitment to elections as a path to authority. They summarily dispensed with everything that actually made democracy.

The day after el-Sisi took power, Moaz visited Rabaa and its sister sit-in across town at Nahda Square for the first time. He found his old comrades struggling to accept their precipitous fall from grace. At the square, Moaz saw the man who had presided over his expulsion hearings from the Brotherhood. Setting aside his own feelings, Moaz hugged him. The man had spent four years in prison under Mubarak, but until a few days before had been a senior adviser to the minister of health. That morning, his colleagues at the ministry had taunted him.

"Pack your bags," they hooted. "You're going back to prison."

That day, a few dozen Brotherhood supporters were killed in clashes with the army at Rabaa and Nahda Squares. There wasn't much room for maneuvering between the absolutes of the Islamists and the military. Basem's concern with the law, and Moaz's with civilian rule and democracy, were secondary niceties in this struggle. Few others cared. Ceaseless patter on TV, in newspapers, from the mouths of generals and businessmen and politicians, had intensified fear. The prospect of anarchy was real. You could feel it in the snaking fuel lines, in the wild-eyed threats of the clerics, in the screaming dirges at the funerals of martyrs killed by police or in clashes between Islamist and secular protesters. The simple reactionary slogan "Stability or chaos?" spoke to a universal yearning. No one wanted to live in transition forever. Even the revolutionaries hoped that now, after two and a half years of tribulations, Egypt would be enjoying stability as well as democracy. On July 8 more than fifty Brotherhood supporters were massacred by the army outside the presidential guard barracks, where they had demanded Morsi's release.

Now that they were on the defensive, the Brotherhood was willing at least tepidly to accept sympathy from those it had rejected. Moaz was invited onto the stage at Rabaa al-Adawiya, where he admonished the Brothers in the audience to back away from their impossible demands and seek common ground with the supporters of el-Sisi.

"People were right to protest against Morsi, because he failed. Protest is a right we won in the revolution," Moaz said.

The crowd booed. "Don't call him Morsi, call him President Morsi!"

Moaz continued. "You carry the historical responsibility to resolve this problem and avoid leading our country into hell."

Afterward, he met with some of the Brothers' top strategists, Mohamed el-Beltagy and the former minister of youth, Osama Yassin. "You need a new strategy," Moaz told them. "You need to apologize to the people and clearly say that Morsi failed. You need to say that you made many mistakes and that you will work to correct those mistakes."

Even deposed and on the run, the Brothers found it difficult to comprehend their own responsibility for their failure. "I will take your message back to the leaders," el-Beltagy said. "It's worth discussing."

Extremism was flourishing in the ranks. An old friend of Moaz's hectored him. "How dare you criticize Morsi in public!" he shouted.

"You're making a huge mistake," Moaz said. "You should support Egypt and democracy, not Morsi."

Each time there were clashes, the media portrayed them as Muslim Brotherhood terrorism or aggression against the armed forces, even though it was usually soldiers murdering unarmed Islamist civilians. Attitudes hardened. Basem blamed the continuing deaths on the intransigence and fanaticism of the Muslim Brotherhood. The group's leaders ordered their followers into clashes with the military that were certain to be fatal. Even if Basem had once fought for the Brotherhood's legal right to continue nonviolent protests, he now felt that the Brothers were misusing protest in an effort to drive their base into a frenzy and the nation to civil war. "They are just a mob whose goal is to occupy the country," Basem said. "The strict security solution is the only solution."

El-Sisi crudely stoked the fear and nationalist frenzy. He asked for a "popular mandate" to fight terrorism, in the form of mass demonstrations on July 26. Millions heeded the call, many of them carrying banners imploring the general to run for president. "Finish your good deed!" they proclaimed. Right after the July 26 "Mandate Day" demonstrations, el-Sisi's army tested the political tolerance for casualties, confident that the general's public reputation was now unassailable. Soldiers made a few probing attacks on Rabaa Square, killing between 70 and 130 people. Most Egyptians cheered el-Sisi's resolve, opening the way for a massive bloodletting.

There were some final efforts to avert catastrophe. Diplomats from the United States, the European Union, and some Gulf monarchies sponsored talks between the government and the Brotherhood to find a peaceful solution. Inside the Egyptian cabinet, ElBaradei and the deputy prime minister pushed for a political compromise rather than a violent clearing of the sit-ins. But by early August, the hard-liners had won out, and the transitional government ceased any more talk of reconciliation. Instead, the government began describing Rabaa as a den of violent terrorists bent on overthrowing the state. Egypt wouldn't ignore the protest or negotiate with its leaders, but would treat it as an insurgency and fight with full force.

A few days after the end of Ramadan, on August 14, the police and army closed in again on Rabaa Square. For days, el-Sisi's government had talked of the need to clear the Brotherhood protests once and for all. The sun had not yet risen when officers drove directly into the sit-in with armored bulldozers and began firing into the crowd with tear gas, birdshot, rubber bullets, and live ammunition. The death toll was staggering and indiscriminate: children, teenage boys and girls, and the elderly fell alongside the adult men trying to protect the sit-in with their futile wooden clubs. The military had shown before that it knew how to clear a protest without killing; this time it put the police in the forefront and pursued tactics that maximized the death toll. It wanted more than to merely end the Rabaa sit-in, the final vestige of the Brotherhood's electoral success; it wanted vengeance and to break the Brotherhood.

Moaz's father pleaded with him to come home. At every major protest or massacre, Moaz had worked in the clinic treating wounded protesters. His political ventures didn't always work out, but his expertise in the combat-like conditions of protest hospitals was indisputable. He had no intention of staying away from Rabaa while hundreds of people were being gunned down.

"You weren't killed on January 25," his father said. "You will be killed today."

"We are trying to solve problems," Moaz said. "You should support me."

Rabaa was awash in blood. Tanks blocked all the main thoroughfares, but people could escape through small alleys. At the same time, the army swept through the other, smaller Muslim Brotherhood sit-in at Nahda Square on the other side of the Nile. Pro-Sisi plainclothes thugs, working with the police, erected checkpoints all over the city to harass anyone who looked like a Brotherhood supporter. Scattered gunshots echoed all over Cairo, even far from Rabaa and Nahda Squares.

In the wake of these massacres, Moaz felt his last hope slip away. He railed aloud against its perpetrators. "What do you think the families of the people you killed will do? Don't you think they will kill your families? You are writing your own future. No matter how many times you hit the people, it won't solve the problem."

People screamed and ran away from the gas and bullets. Some took refuge in the nearby apartment buildings, hiding in garages. Moaz loaded the wounded into his car and ferried them to hospitals. One man bled to death in Moaz's backseat. Around Rabaa Square, it seemed like everything was on fire, including the field hospital. Soldiers weren't letting anyone pass, even medical volunteers like Moaz. Almost twenty-four hours after they began, soldiers and police were still shooting stragglers in Rabaa. Exhausted, Moaz was crying as he drove. He could smell blood on the street. He tried to return once more to the center of Rabaa, where he knew a wounded man was trapped in a building that had once served as the sit-in's clinic. So far, he had successfully passed through checkpoints with his pharmacist ID. A soldier pointed his rifle at Moaz and forced him from his car.

"What are you doing in a military area?"

"I am a pharmacist," Moaz told his interrogator. "My job is to help people."

"Go to the Iman Mosque," the officer said. "That's where all bodies are. We will let you pass this time, but if you appear again, there's no saying what might happen to you."

"But there's a man in a building in Rabaa, and he has phoned me for help," Moaz pleaded.

"No one here is alive," the officer snapped. "Everyone is dead. If anyone is still alive, he will be dead within an hour."

Moaz gave up and joined the effort in the Iman Mosque to identify the hundreds of corpses. The military soon attacked even there, arresting the family members who had come to claim their dead. The military was sending a clear message: it would do anything, even disrespect the most basic Islamic funeral rites, to destroy the Muslim Brotherhood. The government stopped counting the dead after the number exceeded seven hundred. The Brothers estimated that more than a thousand people were killed that day, including many children of senior Brotherhood leaders, apparently singled out by snipers. Many leaders were caught, but a few escaped the country or found hiding places. From there they delivered menacing threats. Now, they vowed, Egypt would burn.

The massacre at Rabaa would be the pivotal litmus test that separated the masses praising el-Sisi from the small community of Egyptians who decried any abuse of human beings. Some activists, such as Ahmed Maher from the April 6 Movement, had been relatively quiet about the military's return to power in July but reacted swiftly to condemn the crime of Rabaa. Mohamed ElBaradei belatedly developed a conscience. In the wake of the violence at Rabaa, he resigned from the post of vice president that he had held for just a month. For his act of decency, ElBaradei was investigated for the criminal offense of "breaching the national trust." Instead of staying to challenge the increasingly fascist political atmosphere, ElBaradei chose exile. He had taken a lead role as a political enabler of el-Sisi's rise, but he was not alone. The Social Democratic Party, the chosen home for many of the secular revolutionaries, wholeheartedly cast its lot with the military. Dr. Mohamed Aboul-Ghar, the leader of the Social Democrats, busily defended the massacre on television as a necessary evil. Ziad Bahaa el-Din, considered one of the smartest members of the party, had accepted a position as deputy prime minister in the transitional government and used his position to reassure foreign governments and Egyptian liberals that there was no reason to fear the military men in charge. These were the most liberal members of the mainstream political elite; their embrace of the coup and massacres paved the way for public opinion to follow.

Like many secular or liberal Egyptians, Basem was willing to blame the Brotherhood for the massacre in which so many of its members perished, especially when in the aftermath the Brotherhood appeared to endorse a jihadist insurgency in retribution. "Everyone now knows that the Brotherhood is a terrorist organization," Basem said. "There can be no more talk about reconciliation."

For five days, Moaz had been living out of his car, driving from massacre, to clinic, to mosque, arranging clandestine meetings with friends who were on their way to prison or hoping to sneak across the border to exile. Thugs had beaten him and ripped his clothes. He was wearing a red tracksuit he had bought from a street vendor. On Saturday evening, he was stopped at yet another checkpoint, down the street from Basem's parliamentary office in Shoubra. He shuddered with fear that he would be recognized. Suddenly Moaz realized that his time was up. He had to leave Egypt. He made it through and finally drove home. There he found his mother crying. She hadn't seen him in almost a week.

"I was worried," she said.

"I had no problems," he said. "I was just keeping my friends company."

"You're lying," his mother said, holding him tight. Without discussing any of the details, they agreed it was wise for him to leave the country—and to sleep in his car, far from his family, until his departure. State Security knew the house on Sudan Street. On August 22, Moaz's brothers drove him to the airport. Moaz knew, thanks to a sympathetic contact in the government, that he had not yet been placed on the no-fly list. He had packed a duffel bag with his most important tools: multiple laptops and tablet computers, a stack of external hard drives, and a bag of smartphones. The route to the airport took them past the sites of all the revolution's triumphs and massacres. They passed the Mostafa Mahmoud Mosque, where so many promising revolutionary marches had begun. From an overpass, they looked down on Tahrir Square, and then a moment later the Coptic Hospital and the road to the Coptic Cathedral and Ministry of Defense, where revolutionary promise had first lapsed into sectarian murder. Then the airport road passed through Nasr City, near Rabaa Square and directly in front of the presidential guard barracks, where Egypt's faltering experiment with democracy had plunged to a bloody halt.

"We are living a bad dream," Moaz said to his younger brother Bilal. Moaz was headed to Istanbul, Turkey, where he had no friends, no job, and didn't know the language. "Where am I going?"

"For now, just focus on getting out," Bilal said.

The security officer at the airport recognized Moaz and questioned him for an hour, but his papers were in order. As much as the officer didn't like Moaz, he had to let him go.

Within weeks, he was joined by dozens of acquaintances and former Brotherhood comrades. Ayyash also managed to slip past airport security and fly to Istanbul, where, despite his tense relations with the Brotherhood, he took a job with a Brotherhood-linked website. He worked as well on medical relief for Syrian refugees and also applied to master's programs, still mindful of his dream of working as a presidential adviser.

"This is our life now," Ayyash told me over Skype. "We will wait for another chance."

Only a trace now remained of Tahrir's conscience. Most Egyptians applauded the bloodbath and shouted down as a traitor anyone who questioned the military government's violence. Almost alone in the secular political class, ElBaradei had spoken against the massacre at Rabaa. Even his timid critique, too late to make any difference, had disqualified him from public life in Egypt as voices began to converge into a single hor-rifying chorus. The public figures critical of the coup numbered at best in the hundreds: a tiny community of conscience. Abdel Moneim Aboul Fotouh, the ex-Brother, never wavered. Nor did Amr Hamzawy, the liberal academic who had refused to join the mainstream revolutionary parties at the outset in part because he recognized the tenuousness of their commitment to liberalism. Among the youth, the Revolutionary Socialists and some well-known figures such as Alaa Abdel Fattah had maintained their integrity. The April 6 Movement had succumbed briefly to el-Sisi fever but by the time of the great massacre at Rabaa Square had regained sanity. Alaa, Ahmed Maher, and some others founded a new movement called "the Way of the Revolution," a third front between Islamist and military rule. Few people paid it any heed. This small group included the only voices raised against military rule, against the idea that the correct response to the Brotherhood's mistakes was to kill its leaders and outlaw its beliefs.

El-Sisi declared a preemptive war on terror, and jihadists obliged by providing terrorism for him to fight. Assassins tried to kill the interior minister. Suicide bombers struck for the first time in Egypt. The Mus-lim Brotherhood condemned the attacks, but it made no difference; the organization was blamed all the same. *Takfiri* jihadists from Sinai took responsibility for a series of bombings that targeted police in Cairo and other cities. In a perfect mirror image of what the Brotherhood had done when it was in charge, el-Sisi's government convened a new Constituent Assembly that completely shut out the Islamists. Led by Amr Moussa, no enemy of the *felool*, a group of fifty establishment secularists wrote Egypt's third constitution since Mubarak. This one preserved the secular nature of the state but spelled out the broadest protections yet for the military. The SCAF was snapping up lucrative contracts from the interim government, including hundreds of millions of dollars in construction projects.

The military was openly pursuing naked political power and crass riches while el-Sisi's cult of personality blossomed. Anyone who didn't like it was silenced. The popular comedian Bassem Youssef, who had been hounded by Morsi's prosecutors but never taken off the air, found his show cancelled suddenly when he mocked the public obsession with el-Sisi's manliness. Apparently it wasn't acceptable to make fun of the ladies who proclaimed they wanted to leave their husbands for el-Sisi, or the bakers who decorated their pastries with the general's portrait. The only politics allowed were el-Sisi's politics. His emerging regime enjoyed tremendous popular support. For all the state-orchestrated propaganda and anti-Islamist hysterics, the acclaim for el-Sisi was genuine. Each of his repressive measures was welcomed and applauded. After three years of disappointing leaders, Egyptians were hungry for more than just charisma: they wanted someone who could get things done, and despite his flimsy record, they thought el-Sisi could be that man.

Basem only snapped out of his lethargy in late November, when the transitional government, whose prime minister hailed from Basem's own Social Democratic Party, passed a law criminalizing protest. This was too much even for Basem and others who had been willing to team up with the military against the Islamists. He went downtown to protest the anti-protest law and narrowly escaped arrest. The last remaining activists at large were locked up, first for protesting without a permit, and then for a variety of incredible charges of fomenting violence. Alaa Abdel Fattah, Ahmed Maher from April 6, and most of the widely recognized faces of Tahrir were imprisoned, accused of undermining national security.

Zyad had been laying low since the events of the summer. His sponsor, ElBaradei, had been drummed out of politics. Zyad had always been a more pointed critic of Islamists than Basem and the other liberal revolutionaries were, but he didn't want to appear to condone the massacre at Rabaa or the restoration of military rule. He had escaped a prison sentence for his comment about the field marshal and the donkey, so now he was biding his time. He tended to some duties in the Social Democratic Party, visited his son and ex-wife, and hung out in his small bachelor apartment. When el-Sisi's constitution came up for a vote, Zyad tried to convince the Social Democratic Party to campaign against it. The protections it gave the military weren't worth any of its good points, Zyad argued. True to its liberal charter, the Social Democratic Party hosted an internal debate on whether to endorse or oppose the charter. Zyad made his case, but the party members were eager to move on and get out on the stump; it was a chance to increase their visibility. They voted against Zyad and for el-Sisi's constitution.

Dissent was silenced at a dizzying speed, crossing boundaries that had been respected even by Mubarak, the SCAF, and Morsi. Well-known human rights activists retired or took sabbaticals. Sally left Egypt for a spell. Supporters of the revolution renewed applications to study or work abroad. El-Sisi meant to remake Egypt, and quickly. Every week, Brotherhood supporters were killed and arrested. A group of teenage girls was sentenced to eleven years in prison for protesting in support of Morsi. A team of foreign correspondents for Al Jazeera English was arrested, accused of operating a Muslim Brotherhood terrorism cell; until now foreign journalists had almost always been left alone by the state. Members of Aboul Fotouh's party who campaigned against the latest terrible constitution were arrested. Recordings of the private phone calls of activists began surfacing on proregime television channels. Some were blackmailed privately with threats that sex tapes or other embarrassing conversations would be leaked. The regime's message was clear: criticizing el-Sisi was a crime. Independent journalism was a crime. Talking to Muslim Brothers was a crime. Opposing government policies was a crime. El-Sisi would do what he could to put the revolution to an end. Among Egypt's fatigued citizens, he found millions of willing accomplices.

All that was left was to draft the revolution's obituary. Those who still dreamed of revolution sought to figure out where they had gone wrong, how they had failed to persuade enough Egyptians that liberty and security weren't mutually exclusive. Alaa Abdel Fattah sent letters from prison, which were published on the dwindling number of critical websites that remained. Moaz wrote passionate essays, which were occasionally accepted by newspapers; otherwise he posted them on Facebook. At the beginning of the revolution, Mubarak supporters had formed a group called "Please Forgive Us, O Leader," apologizing for the Tahrir youth who were rudely disputing his rule. As el-Sisi promoted himself to field marshal and prepared his inevitable presidential campaign, Moaz recalled the firestorm that had engulfed Zyad when he likened the previous field marshal to a donkey. Moaz penned a parody of the *felool* credo: "Please forgive us, O donkey," he wrote, a flowery apology to beasts of burden everywhere. The craven Egyptians who were voluntarily surrendering to the yoke of military fascism, Moaz wrote, did not deserve to be compared with the oppressed but dignified donkey.

El-Sisi's constitution passed with 98 percent support in a referendum in January. Weeks of smothering propaganda had urged a "yes" vote, and the last stragglers who urged people to say no were jailed as spies, traitors, or vandals. In a vast show of force across the nation, representatives of all the different security branches surrounded polling stations, outnumbering civilians on the street at any given time by a ratio of two to one. They meant to thwart any Muslim Brotherhood protests, and also to signal to the citizenry that the deep state was in better condition than ever. "The army and the people are one hand," banners everywhere proclaimed while sound trucks played the promilitary anthem "Bless the Hands."

Only the details of the restoration remained to be sorted out. Field Marshal el-Sisi would assume the presidency, the Muslim Brotherhood would weather another generation underground, and Egyptians would bow again under an incompetent authoritarian government that would promise stability and growth while delivering neither. For sixty years, the generals had controlled Egypt, and they'd never managed to provide liberty, economic prosperity, or dignity. On the third anniversary of the revolution, January 25, 2014, Tahrir Square was closed to revolutionaries. Only el-Sisi supporters were allowed, and they threw a grand coronation party funded and organized by the army. First-rate sound system, banners, and refreshments. Dissenters, real or perceived, were beaten. No one had to give an order. The people were fired up enough to do it of their own accord.

Basem had given up on his bigger dreams. His architecture business had dried up. His savings would last another few months. He didn't know how long el-Sisi would permit political life to continue. His dreams of revolution had faded into something much more meager. Power lay out of reach, and so did the people. Now all that was left for him was to build something in politics that might serve the next generation: no longer the ambitious blueprint of a revolutionary architect but the workaday routine of an engineer. From now on, he was dedicated to training party members, giving them management and logistical skills, and a curriculum in social democratic political theory that he had spent a year developing. Many of the other party leaders were lazy, turning up only to give speeches or appear on TV. Basem thought the next opportunity would come in eight years or so, when el-Sisi would be wrapping up his second presidential term. That's when a finely trained political party could compete for elections and public opinion as the Muslim Brotherhood had been able to do in the first rotation after Tahrir.

"You cannot have any more expectations of voters," Basem said, slumped over the fading conference table in the Egyptian Social Democratic Party headquarters downtown. "We have struggled for three years against four different regimes," he said. "All this time, we have been against the regime, but the people are against us. There is no way to succeed without the people's support. The problem is not with the regime, the problem is with the people."

The Social Democratic Party's shabby headquarters never had been refurbished. I had sat in this corner room countless times in the three years since the revolution began, as the liberal brain trust hashed out its response to the different crises and opportunities it had faced. Now the office was quiet; nearly deserted. Basem's eyes were swollen with tiredness, and his skin had dried into an ashen hue. He smiled less frequently, and his affect had flattened. The revolution had aged him visibly.

"I have changed my thinking," Basem said. "We must not fight the dictator. We must fight to change the people. If they are hungry, they will not speak about democracy."

It was time, again, for patient work. "People say I should go back home, to work, focus on my kids, but *haram*," for shame, he said. "We shouldn't lose all the investment we have made."

Basem didn't seem capable of facing the implications of his support for Tammarod. He despaired that el-Sisi would outlaw all dissent, but went about his business as if he and his Social Democratic Party bore no responsibility for the coup, the Rabaa massacre, and the political dead end that followed. "I didn't support Sisi, I opposed Morsi," he said. "Whatever we are now, it is better than the Muslim Brotherhood."

For three years, secular and Islamist revolutionaries had failed to forge a shared vision of liberty and rights. Now they were all consigned to the same dreary fate. When and if they managed to create another day of promise, another January 25, 2011, another Tahrir Square, they would once again confront the same divisions. If they couldn't square their divide, they would be doomed to another chapter of dictatorship.

After three years, Basem was no wiser about how to reach this promised land. His sense of mission burned steadily. He still wanted to build the political future he had envisioned while surfing Facebook years ago, but he had no clue how. He knew murder wasn't the way, but the failure of Tahrir had nourished in him an abiding loathing for the Brotherhood. Unlike so many of his peers, however, he knew the Islamists had to be part of Egypt's future.

"The Muslim Brotherhood cannot be finished in Egypt," he said. "How can it? Can you kill Moaz?" He rattled off the names of other friends and activists, men and women who had come to the revolution from the Brotherhood.

"Can we kill all of them?" Basem mused. "If yes, then okay, the Muslim Brotherhood is finished. But we will not allow it. They are Egyptian, after all. They have the right to express themselves."

In Istanbul, alone at a small desk, Moaz witnessed his first snowfall. He watched through the window as a drift piled in the alley by his apartment, while on his computer screen instant messages informed him that his last friend in Cairo was being snatched by police. The terrorism case against him was proceeding through the Egyptian courts. Moaz could face a serious prison sentence, depending on the whim of the prosecutor and the corrupted judiciary. He drafted a power of attorney so that his father could pursue his legal defense in his absence. Every thirty days, his tourist visa expired, and he had to travel for a few days to the only countries that would allow him entry: Lebanon and Qatar. Moaz was rattling about, unwanted in his homeland, undesired by the countries in the region, and distrusted by many of the exiles in Istanbul. Through everything, some had maintained their mindless obedience to the Muslim Brotherhood and considered Moaz a traitor to the supreme guide.

On one of his visa trips, he came to see me in Beirut. When we met, he was wondering how and when he could return home, back to Egypt and back in time to that alchemic moment when Tahrir Square had banished the dictator and rolled back the deep state. Before the quest for power had unraveled the revolution. It hadn't been a dream. It really had happened. People had done it. They had changed. They had defied their own fates. They had rejected the status quo with utter bravery. Millions had revolted. Their psychological transformation had been complete. They had been nobody's puppets. All this had happened. It could happen again.

For the first time, we enjoyed a stretch of time together uninterrupted by tear gas, mayhem, or political demonstrations. We sat in the garden. Paralyzed, following the deep state's reemergence from a remove, Moaz was philosophical. He had always thought Egypt's greatest problems were poverty and repression, and that democracy was the beginning of any solution.

"I thought we had transcended the fight between the Muslim Brothers and the liberals, but it is transmitted from generation to generation," he said.

He whispered a short prayer before raising a forkful of food to his mouth. He had spent a long day recalling the massacre at Rabaa, enumerating crimes and betrayals great and small, including the revolutionary comrades who had countenanced the killing and the restoration of military rule. Many of them had regrets now, and Moaz, still able to slip into a Tahrir reverie, was ready to forgive and begin anew. "Democracy is for everyone," he said. "I cannot judge people. Anyone who feels he is an angel should not live here on earth with the rest of us. If we want to cooperate with other people, we must cooperate with people who have made mistakes."

He planned to stay close to Egypt and return the first moment he could, ready to make revolution again.

"We should respect anyone who wants to change the world for the better," Moaz said. "The same things that united us before the revolution could collect us again."

11.

THE REVOLUTION CONTINUES

The world seems to move faster now than it did a few centuries ago, but societies still change at a glacial pace. The marquee events of history give their yield slowly. America's founders based the Declaration of Independence on the inalienable rights to life, liberty, and the pursuit of happiness; yet it took nearly one century for America to end slavery and another for it to establish equal legal rights for people of all colors. Similarly, in Europe, the 1848 uprisings challenged the anti-democratic ruling order at its core, but their ideals only ripened into practice a century later, once the Continent had hosted two catastrophic world wars. Maybe that's how Egypt will turn out. January 25's moment of promise might eventually translate into a new order of rights and dignity, after many decades. Power takes a long time to dislodge, and old attitudes even longer.

The most startling aspect of the Republic of Tahrir was the speed with which common people with no history of activism shed their fears of authority. The most startling aspect of the military coup of July 2013 was the jubilation it elicited from many of these same people. It was no surprise that the old regime returned with such vengeance, but it was a surprise to see who cheered. Among the throngs who anointed General el-Sisi savior of Egypt were people who had braved many army bullets during the past three years. Sure, many of the new junta fans were conformists, Mubarak remnants, stability addicts, uncritical parrots hungry for the structure of a strongman. Many, but not all. Those who dabbled in revolution and then supported the regime's return remain a mystery.

Why did they break the wall of fear in January 2011, and why did they decide three years later that they'd rather live under military rule again? Time will show us whether they really prefer dictatorship, in which case Egypt is doomed to a dark fate, or whether they have made a tactical choice (or are experiencing temporary fatigue) and will attempt to defenestrate el-Sisi in a matter of months or years rather than decades.

Just before he retired from the army, el-Sisi had himself appointed field marshal. Perhaps he was as vain as he was ambitious, or perhaps he calculated that the credential was necessary if he was to retain power. A year after the coup, el-Sisi ran a presidential campaign notable for its scolding, detached tone. There were no public events, only a handful of television interviews in which el-Sisi declared that as president he would be beholden to no one. The *felool* fat cats delivered their own volunteer ad campaigns on el-Sisi's behalf, but the candidate told them not to expect any favors in return. He refused to publish a platform or describe his economic plan beyond several hectoring references to the sacrifices he expected from Egyptians rich and poor. The election followed the script of dictatorial referendums from times past. There was a nominal challenge from Hamdeen Sabbahi, but el-Sisi won with 96.9 percent of the vote in May 2014. Even dictators have constituencies and need support, but el-Sisi seemed to equate any form of coalition building with pandering. He refused to court Mubarak's old elite. Saudi Arabia and other Gulf countries spent more than $12 billion to bring el-Sisi to power and promised further payments to keep him there. Beyond the foreign cash, el-Sisi offered no hints on how he planned to govern.

At the time of this writing, Basem and Moaz are studying their mistakes, each seeking another path to his goals. So are the scores of thinkers and activists in prison and exile who have not discarded their ideas but who recognize that their efforts in the first three years after Mubarak did not suffice. We who chronicled the uprising have a responsibility to try to be honest and fair. In my estimation, Egypt's revolution was defeated so readily because it wasn't organized, it wasn't political enough, and, most fatally, it didn't have a compelling, constructive idea at its center. It had many other significant ingredients and was led by inspiring, brave individuals. What took place was rare enough: a population pushed to the edge lost its fear and challenged a rotten regime. That alone commands admiration and emulation. But it wasn't enough to make a revolution. It wasn't enough to change a country.

Many Egyptian activists and revolutionaries have blamed this miscarriage on the revolution's internal tactical choices or its external circumstances. On the tactical level, the revolution never developed any alternative or supplement to street protests. Crowds were its only tool and only measure, and revolutionary fervor is always just a stroke away from the frenzy of the mob. There are arguments about whether the revolutionaries used too much violence, alienating the public with their street fights, or not enough, because a street militia might have won bigger concessions. Many said that if protesters had remained in the square after Mubarak quit, his regime would have followed suit; but the fact is there was no will at the time to continue testing authorities after people got most of what they thought they wanted. Some reasonable theories focus on the private deals between secretive elites and the military that left little opportunity for a revolutionary agenda. The guiltiest party on this front was the Muslim Brotherhood, followed by some of the secular politicians and the bureaucracy of the state.

These critiques all have some merit but limited explanatory power. Ultimately, the status quo is not an immutable law of nature; it is the result of inherently malleable quantities: political circumstances and institutional power. Perception and personality matter in politics. A single man's momentary lapse of confidence can alter the course of a dictatorship. Popular momentum can swamp even a force as potent as Egypt's deep state. For a while, perhaps for as long as a year, that's what appeared to be happening in Egypt. All the status quo powers teetered on the defensive, unsure how they might survive: the military, the Muslim Brotherhood, the *felool*, and the established politicians. Slowly, however, the legacy powers regrouped as they sized up the popular force and recognized its incoherence. The kings and kingmakers realized that their fearsome adversaries were easily distracted and fragmented. It might take time, but the revolution could be defeated, brought back to earth, fattened, manipulated, silenced. Charged with energy, the revolution agitated against the abuses of the state but aspired to no single aim. For what did it stand? That depended on whom you asked, and the overwhelming majority of the young people who gave the revolution its striking force also rejected its would-be leaders.

I am not saying that the revolutionaries are at fault for the horrible things done by those in charge. No, responsibility for Egypt's terrible condition lies in the hands of those who held power and trust, and abused it: the military, the Muslim Brotherhood, and the old ruling party, in that order. They did the damage; they ruined the country. But the revolutionaries are to blame for failing to make a coherent, plausible revolution. Had they done so, they might still have been defeated, but they would have contested the established powers to a degree that they never managed.

The revolutionaries collapsed on three different levels: their organization, their politics, and their ideas. They were constrained by their society, with its terrible education system, endemic poverty, and lack of resources. Yet their failures weren't inevitable, as evinced by the successes within the revolution.

Organizationally, revolutionaries performed their best on narrow, tangible issues. A group called No to Military Trials did incredible work tracking and trying to represent the thousands of civilians detained by the military. A collective of videographers called Mosireen documented Egypt's struggle better than any media outlet. Resourceful and brilliant Egyptians weathered a concerted state assault to work as human rights monitors and defenders, and as independent journalists. They displayed fabulous inventiveness at protests and in clashes with police. In those ventures, revolutionary efforts were disciplined, organized, and sustained. But the best revolutionary organizations were one-person shows or tiny collectives; they never were able to transcend the small cell and organize adaptable institutions that could transcend and survive individual personalities.

Politically, the revolutionaries shied away from compromise. They displayed surprisingly little interest in crafting a platform or dogma to market. Initially refreshing, the absence of political thought and planning over time came to seem pathological. A century-long propaganda assault against the very idea of politics had paid off for Egypt's rulers.

The activists who chose politics as their field of play fared poorly. Even the activists who understood the utility of building coalitions never succeeded, perhaps because they didn't know how to do the work or because they lacked the resources to entice various constituencies. For example, several revolutionaries desperately tried to form a united front with labor unions; their failure to do so wasn't through lack of trying, but it was a failure all the same.

The failure of ideas is perhaps the most painful. At the beginning in Tahrir Square, revolutionaries spoke in bold strokes. They believed the end of the age of Arab authoritarians had come, and that the popular revolts were ushering in a dawn of Arab democracy. Their initial thoughts were profound and creative. Activists in the square spoke of a democracy built on justice and responsibility. They didn't intend to fetishize elections. Their first priority was to choose a government charged with providing freedom but justice as well, and by justice they meant a life of dignity: rule of law, employment, food, and health care. They imagined citizens who exercised rights while enjoying new freedoms. They borrowed some elements of European social democracy, and some from the American system, but they drew heavily on Egyptian and Arab history as well. As a starting point, they couldn't have been more ambitious. But that creative energy ebbed during the first year and failed to coalesce. The aspirations never distilled into something actionable.

It feels disrespectful, almost sacrilegious, to put it this way, but in the ripeness of time, it becomes clear: Tahrir was bursting with ideals, but it had a surprisingly small number of fully baked ideas. What did Tahrir want? The people in the square couldn't even agree on a starting slogan like "Freedom." No, even at the vaguest level, they wanted everything: "Bread, freedom, social justice." So vast a demand as to be meaningless, even thematically. If you want everything, you focus on nothing. And if, like Basem, you do manage to focus on a single goal (in his case, the pursuit of power through a viable political party), your journey will be tainted if it lacks a coherent ideological focus. There the revolution failed, and over time, it did not adapt and grow.

There were thinkers who tried to expand the complexity and thoughtfulness of the revolutionary political program, like the blogger Alaa Abdel

Fattah and the academic-turned-politician Amr Hamzawy. There was a larger group of people such as Moaz who sought to keep revolutionaries focused on ending the old regime before squabbling over its replacement. None of them, however, managed to dominate even their factions, much less the revolutionary space. Even after a year or two, when I asked revolutionaries what they wanted, I would get a laundry list. The Egyptian system was rigged to marginalize and discredit political thinking, and the leaders who did emerge in the different islands of the revolution never tried to make themselves into leaders of the entire archipelago. Each member of the Revolutionary Youth Coalition aimed only to represent a tiny slice, and the modesty of those ambitions, along with the lack of a coherent idea, spelled doom.

Furthermore, like destructive germs, Egypt's excessive nationalism and pride in the army festered within revolutionaries, like within most Egyptians. Even faced with overwhelming evidence of the military's malfeasance, too many revolutionaries were willing to trust the military as an impartial referee. The revolution never sought to dispel the shibboleth that Egypt's army was sacred. Far too many revolutionaries succumbed to a belief in historical exceptionalism: Egypt, the mother of the world, was crafting its own history, immune to the forces that affected other nations. They avoided studying parallel cases of revolution and militarism, and were blindsided by predictable developments such as the machinations of the military, the return of the *felool*, the breakdown of the economy.

I say again, because it is worth repeating, that the revolutionaries bear no responsibility for the torture, murder, and miscarriage of justice that persisted from the rule of Mubarak through the periods of the SCAF, Morsi, and el-Sisi. However, the revolutionaries are responsible for their own shortcomings: their incoherence, their absence of tactical innovation, their inability to forge ideas. When and if the revolutionaries repair these deficiencies, they will be able to bring to life the notional Republic of Tahrir.

Moaz tried his best and preserved his moral integrity. Basem tried his best and preserved a sliver of his political project. There are a few thousand like them who honorably gave their all in an attempt to change their country, and who still are trying. As they do their time in exile, in prison, or under the corrosion of a reconstituted dictatorship, perhaps they'll find a way to speak of politics with a vocabulary that is equally open to Islamist and secular freedoms. Perhaps they'll find themselves able to choose just one goal to begin with, and to think through the types of morally ambiguous choices needed to reach it. Bread, freedom, *or* social justice. One day, perhaps, they'll agree on a single idea, and a plan will follow. Then they might change the course of history even more than they did in those first eighteen days in the square.

Almost two and a half millennia ago, in the midst of the Peloponnesian War, the Athenians landed on the neutral island of Milos and ordered it to surrender. Otherwise Athens would slaughter the men and enslave the women and children. Even by the standards of the time, the ultimatum sounded like a war crime. The leaders of Milos appealed to justice and morals. They had a right to remain neutral in the war. As the ancient Greek historian Thucydides tells the story, the Athenians, self-styled progenitors of democracy and moral philosophy, laughed away the objections of Milos. "The strong do as they can, and the weak suffer what they must," they said. Milos stood by its convictions and was destroyed.

Tahrir, like Milos, was right and just and moral. Victory always needs something more than that, even today. The internet age hasn't reconfigured the calculus of power. Guns and money trump words alone, even if those words are published on a brilliant and flexible open-source web platform. Revolution comes when a narrative persuades the guns and money to change sides. Egypt's revolution and counterrevolution reminded us of the power of words, as well as the limits of that power.

The Tahrir Revolution reminded the world that authoritarianism isn't preordained. Some had argued that the Arab world was destined to live under dictatorship, or preferred it. The Arab uprisings of 2010 and 2011 dispelled that lazy and racist idea for good, hopefully. Egypt's revolution reminded us of some other truths. History never stops. There is no such thing as universal agreement. Power is never static. Three years after Tahrir, many revolutionaries are in prison, in exile, dead, or otherwise silenced. A few are still striving in the claustrophobic confines of political space not yet destroyed by the deep state. El-Sisi won control, and he won fawning love. But his victory still doesn't mean that authoritarianism will prevail forever. It isn't culturally determined. Its tide can be turned. It can be destroyed. That's what Tahrir proved.

Demonstrators in Egypt pushed aside three regimes in three years. It wasn't entirely the same crowd that bayed against Mubarak, the SCAF, and Morsi, but during that three-year stretch, probably every thinking person in Egypt took to the streets and demanded that one ruler or another leave. That public ownership of the political process didn't disappear with restoration of a military despot. The very nature of the governed has changed unequivocally. The overwhelming majority of Egypt's citizens came to feel entitled to decide who ruled them. Their consecration for el-Sisi carried a tinge of poison, whether he recognized it or not: the people made him, and they could break him. That connection was without precedent in Egypt and in most despotic countries. In such places, "the people" is a concept in which the sovereign's power is vested; it is not supposed to act as a force in its own right. But through revolution, all these different Egyptians had acquired an awareness of their agency: revolutionary and *felool*, young and old, thuggish and bourgeois. They had also sharpened their sense of historic destiny. Egypt's revolution prompted uprisings across the Arab world, and caused anxiety among authoritarians in faraway China and Russia. The square resonated as a metaphor and a cautionary tale. Antigovernment protesters in Kiev in early 2014 studied the Egyptian revolt, determined to emulate its strengths and avoid its mistakes. Egypt's revolutionary ideas reverberated on the world stage even as they were ghettoized inside Egypt.

As I write these words, a smothering majority of Egyptians are choosing to return to military dictatorship, welcoming violence and the repression of dissenters. Does this mean we should understand the idealists in Egypt as some endangered species in a culture that is primed for fascism? I believe that the uprising, with its deep historical roots and its implications stretching far into the future, teaches us the opposite. Egyptians propelled their revolution with their own unexpected agency and bravery. They opposed epochal injustice, and although it remained

inchoate, they conjured a vision of Arab democracy that was compelling
and authentic. That seed remains, as do the manifold impediments to its
taking root.

I think we have to acknowledge that, in Egypt's case, love of the military and comfort with authoritarianism run deep. The dominance of
authoritarians is not guaranteed, but their presence in the political discourse is. Any future change will have to make some accommodation for
them, just like it will have to find some space for Islamists. Throughout
history, many people have freely chosen juntas (and later came to regret
it), and many countries seemingly conditioned for life under abusive caprice have somehow raised themselves into a more just condition. Egypt
is neither doomed nor condemned, though for the time being it has
reached an impossibly sad juncture. After Tahrir, Egypt is a much harder
nation to subordinate. In just his first year in control, el-Sisi killed and
arrested more people than Mubarak did in nearly three decades. He faced
only token opposition on his way to the presidency, and he refused to
campaign, make promises, or even publish a platform. He chided Egyptians for asking him questions. With a heavy hand he brushed off the
few remaining dissidents as well as the *felool* businessmen who supported
him. His imperious style could be a sign of el-Sisi's Machiavellian fierce-
ness, or it could be evidence of weakness. The uprising against Mubarak
and the events that followed were not a dream. Everyone involved said
and did things of consequence. Even those who surrendered did so as
changed individuals. None of them was the same person he or she had
been in 2010.

We also ought to reserve some empathy for the stability crowd. I find
it impossible to approve of someone who condones torture but find it
possible to relate to the desire to live under a predictable, centralized
state—even a problematic one. Among those relieved at el-Sisi's rise,
we find reasonable people who have grown tired of uncertainty. Critical
thinking and political experimentation lead in the short term to more
questions, more criticisms, and more open-ended changes: an unset-
tling condition even for those who crave the democratic experiment. In
Egypt's case, even mere reform entails the loss of stability. If the familiar
framework of paralysis is cast aside, no one can predict the path forward.

As a result, some reasonable people choose stability and the familiar, even if it means repression or even fascism.

Those who accept authoritarianism aren't all maniacs and extremists. Some are reasonable people such as Basem, or, for that matter, my grandmother, who welcomed the 1967 coup in Greece because it resolved national fears and anxieties stoked by decades of privation, war, and civil strife. To those convinced that their country is sinking into civil war, military rule can seem a bracing antidote. I believe that pluralism and due process are the only guarantees of liberty and security in the long run, but I can comprehend if not accept the opposing view, that freedoms are luxuries to be enjoyed only when existential threats have been tamed.

"I'm tired of people telling us we failed," a friend still working against the regime in Egypt told me with a flicker of irritation. My friend is right to be irritated; the revolutionaries didn't fail so much as they were defeated, more than anything else by the shallow fetishism of the crowd that brought President el-Sisi. Nothing bothered me more than the unabashed zeal with which proponents of the old order set about demolishing and humiliating the legacy of Tahrir. Judges sentenced hundreds to death after a day's hearings. Sycophantic journalists broadcast the private conversations of revolutionaries, illegally wiretapped by State Security and hoarded for the moment they could be used for blackmail or revenge. Policemen shot to kill, *felool* resumed their old plunder, and, worst of all, all the revanchist forces assumed an air of wounded moral superiority. They behaved as if none of what happened during the first three years of the Tahrir Revolution made them reconsider their lying, killing ways, as if they hadn't feared for an instant that the game was up and they'd have to treat people better. Now they were winning again. The old regime was in control.

Yet how could they imagine that they hadn't narrowly escaped, that the lesson of history was that you can't take power for granted, especially if your power is built on mutually exclusive pillars of injustice and incompetence? The Egyptian Revolution that erupted in 2011 was interrupted two years later. El-Sisi might rule for a long time, curtailing freedoms while pillaging the national economy. But he might also be swiftly undone by a population accustomed to revolt. "Do you remember the tomorrow that never came?" asked a graffito on Cairo walls in 2014. It speaks of a tomorrow that glows warmly in people's minds, for which they fought and will fight again. Only an unimaginative mind would believe the Egyptian Revolution was an evanescent fancy that can be dismissed or erased.

I don't want to end this story, because I don't like the way it turned out. The heroes were all flawed, and the best of them compromised too much, like Basem, or achieved too little, like Moaz. Their extraordinary accomplishments didn't convince enough of their neighbors and fellow citizens that freedom is worth the trouble it causes. The ending is not all gloom, however. The men and women who did these brave things leapt across a threshold. They contributed something invaluable to the moral fiber of the universe, and, less abstractly, they learned to organize and command substantial power. They might well find a way to change their country. And so, until then, if I must end this story, I might as well end it with Moaz's words, as apt a coda as any to a struggle that never ends.

It's hard to draw moral lessons from such fresh history, but as I tried to make sense of the place to which Egypt seemingly had returned just a few years after the Tahrir uprising, I wrote to Moaz in the spring of 2014. El-Sisi was building a dynasty, and the revolution already seemed a subject for historians. "Were the last three years a dream, an interruption of what is truly normal?" I asked. "Or is it normal for people to feel free and respect each other, and dictatorship has been the sixty-year interruption?"

The email reached Moaz in Qatar, where he was appearing on Al Jazeera television, arguing still about the events of 2011 and their continuing repercussions for the Arab world, and for revolutionaries and despots all over the globe updating their calculations about how to keep power or seize it. He didn't know where he'd land, whether he could secure legal residency in Turkey, or in Qatar, or somewhere else, but he was trying everything, and, oddly, didn't seem demoralized or exhausted.

Moaz reminisced about the years that had passed and about Tahrir, which for him never would.

"It was the happiest dream of my life," he wrote. "I felt freedom and safety, and also that I am part of this country and we can change everything to reach the dream country. I had a dream, and I still have the same dream."

Beirut, Lebanon, June 2014

ACKNOWLEDGMENTS

Most importantly I want to thank the people who shared their time and stories with me during a transformative and busy period of their lives. Without them, there would have been no story to tell, and no book. Moaz, Basem, and Ayyash were exceedingly generous in extending their trust. I am grateful to all the individuals who spoke with me and let me accompany them at close quarters. Many of them do not appear by name in these pages. A partial list of those to whom I owe a debt of gratitude includes Ahmed el-Gohary, Sally Toma, Abdelrahman Fares, Zyad el-Elaimy, Sara Mohamed, Mohamed el-Qasas, Alaa Abdel Fattah, Bothaina Kamal, Ahmed Sleem, Hala Moustafa, Sally Sami, Maha Abdel Nasser, Asmaa Mahfouz, Ahmed Abdrabo, Mostafa Shawqi, Ayman Abouzaid, Khalid Hamza, Nazly Hussein, and many, many others.

Many friends in Egypt provided insight, moral support, shelter, and care of all sorts. Shawn Baldwin went above the call of friendship and welcomed me as a housemate. Scott Nelson and Rawya Rageh served pancakes, fresh cookies, and unending moral support. Borzou Daragahi, Delphine Minoui, and Samarra welcomed me as always into their home. Many others provided companionship at election rallies, riots, and demonstrations, over meals, and on felucca rides. I enjoyed invaluable conversations with acute observers of Egypt, including Abby Hauslohner, Ursula Lindsay, Issandr ElAmrani, Ashraf Khalil, Rola Zaarour, Elijah Zarwan, Hisham Hellyer, Shereen Zaky, Lina Attalah, Sarah El Deeb, Heba Morayef, Leila Fadel, Erin Evers, Kareem Fahim, Max Becherer, Rebecca Santana, Giovanna dall'Ora, Asmaa Waguih,

Rolla Scolari, Max Rodenbeck, David Kirkpatrick, and too many others to name.

Countless individuals donated their time and energy to give feedback, explain things I didn't understand, and correct me. They accompanied me on tiring days. They worked thankless hours and performed nitpicking tasks. They read notes and drafts, and shared their thoughts, feelings, and conjectures. Joe Gabra was a loyal and enthusiastic colleague, critic, translator, and friend. Gaser el-Safty and Ahmed Ghamrawi provided eyes, ears, company, and translation for the better part of a year. Yasser Halawa stayed awake late at night on bumpy roads and brought us home alive if sometimes in a stupor. Many others contributed research and journalistic work: Dana Kardoush, Dahlia Morched, Brandt Miller, Mohamed Magdy, Marwa Nasser, Refaat Ahmed, Heba Naiem, Mona el-Naggar, Samar Awada, Therese Postel, and others. Shereen Zaky, Charles Levinson, Brian Katulis, Michael Hanna, Neil Bhatiya, Nathan Deuel, and Ursula Lindsay commented on drafts of the manuscript. Shereen Zaky was a detailed and committed critical reader, catching errors and arguing interpretations; her feedback crucially shaped the manuscript. Charles Levinson introduced me to Moaz and Basem in Tahrir Square, for the second time in our friendship planting the seeds of a book for me.

I owe a debt of gratitude to the many journalists and researchers who chronicled, quantified, and analyzed events in Egypt, often in real time and at substantial personal risk. I relied especially on the work of Heba Morayef, Sarah El Deeb, the marvelous reporting team assembled by Lina Attalah at *Egypt Independent* and then at *Mada Masr*, and Hani Shukrallah's team at Ahram Online. My daily reading began with the blogs *The Arabist* and Zeinobia's *Egyptian Chronicles*.

Colleagues and editors gave me crucial help along the way. Jim Smith at *The Boston Globe* and then Susan Chira at *The New York Times* dispatched me to Egypt before the revolution. Much of my initial reporting from Tahrir Square and its aftermath first appeared in *The Atlantic* in the able care of Max Fisher, and in *The Boston Globe*, where I had enduring support from Steve Heuser. The Century Foundation, especially Janice Nittoli and Greg Anrig, provided the support and structure that enabled me to breathe freely while drafting and completing the book. Waleed

Hazbun and the American University of Beirut supported my research. Peter Canellos, Alessandra Bastagli, and Dominick Anfuso were early editorial believers in me and this project. Brian Katulis has kept the faith since I was writing about fire engines. Anne Barnard has remained my most important editor.

Editing the book itself has been a most rewarding if grueling labor. My agent, Wendy Strothman, has been a lodestar, and in the clutch cooked a pivotal bowl of soup that might have saved the entire enterprise. Without her and Lauren MacLeod, this book would have remained but an idea. Priscilla Painton and the rest of the team at Simon & Schuster, including line editor Sophia Jimenez and copy editor Philip Bashe, did artful and thoughtful work, improving the manuscript immeasurably while investing copious labor.

Anthony Shadid taught me constantly and transmitted an infectious excitement about the uprisings. Through him, I first came to love Egypt. In the early days of Tahrir, we reported together, and as he mused out loud, he convinced me that we were living a moment of irreducible historical importance and that we could have fun covering it. I miss his friendship, and his death leaves us all poorer; I still wish I could read his take on every day's news.

I can't imagine these years reporting and writing about Egypt without Michael Hanna. He has been a friend, mentor, colleague, companion, reveler, and much more. He put enormous time and energy into helping me, with good humor and uncommon insight. Whether he was talking our way through a checkpoint manned by jumpy xenophobes in Nasr City or arguing a tiny detail in a New York office, he was selflessly committed to this project.

I know I have not mentioned many people who were crucial to this book, which has been four years in the making, but know that I am grateful. I owe much to this supportive community, but all shortcomings and mistakes in the manuscript are wholly my own.

My friends and family held things together when I went AWOL to Egypt and at various times when I had to withdraw from the world to immerse myself in the manuscript. Martha Arnold, Deborah Hallam, Kenrick Cato, Jenny Castillo, Helen and Russell Barnard, Gretel Neal, and my mother, Miranda Cambanis, enabled our family to thrive during the toughest stretches. My wife, Anne Barnard, embraced this project from the very start, encouraging me to go to Tahrir Square in January 2011. Without her advice and unflagging support, there would be no book. Without the love I share with her, Odysseas, and Athina, I never would have wanted to write it.

INDEX

ABOUT THE AUTHOR

Thanassis Cambanis is a journalist who has been writing about the Middle East for more than a decade. His first book, *A Privilege to Die: Inside Hezbollah's Legions and Their Endless War Against Israel*, was published in 2010. He is a fellow at The Century Foundation in New York City. He writes the "Internationalist" column for *The Boston Globe* and regularly contributes to *The New York Times*, *The Atlantic*, and other publications. Thanassis lives in Beirut, Lebanon, with his wife and their two children.